The Path Is Everywhere

The Path Is Everywhere

Uncovering the Jewels
Hidden Within You

Matt Licata, PhD

Wandering Yogi Press

Cover art and author photo by Krista Ahlfors

Interior design by Meadowlark Publishing Services

ISBN 978-0-9990569-0-5

Published by Wandering Yogi Press
Boulder, Colorado

Manufactured in the United States of America
Published 2017

This book is dedicated to all lovers of truth. To your deepest longing for aliveness, meaning, and depth, and to something sacred that you may have lost contact with along the way.

It is also offered to your heartbreak, homesickness, hopelessness, and despair: unexpected allies on the path of wholeness.

May your journey unfold with compassion, courage, and clear seeing as you explore the forests, oceans, and starry universes of the heart, a voyage that by its nature is one of endless revelation.

Contents

Foreword by Jeff Foster

IN ANY MOMENT OF OUR LIVES, THERE EXISTS A WONDERFUL POSSIBILITY: to take a sacred pause. To stop running toward the next moment and become truly fascinated with *this* one. To drop out of the complex and compelling narrative of our lives, the dramatic story of "Me, Myself, and I" that exists in memory and imagination and dances those strange and distant worlds called Past and Future, places we hear so much about but can never actually touch. And instead, to invite a curious attention into our real-time, moment-by-moment, embodied physical experience.

For just a moment, can we stop thinking *about* our lives and instead find the courage to actually *inhabit* them? Can we begin to feel our feet on the ground? Notice what's happening in our thinking? Sense our bodies instead of running away from them into addictive, distracting behavior? Hear all the sounds happening around us? *A bird singing. The buzz of the refrigerator. An airplane in the distance.* Feel a fluttery sensation in the belly, a tightness in the throat, a pressure between the eyes? This is true meditation: not trying to enter into some altered state but finding the courage to live—to hear with fresh ears, see with unprejudiced eyes, taste the moment as if it were the first and only one in existence. And then, underneath the cacophony of our lives, perhaps we can touch that sacred place that has remained unchanged since we were born. Being itself. Our own presence. This awesome, inexplicable sense of being alive.

In Matt's beautiful book of love songs to the exquisite fragility of our humanness, you will learn to trust life again (because even your doubt is trustable). You will learn there is never anything wrong with you, and it's not actually possible to be having the *wrong* experience, ever. That you were never meant to get *there*—the far-off Utopia, the enlightened self, the perfect bodymind—you were always meant to be *here,* in all your messy and glorious imperfection. Here, in this moment as it is, is the Garden of Eden you've always tried to find. And you—as you are, even with your human flaws and failings, longings, and sorrows—are the Gift. Your humanness is not less than your divinity; your humanness *is* the divine expression itself. Your confusion, your pain, your fear, your anger, your sorrow, even your feelings of shame and guilt and unworthiness are all drenched with intelligence, saturated with wisdom, infused with the same power that makes the sun shine and the grass grow in springtime. And however painful, however uncomfortable, however intense the present moment gets, you are always exactly where you need to be.

Your true path is everywhere. Your true path is not separate from the one who walks it. Your true path is right here, in the intimacy of your embodied human experience. Your true path is alive; it is every sound, every sensation, every feeling as it surges in your body, every throb, every flutter, every ache, every pulse, thump, and tingle. No feeling is a mistake or "unspiritual" or a "low vibration" or a sign of your failure; each feeling is only looking for sanctuary, acceptance. No thought is an aberration either—even your most "sick" or "shameful" thoughts are beloved.

Matt's invitation is exquisitely simple but shockingly powerful. *Be profoundly what you are, as you are, where you are.* Let go of all the images of how you "should" be, for there are no "shoulds" here in the heart. Bow to whatever arises in your experience and bow to your inability to bow to what sometimes arises! Yes, sometimes you have to begin by allowing the part of you that doesn't know how to allow.

Foreword

The part that feels frightened. The part that doesn't trust. The part that feels far from home. Yes, even these parts of you are your spiritual children, worthy of great kindness.

Matt's rare gift is his ability to stay present, curious, and empathic no matter what you throw at him. I have found this to be true in my friendship with him as well as during the workshops and retreats we hold together around the world. Matt effortlessly creates a holding environment, a warm, safe space in which even our strangest thoughts, our deepest fears, longings, sorrows, pains, and joys are given permission to be. I believe this is the greatest gift we can give each other as human beings, this sacred field of unconditional friendship where we allow each other to be imperfect. It is the space in which we give up trying to fix each other and instead *listen* with our entire being. It is the space in which true relaxation can happen, where the frazzled nervous system can breathe a sigh of relief.

I have witnessed countless people over the years relaxing deeply in Matt's warm and loving presence. I have seen old narratives melting away, childhood wounds being flushed with love and understanding, seemingly unbearable feelings finally able to be borne. Matt does more by doing less. He heals by never pretending to be a healer. He awakens by treating us as though we are already awake. He teaches by *not* teaching, by simply sharing with the greatest integrity and sincerity from his vulnerable, powerful human heart. Ironically, I consider him to be one of the clearest and most authentic teachers of our time.

The Path Is Everywhere is a friendly guide to unpacking, understanding, and unravelling the shame that has been holding us back from feeling fully alive. When we were young we were judged, criticized, even punished for having our own unique thoughts, feelings, perceptions, desires. We were shamed for being ourselves, looking how we looked, walking how we walked, dancing how we danced. We were shamed for our urges and impulses or our lack of them. We were taught by those who had been taught to hate themselves and hadn't yet learned to love themselves. Now is the time to reclaim the love that is rightfully ours, to reclaim it from deep within.

Foreword

You've been on such a long journey, friend, an ancient journey from the stars. The self-improvement project, while noble, has worn itself out. Today is the day to break once and for all the core belief that there is something wrong with the way you are. Dive now into Matt's beautiful poetic prose that weaves together elements of psychology, nonduality, tantra, and loving common sense into an intoxicating whole. Dissolve into his words and into the silences between and underneath them. Discover the paradoxical secret that has never for one moment been hidden from you: that the One you sought was always You. That there is beauty in your brokenness, grace in your sorrow, brilliant light in your shadow. That the true path can never leave you, because it is written in your very bones.

—Jeff Foster, author of *The Way of Rest*
Brighton, England, January 2017

Preface

I WROTE THIS BOOK WITH THE INTENTION THAT IT SERVE AS AN ATTUNED yet provocative crucible in which a sacred confrontation might occur between you and the mystery that is your own heart, and to remind you of something you may have forgotten in the busyness of our modern world. Whether owing to external commitments or by way of the inner project of self-improvement in all its forms, many have grown weary, longing for rest and an aliveness they sense is possible but somehow continues to remain just out of reach.

Everything that you are is welcome on this journey we will take together, including your confusion, heartbreak, joy, and bliss. The invitation presented here is radical and nonconventional in its nature: it is that there is nothing wrong with you and you have everything you need to live a life beyond imagination. Your sensitivity, vulnerability, and even your confusion about who you are and what this life is all about are not obstacles on your path but *are the very path itself,* drenched with energy, information, and guidance for the way ahead.

This is not a book for you to read cover to cover in one sitting or struggle to understand conceptually, but one to pick up from time to time in response to a call from within. While at times it may appear you have lost contact with your inner guidance system, love is relentless and will continue to take the most unexpected forms in order to reach you. With curiosity and courage—and guided by the innate bravery

Preface

and confidence of the open heart—you can train yourself to listen and attune to this wisdom as it unfolds inside you, opening you to the sacred world that is always already here, awaiting your participation.

The Path Is Everywhere is more *poetic* than it is *prescriptive*. It does not offer a prefabricated set of instructions, five or seven clear steps for you to follow, or a predetermined way through the dark wood and into the golden world of mystery, meaning, and aliveness. While I hope to invite deeper levels of awareness of the mystery as it appears in and as your life, I do not have any answers for you. Rather, it is my intention to help you to clarify the immensity and sacredness of the questions. What these questions are will be outrageously unique and in a language only you can understand. The words here are only fingers pointing to a moon that is already rising within you, and their sole intention is to guide you back, over and over and over again, into the luminous wisdom-field that is your true nature. Your journey is unprecedented, and you will never be ultimately satisfied by a partial or secondhand path. The aim of this book is to invite you into a radical new level of trust in your own experience and into the courageous hero's or heroine's journey, which is always shimmering with life as it arises freshly in the here and now.

The essential message of *The Path Is Everywhere* is that there are no *actual* obstacles on your journey, no obscurations to your true nature, and, surprisingly, that you may not even need what is conventionally referred to as "healing." As we make this journey together, you are invited to discover a profound and life-shattering realization: that despite appearances to the contrary, the aliveness you are longing for is available *now*. You do not need to first clean up your past, find your soul mate, resolve all your trauma, discover your life's purpose, or complete some mythical spiritual journey in order to fully participate in the sacred reality that is unfolding within and around you. This world is always already present in your immediate experience yet does seem to require the cleansing of conditioned perception in order to realize that you are already home. This (re)discovery of home does not mean that the journey is over, but only that it is able to truly begin.

Preface

The path of the heart is endless in its depth and there is *always* further revelation. In the heart, the fantasy of some "permanent," "complete," or "full" state of healing, awakening, or enlightenment is burned up in the energy of love itself.

If you look carefully, you may sense a field of permission that co-arises with all of your experience, wrapped around it and infusing it with its qualities each time a thought, emotion, image, or feeling comes into conscious awareness. It can be astonishing to discover the truth that there is so much space around your experience. One of the aims of this book is to catalyze your experiential connection with this field and support its unfolding within you at the deepest levels. As you touch and live more deeply from this field—recognizing your ultimate nonseparation from it—you will discover that despite the challenges along the way you are *already whole*. The journey then becomes less about how to *get to* wholeness, and more about how to consciously participate in what you already *are*. As Jesus reminds us, the Kingdom is *already here*, a revelation that naturally dawns as we slow down and ground in the earth while simultaneously opening into the heavens, and our perception is purified by clear seeing.

As you make your way through the book, you may notice some repetition of the central themes as they are presented in the form of invitations, contemplations, and inquiries for you to engage in experientially. In large part, this is intentional as in my experience it takes many micro-moments of compassion, attunement, and increased awareness to encode new circuitry and shift the momentum of self-abandonment, self-aggression, and conditioned perception.

It might help to view each section of *The Path Is Everywhere* as standing alone, each a unique summons into a particular dimension or aspect of your experience. I encourage you to go slowly as you engage with the words, close your eyes from time to time, feel yourself on the earth, and reconnect with your senses. Read the book for short periods, setting it down frequently to allow the material to sink in and come alive inside you. "Mastering" or even fully "understanding" the concepts is of secondary importance to a direct, nonconceptual encounter with your true nature, realized in the silent spaces around and between the words.

Always remember that the words are only signs, symbols, and lyrical doorways into the great mystery. Let them draw you into your own innate wisdom, when they do; and allow them to dissolve back into spacious awareness when they do not. They are not intended as "objective truths" or as theories to get tangled up or lost in, to prove or disprove, or to overly analyze. Let them penetrate you in a more poetic way, staying connected with your body, your feelings, and the grounding of the earth as you proceed. For the truth is that you do not *need* any new concepts or information to discover the majesty of what you are and to fully participate in the sacred world around you. Engage with the words if and when they are inspiring and helpful, and set them aside when their energy or magic falls away.

The Path Is Everywhere has three primary sources of inspiration: the tantric approaches found throughout the world's religions and spiritualities; the written and oral traditions of the great mystic poets; and the larger relational movement in contemporary psychoanalysis and depth psychology. It is my sincere wish that through a meeting of these seemingly disparate wisdom streams—along with discoveries from my own experience and in working with clients in psychotherapy and spiritual guidance—these words, as limited as all words are, may somehow point you back to the reality of the sacred and who you are at the deepest level.

Throughout the book, I make reference to "the beloved" as a way of calling you into that open, warm, spacious dimension of loving awareness, out of which all form comes and goes. In this sense, the beloved is not a thing or a noun but an *invitation*. This word "beloved" has been used by mystics for thousands of years—Sufi poets, Indian sages, and Christian contemplatives—and is being offered here as an open doorway into previously hidden areas of your body, heart, and psyche, each unique carriers and revealers of the great mystery.

While I usually refer to the beloved in the feminine (as "her" or "she"), this is only my personal preference and a reflection of what is most alive for me. The beloved, of course, is beyond gender and never limited to any form. Please feel free to substitute masculine (or gender neutral) pronouns if doing so is more resonant for you. Or replace the word altogether with "God," "Spirit," "Love," "Life," the "Self," or any other term that is meaningful in your immediate experience. What is most important is not the word or concept itself but the feeling tone it evokes.

Throughout *The Path Is Everywhere,* I speak frequently in the second person, directly to "you," the reader. I realize this is somewhat unconventional and perhaps even a bit presumptuous, as if to imply that I know what you are currently experiencing. Because so much of the writing in this book emerged out of very personal, real-time dialogue with clients, friends, and strangers from around the world, I have retained this usage in an attempt to accurately reflect the source of the material, and also as a way to stay close with *you*, my fellow traveler on this journey.

While this approach can provide a certain degree of intimacy, there is also a risk that you may in fact *not* be currently experiencing what these words are pointing to, resulting in your feeling that they are misattuned to your unique, subjective experience in the here and now. If this is the case, please move on to another section of the book that is more resonant with your current lived reality, share the words with a friend who may benefit from them, or bookmark these sections to return to at another time.

While I am attempting to speak to experiences that are universal in the unfolding and maturation of the human person, such attempts will always fail to meet everyone exactly where they happen to be at the precise moment of our encounter. Your experience is wildly unique and will never be pinned down by the limitations of the conceptual.

It is my hope that these words, as limited as they are, will somehow ignite a fire within you, spreading in the four directions, seeding everyone and everything in its wake with the erupting and outrageously

creative energies of pure love. And that this book will make even a minuscule contribution to the reduction of suffering in our world.
—Matt Licata, PhD
   Boulder, Colorado
   June 2017

Introduction

MUCH IS SAID THESE DAYS ABOUT HEALING AND SPIRITUAL AWAKENING, and the deep joy, clarity, and peace that are the promised fruits of the inner journey. Not much is mentioned, however, about the *disappointment* of awakening and the ways it can shatter our hearts, breaking us open to the reality of the crucifixion, the resurrection, *and* the transfiguration we are likely to encounter along the way.

In the rush to convert the negative to the positive, to manifest everything we (have been conditioned to believe we) want, and to manage our lives into some permanent state of "happiness," we lose contact with the reality that there is no transfiguration without embodiment to the dark cross within. The journey of individuation, of becoming a true human person, is a bit messy by nature as it emerges directly out of the unknown and requires that we come in contact with the *entirety* of what we are. The confrontation with the unconscious is not pleasant, as was alluded to by the great Swiss psychiatrist Carl Jung, but offers depth and meaning beyond what we are capable of knowing ahead of time. Furthermore, we must come to face the reality that the inner journey is not organized around our hopes and fears, or our dreams of the way we thought it was all going to turn out. It is just too extraordinary, too magical, and too alive for all that.

In an inclusive embrace of life—inside the messy and shadowy nether regions of the psyche—we are invited to meet the wholeness

Introduction

that we *already* are, which includes the dark *and* the light, the activity of separation *and* union, and the entirety of what it means to be an open, sensitive, and powerfully vulnerable human being. Paradoxically to the mind, but in ways the heart and the body know natively, inside the core of our vulnerability is a nonordinary gold, a jewel that is found only there. This gold is available to us at all times, though it will often appear in unexpected and unrecognizable forms as our life circumstances, feelings, symptoms, symbols, and the other people who come into (and out of) our lives. Through this appearance and disappearance of form, we come to discover that awakening is not only a creative process but a *destructive* one as well, and the gods of wholeness appear to be equally ready to employ *either* energy in fulfilling their mission here. What that mission is, we can only know through primary experience, bearing witness to the numinous as it pours through us and into the relative world.

As we look carefully and begin to see beyond the veil just a bit, we may sense something longing to emerge out of the mess and the chaos, surging up from the dark, rich soil of the body and out of the earth itself—right out of the core of our deeply embedded sense of unworthiness, disconnection, and loneliness. Even spinning out of moments of anxiety, hopelessness, confusion, and despair. On the path of the heart, the question isn't, how do we stop this material from arising, for it is its nature to do so, but whether we will provide a home for it when it arrives. Will we receive it with our curiosity, interest, kindness, and the warmth of our embodied presence? Or will we pathologize it, conclude it is evidence that something has gone wrong, that we have failed, and that we are somehow not okay? Of course, it is both intelligent and kind to take care of ourselves in whatever ways we are able, and to bring relief during difficult times. But there is another invitation, one that is more alchemical in nature, that is the subject of this book: to *turn in* to the symptom, the feeling, and the symbols as they appear, for they are carriers of profound wisdom and guidance.

While we may long more than anything for the high-voltage

Introduction

aliveness that underlies the path of the heart, a part of us may always remain unsure about fully stepping in, as we sense the implications of living in this new way and what will truly be asked of us, which is *everything*. As Jung so poignantly reminds us, we do not become enlightened by "imagining figures of light, but by making the darkness conscious."[1] He went on to say that the integrating, nonnegotiable journey of the dark *and* the light is by its nature "disagreeable" and therefore would never be popular. In a culture that has fallen under the spell of "being happy" at all costs—and owing to collective pressure to turn from the shadow in nearly all of its forms—we would do well to heed Jung's advice. For in disavowing the darkness we abandon the jewels that have been placed inside it, and without exploration of that which lies in the shadows, the true light will never have any chance here. As we penetrate deeper with our inquiry, we might discover for ourselves whether it is the consistent experience of being "happy" that we are truly after or whether it is something else, something of even greater depth, subtlety, and magic.

Remember: we may never *want* to turn back in to what we have avoided for so long. And it may rarely feel comfortable or safe to do so. But if we wait for the consistent appearance of comfort or safety, demanding that the journey be clearer or *feel* good before we are willing to fully show up, we will likely wait a very long time. It is perfectly natural to prefer one subcategory of beliefs, emotions, and feelings over another, and this reality need not be dismissed nor denied. But at some point the journey seems to demand that we become less interested in our *preferences* than in what is *most true*, a requirement that carries with it not only the embodied experience of deflation, but a power and a freedom beyond our wildest imagination. In this sense, the activity of deflation is sacred as it comes as a harbinger of depth.

The ancient path of the heart may never conform to our most cherished hopes, fears, and dreams, for it is emerging in the here and now as an emissary of the unknown itself. It is an invitation to something

---

1. Jung, C. G. *Alchemical Studies. Collected Works,* vol 13. (Princeton, NJ: Princeton University Press, 1983), 335.

new, mysterious, and beyond what we are able to approach by way of the conceptual. Yes, awakening may always be a disappointment compared to how we thought our lives would turn out. In this sense, the journey is eternally hopeless. But it is in the creation of a sanctuary for our hopelessness—weaved together from the raw materials of our own bravery, courage, and curiosity—that we step into the sacred world that is always already here. In this sense, the disenchantment is holy and the disillusionment is a benediction, both forerunners of a larger reality that longs to emerge within us.

As we journey together as fellow travelers, let us find a way to embrace both the joy *and* the heartbreak of the path, and bear witness to the wisdom shining out of our immediate experience, whether it appears as sadness, bliss, despair, or great joy. It is true that grace will appear in both sweet *and* fierce forms, but irrespective of its particular manifestation, it is still grace, sent from beyond to open us to the radiant fullness of being.

1

The Union of Dark and Light

The Full-Spectrum Nature of Love

IN SPEAKING RECENTLY WITH A FRIEND, I WAS REMINDED OF THE GREAT bias in modern culture toward the light and away from the darkness. When we encounter someone who is feeling down, empty, or flat—or otherwise not beaming, joyful, and overflowing with hope—we can quickly become convinced that something is wrong, that they are broken and we must act urgently to fix them. Sitting in this field with another has an uncanny way of activating this same unresolved material within ourselves. For a moment, we question whether *we* are okay as a sense of restlessness fills the space between us.

The raw, shaky, claustrophobic feelings triggered in these moments usually remain outside conscious awareness unless and until we cultivate the curiosity and openness required to explore them. Ordinarily, however, before we know it we're scrambling to put the other person back together again, rushing to remind them of all the gifts in their life, imparting spiritual techniques and philosophies to provide a larger perspective, and admonishing them to "get over it" and "focus on the positive," all in the attempt to convince them that everything will be better soon and it will all turn out okay.

It is so natural to want to help another and lessen their pain. There is nothing wrong with this intention and employing whatever skillful means we have to bring relief, including sharing our own wisdom and experience. We need not shame or pathologize the movement toward reducing unwanted symptoms and disturbing emotions.

But let us be sure to keep our eyes open. In the activity of prioritizing relief, we might recognize a subtle aggression in our insistence that the other come out of their immediate experience and into the one we believe they should be having instead, especially if that desired state will keep us out of some very vulnerable territory within ourselves. Even as we wish them peace instead of agitation, joy instead of heartbreak, or clarity instead of confusion (clearly a very noble intention), it is possible we are being called into deeper territory. There may be a profound wisdom in the symptoms, an important communication from psyche and from the heart, which is seeking safe passage in the intersubjective field between.[1] In the spirit of open inquiry, we may discover how much of our "fixing" activity arises not from true compassion for the other but from an unresolved relationship with the darkness within.

Possibly the kindest thing we can offer our suffering friend is to sit in the charged energy with them, holding their experience and staying close, removing the burden that they come out of their pain, feel better, transform, or heal in order for us to stay near. This doesn't mean we don't deeply wish their suffering to end; of course we do. But it does mean we are willing to slow down and cultivate a skillful, empathic awareness of what the situation truly calls for. To do so requires that we drop into the wisdom of the body, become more

---

1. I want to thank psychoanalyst and philosopher Robert Stolorow (and his colleagues) for his articulation of the intersubjective field and its relevance in clinical work.

deeply rooted in the heart, and open to the nonconventional intelligence buried within their process. When we prioritize the urgency of relief over the slowness of presence, it is very easy to overlook the dark yet pregnant creativity and guidance that is seeking to emerge. In ways they may not be able to articulate in a moment of pain and confusion, their deepest longing may be to have their experience held rather than "cured," to know that there is someone on this planet who can truly *feel* them, as they are, and that they do not need to become someone else to maintain the connection. Someone who believes in them and the innate intelligence of their experience, who can model and mirror trust in the face of confusion and is willing to stay with them as the wisdom unfolds. As we turn to embrace *our own* unmet disappointment, grief, and despair, we remove the burden from others to care for this material on our behalf, which they cannot do, despite the most genuine, heartfelt intention on their part. Withdrawing this projection is an immense act of kindness that seeds the relational field with presence and compassion.

As we learn to trust and rest in the innate wisdom contained in our present experience exactly as it is, we discern that love is a movement of the totality. It is whole, never partial, and is thundering and alive even in the darkness. In the core of the fear, sadness, grief, and despair there is something real attempting to break through the dream of partiality. But what this is may never support our cultural and spiritual fantasies of a life of certainty, invulnerability, and permanent happy feelings. We can begin to embrace the radical possibility that even depression, anxiety, heartbreak, and rage are appropriate responses to a world that has forgotten, and to a person's embodied loss of meaning, purpose, and connection. These responses are not pathological but have their own purity and are valid expressions of psyche and the heart. But we must reorganize our perception in order to attune to this level of unfolding intelligence.

From the perspective of wholeness, every inner experience is worthy of our attention, ultimately workable, and a pathway back home into presence. From within this new orientation (which may be a bit disorienting at first), the idea of a particular feeling being an "obstacle" falls away and is replaced by a deepening curiosity to know ourselves at the most subtle levels. From the center of what you are, it is then seen that life is not only the joy and the sweetness. At times it will arrive seething out of the darkness to reorder the status quo and shake the very foundation of what you thought you knew to be true. In this surging of your inner family,[2] the transformative nature of your experience will be revealed and the portals to aliveness will appear as they are: infinite. The path is everywhere, even (especially) in the places where we least expect it.

May you stay close to your suffering and the suffering of others, careful not to cut it too quickly, remaining curious and available to the wisdom as it unfolds in unanticipated ways. Before you rush to discard the disturbing symptoms, open to the full-spectrum nature of love in all its forms, turn toward it, and finally see what it has to say.

Only Love in Disguise

What is the hidden part of ourselves we call the "shadow"?[3] Those unwanted aspects of the personality that we spend so much time avoiding in the attempt to maintain the outward persona we have created? Many of us have come to intuit just how exhausting this self-maintenance project truly is: disowning and sequestering the darker (and often more creative) aspects of our personality while cultivating and leading with those parts we wish others to see and identify with us. Especially for those of us interested in things like spirituality and healing, we can see how much energy it requires to keep up the con-

---

2. Heartfelt acknowledgment to Richard Schwartz and his articulation of Internal Family Systems therapy, and his poetic description of our inner parts, complexes, and subpersonalities.

3. I would like to acknowledge the profound work of the great Swiss psychiatrist C. G. Jung, who gave us the concept of the "shadow" and developed its modern-day understanding and relevance in the lives of those interested in inner work, psychological growth, and emotional maturity.

ditioned identities of the spiritual one, the wise one, the one who has figured something out, and the one who has transcended it all. While much of this activity is natural and hardwired, many are discovering that this level of life management has a way of cutting into the sense of fresh, naked aliveness that they so profoundly long for.

Throughout this book, when I use the words "shadow," "unwanted," or "abandoned," I am referring to those feelings, emotions, and parts of ourselves that we very intelligently disconnected, disassociated, and split off from in order to maintain the critical tie to the attachment figures around us. The shadow consists of all those aspects, both positive *and* negative, that we were not able to provide a home for as they arose in our experience and threatened our bonds with others, or otherwise led to a flooding of anxiety and dysregulating overwhelm in our sensitive brains and nervous systems.

For example, if every time we felt sad and expressed this sadness, it resulted in anger and distance from Dad, or generated anxiety in Mom, we learned very quickly that *sadness was unsafe*. If we were somehow able to disembody and place the sadness outside our awareness when it threatened to manifest, we could effectively avoid the rejection and untoward reactions from our environment. This developed capacity of dissociation kept us safe and as connected as possible to the care, attention, and affection we so critically needed as young children in our families of origin. But it simultaneously had the undesired effect of cutting us off from an important dimension of our experience, creating a split in our self-identity, and divided us against ourselves in ways that continue to produce suffering and struggle as adults.[4] Over time, then, whenever sadness arises (a completely ordinary, valid, and normal occasion in the life of any human being), we engage in a variety of avoidant strategies to quarantine the sadness from our conscious experience, distance ourselves from it, and do whatever it takes to refrain from *appearing* sad to others. Because the expression

---

4. I want to thank psychotherapist Bruce Tift for helping me to under-stand experientially the nature of this split, the adaptive function it played, and the importance of exploring it in a somatically grounded way.

of sadness has become associated with aggression, rejection, or a flood of anxiety, we will (usually unconsciously) pretend we are not sad, shame ourselves if sadness arises, talk ourselves out of it, pontificate on how grateful we are instead, or engage in a variety of defensive behaviors to keep it at bay. Obviously, this is not the best recipe for a healthy, mature intimacy, and has a way of wreaking havoc in our interpersonal relationships.

In developing these strategies, we were not *getting rid* of the sadness, but only burying it deeper into the unconscious, where it *will* be sure to leak out in a variety of less-than-conscious ways, in the form of "symptoms" of all kinds, relational conflict, and a growing sense of unease, restlessness, disconnection, and fatigue. The flatness that many report may come from a lifetime of abandoning their inner experience and splitting off from parts of themselves that they associated early on with unworkable states of anxiety and dysregulation. If repressing and stuffing the sadness (feel free to substitute whatever emotion was disallowed in your early environment) eliminated it at the deepest levels, this approach would be an expression of wisdom and skillful means. But the reality is that denying these aspects not only doesn't make them go away, but it keeps us organized *around* them, spinning around a central axis.[5] We continue to remain in relationship with them, though in a way that is fragmented and for the most part outside conscious awareness, where we are unable to integrate and make use of their underlying energy as fuel for our own healing (and the healing of others). Many I speak with continue to wonder why they feel cut off from life but can never quite pinpoint the cause. This ongoing, chronic activity of dissociation is often the culprit. The remedy to this may be obvious but requires ongoing work that is not easy—that of re-embodying, re-owning, working through, and integrating what has been placed into the unconscious and is

---

5. Deep appreciation to psychotherapist Bruce Tift, who helped me to explore the reality of this organization and its developmental origin in dissociation from disturbing feeling states.

one of the essential (nonnegotiable) practices on any mature path of awakening and healing.

For each of us, there were certain features of our experience—feelings, emotions, ways of being, certain forms of creativity, spiritual longings, and so forth—that, when embodied and expressed, led to the withdrawal of contact, mirroring, and attunement from the caregiving field around us. As a result, when these disavowed aspects of our self-experience inevitably arose in our interactions with others, we became flooded with what felt like survival-level anxiety that we didn't have the capacity to digest. Rather than risk complete breakdown and fragmentation in our developing sense of self, we very intelligently disowned and sequestered this material outside awareness and into the unconscious, into that dimension of our psychic experience called "the shadow."

In response to the anxiety that accompanied the shadow material, we brought forward a variety of defensive strategies in the attempt to care for ourselves and prevent the full-scale overwhelm that our inner disquiet foretold. It took a tremendous amount of energy and creativity to isolate this material outside our conscious awareness, a developmental capacity that most achieve around the ages of four or five. Even though these strategies were critical in preserving the integrity of our sense of self—as well as, in some cases, our actual psychic or physical survival—they did not dissolve this material or heal it in any complete or ongoing way. We were able to manage it and keep it from overwhelming the psyche, but it remains active in an unconscious form, operating under the surface. It will continue to seek the light of conscious awareness until its reintegration, usually in less-than-conscious ways that get us into trouble and generate unnecessary suffering, struggle, and conflict for ourselves and others.

We need only look to our intimate relationships as very vivid reminders of that which remains unresolved within us. Owing to the power of intimacy to constellate this material and bring it into the here and now, relationship might be seen as the royal road to the unconscious, a modern-day temple and crucible in which split-off, dissociated material may be most skillfully illuminated and worked through. Especially as we allow another to matter to us, let them into our hearts, and assume the risks that vulnerable, exposed, embodied intimacy always requires, we can count on this material to vividly present itself as it longs for holding and metabolization. As nearly all of our early wounding arose within interpersonal contexts, it makes sense that it will be most powerfully activated (as well as untangled) within a relational field. Many of us have experienced this, often the hard way, in our journeys as lovers, partners, parents, children, close friends, and clients in therapy. We all know the experience of having someone we care about say something rather innocuous, or fail to respond right away or in the way we'd like, only to be flooded seconds later with unexplainable and seemingly irrational feelings of fear, rage, abandonment, and rejection.

The "unwanted," then, are those archaic organizing beliefs and their associated bodily feelings and emotional conclusions that, when arising in the here and now, trigger a subtle (or not so subtle) outpouring of anxiety and sense of urgency. Things just do not feel safe. While on some level we may sense that our terror is not rational, this does very little to calm the storm. Something is happening in our bodies that is primal and not subject to logical analysis. In the language of neuroscience, the cool, relaxed, slow wisdom of the prefrontal cortex is "hijacked" by the urgent, irrational, speedy reactivity of the amygdala. It is clear we must respond and we spin into motion, usually by way of seeking regulation through the ancient pathways of fight, flight, or freeze. It is the undoing and reorganization of these habitual pathways—seeding them with empathic, attuned, compassionate presence—that is one of the core essences of this work.

Rather than turn toward the unmet unknown as it surges into conscious awareness—and confront with loving awareness the very shaky, restless, and claustrophobic energy that surrounds it—we move away, reenacting the young strategies and avoidant behaviors that were designed to return us to safe ground. The challenge, of course, is that by not directly and consciously working with this material as adults with capacities we once did not possess, we keep it alive, burning within us until it is inevitably triggered yet again. We condition ourselves that it is still not workable, that staying with it will overwhelm us as it did at an earlier time, and that urgently seeking relief is our only option. It is as if we've stepped into a time machine and have returned to our lives as young children, doing whatever we must to put the fire out, even if it means abandoning and splitting off from ourselves, attacking our own self-integrity and practicing violence toward our own ripening vulnerability. It is this chronic abandonment of ourselves over time that can lead to a variety of symptoms such as anxiety, depression, flatness, and dissatisfaction of all kinds.[6] This primordial discontent—or core, existential anguish—is what the Buddha referred to in his first noble truth.

The unwanted can take form as sadness, rage, loneliness, or shame; or as a deeply embedded sense of unworthiness, fear, rejection, and abandonment. Without realizing how it came to be, we find ourselves convinced that something has gone terribly wrong that we must resolve as soon as possible, lest we decompensate and lose touch with who we are. In these moments, a very powerful practice we can do is to slow down and inquire carefully what it is above all else that we simply *do not want to feel,* that if we were to allow in would overwhelm us, take us out of our window of tolerance, and result in devastating and life-shattering consequences.[7]

We each have a certain feeling or family of feelings that have come to be associated with danger, overwhelm, and unworkable anxiety of all kinds. For example, you don't receive a text when your partner says she will text you; you receive some feedback about your performance

6. Again, deep thanks to psychotherapist Bruce Tift for helping me to more deeply explore the connection between self-abandonment and symptomatology such as panic, anxiety, confusion, and depression.

7. Deep appreciation for psychotherapist Bruce Tift for introducing me to this practice, which has been so helpful for me personally as well as in my clinical work with others.

at work that is obviously unfair; you get into a heated political or religious conversation that constellates profound feelings of rage; you're misunderstood or not seen as you are, critiqued and called out during an argument; your partner bails instead of listening and processing a difficult situation. Someone questions your spiritual realization or calls you a fraud; questions your business ethics or says nasty things about someone you love. All of a sudden it's as if you are four or five years old, back in your family of origin, fighting and fleeing to get out of the burning energy underneath it all—anything to cut into the panic, groundlessness, and sense of impending danger. It's as if the walls are closing around you, it's getting claustrophobic, and there are no means to escape.

The invitation, of course, is to first of all breathe deeply. Slow down and feel your feet on the ground. Soothe the shock to your nervous system in whatever way works best for you—take a walk, go out in nature, call a friend, lay your hands on your heart, draw or paint, write in your journal, do some yoga, make yourself a nourishing meal. Once you have calmed a bit, you can slowly begin to invite the previously abandoned material back into your conscious experience, where you can work with it and begin the *gradual* process of training yourself to tolerate, contain, open into, and metabolize it with adult-level capacities you did not have as a young child. This is not easy work, it's not usually going to feel immediately peaceful or blissful, and has a way of initiating all sorts of secondary feelings of unsafety, shame, abandonment, and unworthiness. It is often messy and uncomfortable. But you can do it—one second at a time, two seconds, three seconds, and then rest. You can descend underneath the swirling storyline for just a moment (you can return to it later for reauthoring from a more soothed, grounded place) and stay with what was once impossible to hold. Over time, as you train yourself to stay in this way, you may come to discover a certain freedom that is always present, even as you push yourself into uncomfortable territory. Like any muscle, the more you practice, the more the muscle of empathic attunement will grow and develop, and over time it will become second nature and not require a lot of effort to engage. I never cease to be astonished at how those I have worked with have evolved this capacity over time—not years, but weeks and months. Even those with the most profound, deeply embedded trauma and attachment wounding—the plasticity of the human brain and the courage of the human heart to seed new pathways are outrageous and truly awesome.

The reality is that you need not abandon yourself any longer. You are worthy of care, holding, and attunement that you perhaps did not receive earlier on your developmental journey. While the template of self-abandonment and aggression toward your experience may be alive and well in your neural net, you can rewire and reorganize the pathways. It may seem impossible to stay with what *feels* unbearable, but slowly, you can do it. But it does take practice, courage, curiosity, and the cultivating of radical new levels of kindness toward yourself. For many, this sort of self-care is completely foreign and was never modeled in their families of origin, but the good news is that it can be learned and you can start exactly where you are. If you are sequestering important aspects of who you are—isolating them into the shadow and out of conscious, holding awareness—you may always feel half alive, slightly flat and down, and not fully here, even if things are going relatively well in your life.

The entirety of who and what you are is welcome in the miracle of the here and now, and it is only through a fully embodied and compassionate relationship with *all* of you that you can discover and embody the aliveness you so deeply long for. By doing this work over time, you can discover that the shadow, in some paradoxical way, is only love in disguise, come to reintroduce you to the field of space, warmth, and presence that you are. By turning back toward yourself, you lay a new pathway of empathic attunement, hold and metabolize the energies of the somatic and emotional worlds, and become available to yourself and others in wise and loving new ways.

An Unexpected Tour Guide

So how do we make contact with the shadow, with those disowned aspects of ourselves that we have lost touch with along the way, or those more creative aspects that have not yet found the right conditions in which to emerge? At times, we may sense that the mislaid pieces of our psyche and soma are nearby, arising from within, while at other times it can feel as if they are coming at us from the outside. As triggers, hooks, and psychosomatic "symptoms" of all kinds, they can come on display in the most unanticipated ways, leaving us feeling as if we are being attacked by an enemy force.

As we practice turning back toward that which we've lost contact with—holding the orphaned ones of the somatic and emotional worlds—we come face to face with an unexpected truth: that despite appearances to the contrary, the pieces and parts are hidden guides, filled with energy and information. Reorganizing our relationship with the inner family takes practice as well as courage, patience, and curiosity. More than that, what may be most important is the willingness to become our own best friend and practice kindness toward whatever appears. Learning to befriend our experience is a lost art and a capacity that is often overlooked or trivialized. Yes, it might sound trite, too simple, or a little like a spiritual cliché; however, in practice it is a revolution. Opening our hearts to our suffering is not something most of us have been trained in, and it can feel impossible or even crazy to attempt. But within an environment of self-compassion, we can lay down a new pathway that will replace the habitual reenactment of an earlier environment of aggression, shame, and misattunement.

As I mentioned earlier (and will continue to reinforce), it is important that we cultivate the intention to become more interested in the *truth of our experience* than in our demand to *find relief* from our symptoms. It is natural to not want to feel pain, but if our primary concern is relief, we may not be able to allow ourselves to get close enough to the intelligence and creativity that are attempting to break through. As long as there is a subtle agenda to "meet" the material because we believe it is the quickest way to eradicate and escape it, we subtly keep the neural pathways of aggression and misattunement alive, which will interfere with the slower, intimate, and kind encounter that is required. This is not a journey of perfection, but one of wholeness. We can count on these hidden agendas and dynamics to come into play as we do this work. Rather than shaming or judging ourselves for the resurgence of our protective strategies, we can use their appearance as mindfulness bells, as invitations into deeper inquiry. At some point on the path, you may even find yourself *welcoming* the opportunity to be triggered and activated by this ancient material, as it is no longer received as an enemy or obstacle but as a dynamic harbinger of integration. We cannot, of course, pretend this is the case if it is not real for us—out of some sense that this would be a more evolved or "spiritual" response to the material—and we must always remain truthful and authentic as to our actual experience and capacities. Again, the goal is not perfection but wholeness, genuineness, and an uncompromising commitment to what is most true.

To engage with this work at the most profound and transformative levels, we must cultivate a deep love for what is most true *now*. Not what *was* true or what our teacher, therapist, partner, or friend *believes* is true, but what is most alive when we make direct contact with our experience exactly as it is. It can take some practice to discover this for ourselves, as the truth of our immediate experience will continue to deepen and become more subtle over time, as the journey of the heart itself is endless. We must descend underneath our conditioned history knowing that the first responses in the form of thought and emotion are often learned and habitual; as we return over and over into the body and the felt sense of our experience, we will be able to access these deeper and more subtle levels of information and guidance.

The process of sequestering material into the shadow is most often discussed as a historical event that took place at some point in the past, but as we inquire into the moment-to-moment unfolding of our immediate experience, we discover that while our strategies of dissociation may have historical origins, they must actually be *maintained* in the present.[8] This is often hard to allow in: the notion that we are somehow actively working to keep our defensive strategies alive. It is important to remember that this is not something we are doing consciously, because we are bad or unspiritual or neurotic people. Rather than viewing this discovery as evidence of some sort of failure on our part, we can use it as fuel to know ourselves at deeper and deeper levels. It can be very liberating to discover that without this maintenance, these strategies will fall away over time as they simply are no longer needed. From this perspective, healing is not so much a matter of "letting go" of unwanted material as it is of allowing it to *let go of us* when it is no longer necessary, to let it dissolve on its own—not from effort and struggle on our part but out of the nondoing of no longer maintaining it in the present.

Each time we deny or split off from unwanted aspects of ourselves, we reinforce the necessity of our avoidant strategies and keep them alive and operating in the background. From a historical perspective, these strategies emerged not because we were crazy, lost, or had fallen prey to some sort of personality disorder or psychotic break, but in order to protect us from an overwhelming onslaught of dysregulating cognitions, feelings, and sensations that we did not have the developmental capacity to tolerate, contain, and metabolize. As adults, we have access to faculties we did not have at an earlier time. An opportunity has been given for us to turn back toward the displaced inner family and call the members back home.

Until we are able to be in an attuned, mindful, and compassionate relationship with these parts, they *will* express themselves unconsciously—as symptoms, conflict, feelings, dreams, fantasies, and the vivid display of the "others" that come into our lives. This expression seems to be nonnegotiable, as this material does not simply pass away as a result of our choice to disembody from it.

With respect to the journey of integration, it is important to note that the "other" refers not only the *other people* in our lives (the

---

8. Gratitude to psychotherapist Bruce Tift for helping me to deepen my experiential realization of this truth in my own experience.

so-called "external other"), but also the "internal other": those aspects of *ourselves* we have disconnected from. All of those unmet parts, partly felt emotions, and unprocessed feelings make up the internal other that we will at times be called to reenter into relationship with. In a larger, more collective or spiritual sense, the "great other" is another level yet and may be perceived as the entirety of the phenomenal world itself, as an image of a god or goddess, or as seen and unseen messengers, symbols, visions, and archetypes that appear in countless forms, providing an endless stream of information and guidance for the journey ahead. But in order to consciously work with this level of "other," our perception must be cleansed. This purification occurs by way of wisdom and inquiry on the one hand and kindness, compassion, and surrender on the other.

There are a number of ways to access this material and cultivate a present-time relationship with it. One of the most provocative entryways is to ask yourself, Who in your life triggers you the most? Who is it that, just by being themselves, pushes your buttons, catalyzes an eruption of emotion, annoys you, irritates you, and leaves you fuming? Who more than anyone seems to have some secret power over you, shaking you to your core and throwing you off kilter just by a glance, a few words, or the way they walk or carry themselves?

Once you identify this person, you can then inquire—carefully, slowly, and with a new sort of curiosity and self-kindness—and see what it is about them that hooks you so intensely. Specifically, what qualities in them activate and trigger that burning, claustrophobic, seething discomfort? What makes you want to run for the hills, reach out to attack, or curl up in the fetal position on the floor?

Once you get a sense of what these characteristics are, and what beliefs, emotions, and feelings their expression brings alive in you, you can then explore how you may have disconnected from these same qualities in yourself. In what ways have you lost contact with these aspects such that you are reminded in an unexpected way when they appear around you in the behavior of others? One of the really creative things about the psyche is that we tend to attract others into our lives who embody exactly those qualities that we have disowned in ourselves. How annoying. How amazing. This is very challenging territory that is often quite humbling to confront.

This same process also works with those you most admire, become infatuated with, even envious of. Rather than get caught up in the surface personality of these people, you can ask what *qualities* they embody that you may have disowned in yourself. Maybe they are artistic, independent, or able to express healthy aggression, or are able to lead with their vulnerability in an admirable way. Or they are well spoken, intelligent, humble, attractive, wise, kind, successful, or insightful. As you begin to home in on the qualities that activate you and draw you to the "other," you can then explore the thoughts, emotions, and sensations that arise as you open to these dimensions in yourself.

There are likely some very intelligent, adaptive reasons why you chose to disconnect from those qualities in others that annoy (or fascinate) you. If in your family of origin, you were met with misattunement, aggression, or anxiety in response to the expression of certain aspects of your developing personality, you learned to split off from these attributes in your best effort to take care of yourself. You are wired to do whatever it takes to hold on to and maintain whatever limited degree of affection, contact, and mirroring was available. In a way that is both intelligent and creative, you cultivated aspects that were not necessarily native to you while abandoning others in order to keep the tie alive. It was simply not an option to consciously choose to act in a way that might sever the connection. As I noted earlier, however, these abandoned qualities remain buried deep within you—in your body, your cell tissue, and your nervous system—and may not rest until you receive them back into conscious awareness.

In other words, those qualities that repulse, trigger, or infatuate you represent parts you have deserted into the shadow and that to this day you work creatively (though usually unconsciously) to keep out of awareness through avoidant activity of all kinds. When these unmet parts and pieces are triggered in a variety of unique relational configurations—which they inevitably will —your defensive strategies will kick in, resulting in a whole range of anxiety-related feelings and bodily sensations. From this perspective, the anxiety itself is a heads-up (a mindfulness bell) that material you're usually able to keep unconscious is now threatening to erupt into conscious awareness. Not to work against you but as an opportunity for integration. In this way, even the anxiety itself can be seen as a harbinger or forerunner of the realization of wholeness.

You can count on those in your life to relentlessly remind you of what you've disowned in yourself. While this may appear to be bad news, it offers a unique opportunity to reconnect with the lost parts and provide safe haven where they can reclaim their rightful place in the landscape of your inner family. In order to reframe the activation in this way, it is vital that you cultivate the intention to know what is true more than *anything*: more than feeling good, more than appearing spiritual, more than being untouchable, more than being happy all the time, and more than needing to keep up the appearance that you always have it together. You can make a commitment that each time you find yourself irritated, annoyed, triggered, enamored, or enchanted, you will stay close. Sacred data and information are being presented that are ripe for your holding and attunement, a rich opportunity to befriend and take care of yourself in a radically new way.

The invitation during these times is to move *toward* what is coming up so that it can be met, at first for very short periods of time. Move toward, and then rest. Move toward, and then rest. Touch, and go. Push yourself a bit, but not so much that you traumatize yourself or become fragmented or fall too far outside your window of tolerance. It can help to do this work with a trusted, attuned other who knows you well and is familiar with your core vulnerabilities and defensive organization so they can help you dance in the middle, neither letting you off the hook prematurely nor falling into unproductive reenactments of shame, blame, and self-aggression.

Yes, it can be annoying. But these "inner" and "outer" others are your true teachers, pure wisdom guides sent from beyond to remind you of something important that you've forgotten. In this sense, they are unexpected tour guides into your true nature, and for this they are worthy of honor and a few moments of your undivided, warm attention.

There is never an end to the path of the heart. There is no final, safe landing place, no mythical fairy-tale ending, no completion, and no resolution. Only endless unfolding. Your heart is endless.

2

Into the Holding Environment

Rest in the Mystery of Being

THERE IS A PRIMORDIAL LONGING WIRED INTO US AS INFANTS TO BE seen: for our subjective experience to be held, mirrored, and validated by another. In an environment of empathic attunement, we are able to rest in the mystery of who and what we are. Grounded in this environment, it is safe to explore unstructured states of being and engage courageously and skillfully with the world around us. We can take risks in relationship, choose at times to lead with our vulnerability, and explore deeply in the realization that we are both separate *and* connected. We can flow with our separateness and then change course and fully embrace our nature as utterly interconnected. We can move between these realms seamlessly and with our hearts open. In this sense, love is an alive field of presence in which our subjectivity can unfold into more integrated levels of organization.

From this perspective, "I love you" equals "I allow you." I allow you to have your own experience—to organize and make meaning in the way that you do—and I will offer you my presence and warmth even if I do not understand you or agree with your perception or conclusions. Even if your being yourself triggers within me surges of emotion, vulnerability, and unmetabolized feeling, my vow is to allow you to be what you are. While I will not allow you to abuse me or to act violently or break the agreements and boundaries we have established, I will allow your *inner* experience to be what it is. Even if I cannot allow your behavior, I will not demand that the flow of feeling or emotion within you be reorganized to fit my own preferences, hopes, or fears. While I may turn from you in the external world, I will not turn my heart off—because I love you. This refusal to turn our hearts off is not something we are asked to perfect and then shame ourselves when we inevitably "fail." Rather, it is an intention and an aspiration, to care deeply for ourselves and for others as we are able.

Many have heard the term *holding environment,* introduced by the great British analyst Donald Winnicott, to describe this field of presence. Any effective holding environment consists of the essential qualities of good *contact* and an ideal amount of *space.* Through making close, empathic contact with another as they are, and offering a spacious home in which their experience can unfold, we become vehicles of love in action. We are willing to allow the other to matter to us, to care deeply about them, and to take a risk in moving toward them while simultaneously offering ourselves these same qualities in a system of mutual interaction. We seek intimacy with the other and their unfolding experience as it is, but without coming so close that we lose perspective and become emotionally fused. In this sacred middle territory—in between the extremes of cold, passive, disinterested witnessing and sticky, unboundaried identification—we bestow the gift of our attuned presence.

Simultaneously, in addition to making good contact, we permeate the other and their subjective experience—as well as the relational field we are a part of with them—with the offering of pure space. In this context, space isn't something that we "give" or "do"; it is what we *are*. By resting in the organic space of being, we plant the seeds of a cosmic trust that their experience is valid, that we do not need them to transform in order for us to stay close. We commit to not flooding them with our requirements and agendas, but will honor their unique process and path by being there for them if (and only if) we are needed. We will not impinge upon their journey, we will allow them to fail and to succeed, and we will walk side by side with them into the dark *and* the light. But we will not try to make the journey for them. We will not give them answers to questions that are theirs, nor will we protect them from falling apart when that is what love has in store for them. We will do whatever we can to support their unique and unprecedented path of individuation. But we will allow them to walk it alone, to fall to the ground and get back up, to know the full spectrum of the opportunity they have been provided.

Additionally, we can give *ourselves* these same qualities of good contact and attuned space. In many ways, this is one of the essences of true meditation: to meet our immediate experience exactly as it is, in a warm but provocative, curious, and intimate embrace, without any agenda that it be shifted, transformed, changed, or healed. As we deepen in our practice, we come to discover that what we *already* are—as warm, open awareness itself—is in fact the ultimate holding environment. We do not *become* our true nature in time, or produce it by way of process or struggle. Rather, we train ourselves to recognize, open into, and participate in it, in ever deepening and more creative ways. In this way, we discover that we are *already* held and do not need to seek this holding by way of any external form, or through any inner process in time. In other words, it has *already* happened.

While as infants we depended upon another to provide the environment in which we could rest in primordial beingness, it is actually always here. From this perspective, we have *always* been held and could never *not* be held, for this ultimate holding is wired into us as our true nature. It is the substance that forms the synapses in our brains, the cells in our hearts, and the breath that passes through us. It is not something we will achieve one day by way of a searching and exhausting journey of self-improvement. It is not conditioned or caused. While we can cultivate a profound appreciation for the ways in which the "other" can remind us of this, it is an important milestone along the way to come to the embodied discovery of the ultimate ground of this holding.

We may not always understand our experience—and it may never conform to our ideas, hopes, and dreams about the life we were "meant to live"—but we can come to trust that it is unfolding according to a unique blueprint that emerges out of the unseen hand of love. Let us make the most radical commitment to no longer abandon ourselves, exiting into our conditioned stories and unkind judgments, and instead inquire with space and a fiery sort of compassion into the habitual belief that there is something fundamentally wrong with us. As we open our eyes and our hearts to the always, already present holding environment that is our true nature, we behold the drop of grace that pours through the eyes of everyone we meet, including that unknown precious one we see when we look in the mirror.

Archaeologists of Love

As little ones we came to know ourselves through relationship, as our unique nature was mirrored back to us by those we interacted with. We carry this blueprint into our lives as adults, and even though this longing often falls out of conscious awareness, in most cases it doesn't seem to ever truly go away. Even as we evolve spiritually and increasingly disidentify with what is not ultimately true—transcending and including what is partial and less than whole—this longing still somehow dances and plays within and around us. For better or worse, it seems to have its own way of coming back into conscious awareness from time to time: in the dream world as we sleep, by way of imagination and fantasy, as we find ourselves in awe of the colors of an early evening sunset, as we step into exposure and risk in a new relationship, as we gaze into the eyes of a newborn baby.

When our subjective experience is empathically held, accurately attuned to, and provided sanctuary in which to flower, we come to a natural place of rest, harmony, and homeostasis. From this spacious ground of being, we are free to allow others to matter, to take the risk of being ourselves, and to abundantly participate in the world around us. We know that by assuming these risks we will likely expose ourselves to an avalanche of feeling and sensation, unexpected heartbreak and disappointment, and penetrating vulnerability. But somehow we are willing to move forward, knowing that this risk is the doorway into the intimacy and aliveness we so deeply long for. Holding back, while tempting at times, is no longer a real option, at least not in any sustainable way.

From the perspective of this sort of holding and attunement, when we truly "love" another, we offer them a field of permission in which they can fully be themselves, and their unique expression can come forward and bless those around them. They no longer must become someone different in order for us to stay near and open to them. As we step deeper into the crucible together, we realize in an embodied, real-time way that the "other" is not (and never has been) a mere *object* in our own awareness: someone who may or may not be able to meet our needs, someone we "like" or "dislike," or someone who might be able to take care of our unlived lives for us. No longer is the other an *object* that we project all our disowned qualities onto, or someone we look to in order to take care of our boredom, emptiness, and missing inspiration. Rather, they are experienced as an actual *subject* in their own right, yearning to make meaning of their experience, just like us. Longing to feel fully alive, discover purpose and connection, and live a life of true freedom and creativity, just like us. To allow in the implications of this—that the others in our lives are *subjects* and not *objects*—is to rewire our experience of the relational field in its entirety. This is a profound developmental achievement that has ramifications beyond what we might imagine.

In addition to meeting another in this way, we can hold *ourselves* in such an environment, allow ourselves to be what we are, and offer this same permission field for *our* experience to unfold according to that unique blueprint we came here with. In so doing, we create the conditions for presence and creativity to move through us (releasing tremendous energy to share our gifts with others), discover new and deeper levels of meaning and purpose, and engage in the world guided by wise, compassionate action. On an intuitive level, we know that the degree to which we allow and love ourselves is the degree to which we will be able to allow and love others, especially those aspects of our self we find disturbing, "unspiritual," shameful, and otherwise less than ideal. We are invited into the shadowy, previously sequestered regions of the heart, the psyche, and the body to find life—in *all* of the places where it is hiding and seeking the light of our holding and awareness. In this sense we become archaeologists of love, exploring and excavating it from the realms where it has been buried.

The invitation before each of us is to create a sanctuary in which *all* parts of the inner family can be illuminated and find safe passage on their journey to wholeness. By providing a true holding environment for ourselves and for others—guided by the qualities of good contact and adequate space—we step through the doorway into the sacred world, one that is consecrated with the holiness of awareness, aliveness, and pure creativity.

A Cure Through Love

Freud, in a letter to Carl Jung, said, "Psychoanalysis is in essence a cure through love." It hurts so much when those around us are suffering, but what can we do? How can we help? What is the most effective way to respond to their sadness, restlessness, hopelessness, and confusion? We hear that to truly love another is the most powerful form of healing, but what does this actually mean?

When you are with a friend who is struggling, listen carefully not only to their words but to the hidden language that is emerging from their hearts. Make contact with their longing to be met, to feel felt, to be heard and received exactly as they are. Don't fuse with them or come so close that you are engulfed and lose perspective, but enter into their experience with discernment, empathy, and presence. Close, but not too close. Touch and go. *Intimacy without fusing.* Sustained empathic connection without impingement. There is an art to exploring and working from this transformative middle territory, which you can learn and practice with clear intention.

Once you set aside your requirement that their experience change according to the dictates of the unmet "other" within you, a field of sanctuary will open in which their inner world can unfold and clarify, free of any pressure that they become someone other than who they are in the moment. You can then join with them in a fierce sort of trusting in the validity of their experience *as it is,* neither of you willing any longer to pathologize or shame the uninvited guests of grief, despair, hopelessness, and confusion. Yes, it might require that you get a bit messy, that you be willing to confront your own unresolved material in the process, but the call is into *intimacy with what is* as the ultimate medicine. In this way, you work together with your dear friend to provide a warm, attuned home in which the entirety of their inner experience can unfold and illuminate in the great space of being. From this ground of attuned presence, wise, skillful, and compassionate action will organically emerge.

When we are held in this way, our nervous systems down-regulate, our minds soften, our hearts open, and we come into a primordial sort of rest. While our true nature as pure, open awareness is the ultimate holding environment, as relational beings we are wired to rest within a relational matrix. To enter into this field with another, woven and constructed by the alchemical substances of presence and of space, is one of the great secrets of the intersubjective world. Never forget the transformative power of just one moment of pure kindness and what it can do in a person's life. For it is the activity of revolution.

When we allow ourselves to become the vast space in which the other's experience can be exactly what it is—without expecting them see the world as we do or have only those feelings or perceptions we are comfortable with—we find ourselves in a crucible outside the ordinary and the conventional. There, the wounds of the heart are metabolized and previously unresolved psychic, emotional, and somatic tangles are unwound, illuminated, and reorganized according to a new blueprint crafted of empathy, attunement, and compassion.

While we'll never know exactly what Freud meant in his letter to Jung, I like to think (fantasize?) that it was something along these lines.

What If Love Doesn't Feel Safe?

What if the movement of love never feels consistently safe? What if it was never meant to give you that but comes pouring into your life offering something much more radical, majestic, and creative? What if love continues to appear in your life, in all its forms and expressions, not to offer security and certainty but to reveal wholeness?

What if no matter how many profound insights you have, how many amazingly powerful awakening experiences you collect, or how convinced you become that you have it all together, you will always be at risk of further heartbreak, deflation, and revelation? In the bedroom of the beloved, there is always more humbling to come, as we are all beginners there. There are no experts, no masters, and no final landing place where you are guaranteed a life without vulnerability ... for the beloved has no interest in that. It is by way of your vulnerability that she is able to reach you and fill you from within with her essence. In that crucible where the opposites are at play, the rug is being pulled out from underneath us in an ongoing way, with our personas falling away one by one as they burn up in the fire of pure seeing. Out of this highly-charged and creative field, it is revealed once and for all that your raw, broken openness is not weakness and your sensitivity is not something to be transcended, but portals through which the sacred world is able to come into form.

Of course, there is nothing wrong with having a preference for the experience of safety in relationship with others and the world. It is an act of kindness to demand that others act in a safe way around and toward you. The *feeling* of safety, however, like all feelings, very organically comes and goes, and there will be times when we must move in the world, engage with others, and attend to our own bodies and hearts despite the fact that we do not *feel* safe. To be clear, I am not referring to *physical* safety here, which you will *always and absolutely* demand. Rather, I'm inviting an inquiry into the often unconscious cultural and spiritual contention that the inner life (including our spiritual practice as well as our intimate relationships) is supposed to always *feel* safe.[1]

From this largely unexamined belief, we very naturally conclude that if we do not feel safe, something is wrong with us, we have failed or fallen short, and we must act urgently to return into feelings of safety. The invitation is to discover if it is *actually* true that if we *feel* unsafe this means we actually *are* unsafe. We must explore whether it is an *accurate* perception that we must first feel safe before we can fully show up in our life, lead with our vulnerability, take a risk in relationship or with our work, and otherwise participate with an open heart. This is an inquiry that each of us must engage for ourselves to discover what is most true in the here and now. We must confront this unconscious belief that traveling the path of the heart is supposed to feel safe, and that somehow as we awaken we will transcend the very alive feelings of crushing heartbreak, penetrating deflation, and piercing disappointment of all kinds, that awakening in fact implies a narrowing of the emotional spectrum altogether.

Turning back into the broken and the dark may never *feel safe,* but we must discover if this is still a requirement as it was when we were young children. There is no right or wrong answer here and you cannot take anyone else's word for it: you must see for yourself. Don't assume you know what is most true as your conditioned history is sure to be there to greet you as you begin this inquiry. With curiosity,

---

1. I want to acknowledge psychotherapist Bruce Tift for helping me to clarify this discernment in my own life and clinical work with others.

courage, patience, and compassion, you can slowly drop underneath your history and into the unprecedented aliveness of the here and now, into the body and the felt sense of the situation, where new information and new data may be found.

In this inquiry, you may discover that while safety is a perfectly valid experience and one that you naturally prefer, perhaps it isn't safety that you are *ultimately* after. What if the demand to always feel safe was not actually in support of the deepest longing within you, and was instead an unconscious defense against the aliveness you were sent here to know and embody? What if the demand for safety is a remnant of the past and holding you back from the life of intimacy, connection, and gratitude that you so genuinely long for? What if it isn't safety that will provide the life of purpose, authenticity, and meaning you were born to realize, and instead you were wired for a transforming, reordering, burning sort of wholeness? Perhaps the depth and aliveness you long for will not always feel safe, for it is too vast to limit itself to any one particular feeling state. And at times love will employ the feeling state you might call "unsafe" in order to awaken one of its qualities within you.

In what ways are you waiting to feel safe, secure, sure, and certain before you allow yourself to step all the way in, fully show up here, and take a risk? To allow your gifts to emerge and to give everything to live what you have discovered is your deepest truth? As long as you are demanding that feelings of safety and security be present before you take action, you will inevitably hold back. And the degree to which this requirement operates within you is the same degree to which you will inevitably place a burden on those around you to act in ways that generate these feelings—which they cannot do for you, at least not on a consistent basis, no matter how much they love you. For your deep psychic sense of safety is not their weight to carry.

As an experiment and ongoing inquiry, you can investigate in a deeply embodied, real-time way—one that is grounded in self-compassion and not in shame and blame—whether you must feel safe in order to move forward in your life and take action based upon what you know to be most true. The deeper you go with this practice, the more you may discover that the truth of what you are is cosmically vast. What you are is that majestic, limitless space in which feelings of safety, unsafety, certainty, and uncertainty emerge dancing as one: not as enemies or energies that need to be resolved and healed but as lovers playing and exploring in union. As Whitman reminds us, "I am large, I contain multitudes." In this largeness, safe and unsafe will continue their journey together, with you as their witness, holding them as they each perform their function here.

When you are stripped of unexamined concepts of safety and the known—and of your demand that the movement of love conform to your hopes, fears, and the way you thought it would all turn out—you will be shown what you are. When you no longer require to know what's going to happen next, to somehow remain permanently free of heartbreak and deflation, and to feel safe before you take transforming action in the world, your essence will be revealed.

When the known crumbles away, all that remains is your burning heart. There is nothing more alive than that. There is nothing more sacred than that. There is nothing safer than that.

The Artist of a New World

Something happens and you get triggered. Someone says something, ignores you, or doesn't show up in the way you want and need. You quickly become convinced that no one will *ever* see you as you are, that you will *never* be met, and that you will *always* be misunderstood. Others are not on your side and the world is against you. And on top of that, there is only one explanation at the root of it all: you are unworthy of such contact because something is fundamentally wrong with you.

While you may not be consciously aware of these complexes and organizing principles at work underneath a moment of activation, they are wild and alive nonetheless, functioning outside ordinary awareness.

But if you slow down and cultivate the curiosity to know what is most true, you may discover how deeply your perception is being colored by this family of thoughts, beliefs, and associated feeling states.

In these moments, you are totally hooked. Your body is on fire and you're falling apart. You are shaming, blaming, and raging in all directions. The old voices remind you of how wretched you truly are. The energy is hot and surging through you. There is a panicky, nauseous feeling in your stomach. Your throat is starting to constrict. You are about to collapse, and no one seems to care. Where is your friend or partner, anyway? Nowhere to be found, or semi-there but checked out into his or her own self-absorbed spin. Here we go again.

But wait. Before you fall down the rabbit hole—decompensate, and become lost in the seductive realm of shame, blame, and ruminative thought—breathe deeply from your lower belly. Touch the earth. Feel your heart beating. Return to your body and the aliveness of the here and now. See if things are really as urgent as they seem, and if you can stay close for just a moment before you disembody, go back into the conditioned narrative, and spin out to find relief. The constellation of thought, emotion, and sensation is your new mindfulness bell, a ringing, erupting reminder to take care of yourself in a radically new way. It may feel impossible to cut through and reestablish solid ground, but you are only being asked to attend to *this one moment* that is here, now. Not to take care of a future moment or to clarify a memory from the past. But just *this* moment. Can you care for *this* moment? You can begin wherever you are, no matter what is surging through you, to slow down and surround yourself with the warmth of loving awareness, with the intention to no longer abandon yourself as was required at an earlier time.

Pause, breathe deeply, and bring relief from further fueling of the old storyline of unworthiness. Bring your senses back online. Love yourself enough to stay with the burning sensations, soothe them with your presence, and set aside for a moment the very colorful and seductive narrative about what happened, who is to blame, how wretched you are, how horrible your partner is, and how you have failed once again.

What do you hear? What do you see? What does it feel like to have your feet or your bottom on the ground? Can you touch in with the reality that you are being held by the earth, now, without any sense that you must first deserve this holding, or that you must quickly shift, transform, or heal in order to be held? This is no ordinary moment. The harbingers of integration have appeared. While you may never have much control over what thoughts, feelings, or emotions arrive in a moment of activation, you have a choice as to how you will respond. Recognizing and honoring this choice brings you to the threshold of a new world.

Depending on your early strategies for meeting overwhelm and dysregulation, you flow into motion. While these responses are wired in to your neural net, they are open, flexible, and translucent, awaiting reconfiguration into more integrated and compassionate forms. No matter what is happening, you can start *right now*. You can lay down a new pathway. Over time you can replace aggression with kindness, and abandonment with holding. You can replace rejection with curiosity, and shame with self-care. You can develop a new relationship with your feelings, your emotions, and the beliefs that have become the lenses through which you see your life. You can tell a new story, reauthor and re-imagine who and what you are, and cleanse your perception of limiting, conditioned self-narratives.

You cannot do this all at once, in some wholesale way, but fortunately that is not required. Let go of the pressure to heal yourself, to get awakened, to forgive, to accept, to figure it all out. In *this* moment, you can turn back toward yourself. And then when you become lost again, with kindness, you can return. You only need *this* moment, not a future one, to encode new circuitry. It is not possible to establish a new pathway in the past or in the future, only now. It only takes one moment of meeting your experience with kindness, with space, with presence, instead of abandonment, aggression, and violence. This willingness to return, over and over and over again, will shift your center of gravity over time.

Although the old narratives and emotional strategies emerged as the best ways you knew to care for yourself and make sense of a misattuned early holding environment, you are the artist of a new world. Your canvas is the entirety of your sensitivity and vulnerability, the tenderness of your heart, and the brilliance of your creative body. You can rewrite the story, rewire your nervous system, and find new meaning. It is not easy and will take everything you have ... and more. But it is already written inside you.

It may seem hopeless at times, but you have capacities you did not have as a little one when the original pathways were formed. Call on the seen and unseen worlds to help. Open to the holding and the wisdom of the mountains, the oceans, the stars, and the water around you. You are surrounded now by the heartbeat of the earth. Feel the new pathways emerging.

An Open Field

When you are triggered and your emotional world is crashing down on you, experiment with shifting your awareness out of the *interpretations* of what is happening and into your body, into the life that is surging within you. Your interpretations, while also important to explore, arise from what you *already know.* They have a way of keeping you wedded to your conditioned history and out of the fresh, spontaneous wisdom of the here and now. You may find that your belly, your heart, and your throat are alive with important data, if you will explore them with warmth and awareness, opening the gates to previously hidden guidance that is attempting to reach you. While the narrative is vivid, colorful, and convincingly compelling, it is an act of self-love to slow down and return to immediacy. The storyline will be waiting for you at a later moment, when you have come back online and can engage it with grounded presence and fresh vision.

Allow yourself to travel underneath your conditioned history, your attachment wounding, and the perceptual lenses through which you have come to see yourself, others, and the world. What awaits you is an open field of energy and information—raw, naked, direct experience. This dimension of experience is filled with sacred data, but its wisdom is nonconceptual, which can be frustrating for a mind longing for resolution, relief, and control. What you discover here in this realm does not necessarily provide clarity, solutions, or answers but offers something of tremendous depth and meaning. With practice, you can learn to read the signs of the somatic world, to enter into and receive the creativity and high-voltage guidance they offer.

The old pathway is one of engaging the disturbing energies as enemies coming from the outside, attacking you as obscurations that must quickly be shifted, transformed, cured, and "healed." But as you practice the way of intimacy with your immediate experience, flooding it with curiosity, presence, and warmth, the new way will emerge. *Slowly.* The groove is laid down and strengthened one micro-moment at a time. Each time you turn toward the somatic world with your heart open, guided by self-compassion and holding, the groove deepens.

Every arising feeling, sensation, and moment of activation is an invitation into the completeness that you already are. You are enough, right now. You are worthy of your own presence, right now. You are okay, right now. With the sky and the sun and the moon and the stars as your witness, you are fully alive, now.

The Art of Sacred Return

Though it may seem obvious, there is a profound difference between *feeling* your feelings and engaging with them at an interpretive level. Staying embodied in profound sadness, rage, rejection, or despair—as feeling and sensation—is not the same as talking to yourself about *why* you're sad, *when* it's going to go away, *who* caused it, and *how* it is evidence that you are not enough, that you have failed, or that something is wrong with you. There is a time, of course, to engage at the level of thought, inquiring into conceptual structures and beliefs in the understanding and making sense of your emotional experience. But this inquiry will be much deeper, more penetrating, and more effective if the underlying energetic display is first held, contained, and allowed to illuminate in the freshness of the here and now, outside the denser structures of conceptuality that are often oriented in the past. As we learn to rest in the nonconceptual nature of the felt sense of our situation and descend underneath our habitual thinking and reactive emotions, we are able to contact a new level of information and guidance. As Einstein reminds us, we will never be able to solve a problem at the same level of consciousness from which it arose. As we become more familiar with the intelligence of the somatic field, we can inquire from this creative state of nonconceptual knowing, articulate our experience in fresh way, and discover new meaning and purpose in our lives.

Often we will say, "I'm fully in my body. I'm in pure, direct contact with the raw feelings and sensations of anger, sadness, hopelessness, and shame. Don't tell me I'm not feeling all that! *I've been sad for so long! The shame has been there my entire life.*" But if you pause, slow way down, and get curious about the *actuality* of your experience in the present (rather than in your *interpretations* of it), you may discover that often what you are in touch with is a subtle narrative you have wrapped around your immediate experience that is now orbiting around the aliveness. There is nothing inherently wrong, problematic, or "unspiritual" about the narrative. It is just one degree removed from the transformative fires of the here and now, and usually an expression of our past, conditioned history.

As we engage the art of sacred return, we may discover that one of the primary functions of the storyline is to keep us out of vulnerable and shaky material that threatens to erupt under the surface. There is some messy, sticky, raw, hot, panicky, restless energy that has long wanted to be met but until now has not located an environment of kindness in which it was safe to emerge. In this way our interpretations of immediate experience serve to protect us from the intensity of the feelings underneath: there is a deeply ingrained sense that we do not have the capacity to stay with and integrate that underlying material. The invitation is to discover whether this sense is in fact accurate. Perhaps it was at an earlier time, but to what degree is it true *now?* As always, you cannot take *anyone's* word for this but must make the journey and see for yourself. It is an act of tremendous kindness to set aside the theories and opinions of others and finally see for yourself what is most true … for *you.* While there are many who will insist that they know "the" truth about your inner experience, a true teacher, therapist, counselor, or friend will always insist that you make the journey yourself.

You can continue to honor the security these defensive strategies have provided, but you might also ask whether you need continued and ongoing protection from the life that is attempting to make itself known within you. While guarding against disturbing feelings serves a very important function during certain developmental stages, its shadow side usually leads to the experience of an existential sort of flatness, a general sense of numbness, deadness, and lack of spontaneity. For it is within the core of the shaky, vulnerable, tenderness of the body and the heart that our aliveness is to be found. While there is a cultural (and spiritual) fantasy that the freedom and intimacy we long for will be found in the *eradication* of vulnerability, many are discovering that this is not accurate; that, in fact, aliveness is found only by turning *toward* the tenderness underlying our emotional experience, and infusing it with our presence, warmth, and compassion.

Without judgment or blame—but with curiosity and the love of the truth as your primary intention—you can begin to explore how these dynamics may be alive and moving within you. And then, from the reality of your adult-level capacities, you can make a conscious choice in the here and now as to how you'd like to proceed. Not how you can *perfect* this new type of awareness and attunement but how you can begin to hold it as an *intention* around which to orient.

In order to hold, work through, and metabolize that which we've previously disowned, we must train ourselves to come back over and over again into the aliveness of our immediate experience with newfound levels of self-compassion and presence. Often, the inner critic will become involved and attempt to convince us that we must act quickly, storming the egoic castle and removing all our defensive organization at once, as the best strategy to rid ourselves of the so-called "negative" emotions that are obstructing our path. This sort of self-aggression usually has historic origins in early relational experience and rarely proves fruitful. Training ourselves to stay with, tolerate, and contain intense and disturbing feelings for *very* short periods of time is not only a kinder approach, but more effective in the long run. By struggling for long periods of time to "stay with ourselves" at all costs, we usually just end up reinforcing the underlying belief that difficult emotions are evidence of a problem that must urgently be resolved.[2] Even if we stay with the panic, the anxiety, the claustrophobia, and the restlessness for one or two seconds, over time new circuitry will encode. A few seconds, then rest. Then later, a few more, and gradually our tolerance will increase.

We do want to push ourselves a little, as we need to overcome the habitual momentum of self-abandonment and dissociation that has built up over many moments, but not so much that we land outside our window of tolerance in trauma and overwhelm. It can help to explore this safe yet provocative middle ground with an attuned other who can help you navigate your experience when it becomes challenging. It is not realistic to believe that we can turn back toward previously split-off material and not also experience some fear, anxiety, or panic as a consequence, for our protective strategies were put in place to ensure that we never had to confront levels of anxiety that we could not manage. As these strategies are gradually challenged—not with urgency and aggression, but with slowness and attunement—we will

---

2. I want to thank psychotherapist Bruce Tift for helping me to discover the power in metabolizing emotional and somatic material in micro-moments, over multiple instances, as an expression of the activity of kindness.

usually be asked to meet the anxiety that is alive under the surface. But slowly, in small doses, we can build tolerance and learn to contain the intensity in a way that actually aids the process of re-embodiment rather than thwarting it. In this way, small amounts of anxiety can serve as an ally on the path if we learn how to embrace and work skillfully with it at an energetic level.

While there are times when working directly with the storyline can be helpful, doing so prematurely—without first attending to and caring for the overwhelming material at the feeling level—can cause us to become caught up in habitual loops of thinking where we are unable to access the fresh, spontaneous aliveness of what is happening in the body. Before we know it, our awareness is consumed with *interpreting* our experience rather than actually *having* it. Within the crucible of the body is a very alive field of presence, a nonconceptual wisdom and intelligence that can respond to the challenges of our life in a way that is not merely a product of past conditioning. In this sense, healing and integration are in large part *somatic* processes rather than *cognitive* ones. This is not to say that cognitive insight is not important, but in a culture that has become overly focused on logical analysis, conceptual understanding, and rational interpretation—often at the expense of other bands of the experiential spectrum—the return into the body can be profound skillful means for deepening wisdom, compassion, and new types of awareness.

The Purity of Emotion

As open, sensitive human beings, we may never be able to avoid the experience of emotional pain. This fact is not evidence that there is something wrong with us, but that we are alive.

Welcome. You are alive. Thank god you have a body, heart, and mind that allow you to feel, to make meaning of your feelings, and to use them skillfully as a bridge to connect with others. Let us end the pathologizing of emotion once and for all, instead proclaiming together the holiness of feeling.

Sometimes it is as if our hearts are on the outside of our skin, rather than safely protected by the rib cage, hidden away in some fantasy of invincibility. Even the wind blowing, as it makes contact with the raw, tender, exposed flesh, is enough to take us to the ground.

As we somehow take the risk of opening more, we might see that emotional vulnerability is in fact the only response that makes any sort of sense in a world that has gone a bit mad. In this way, we can recontextualize and re-enchant our emotional experience, breathe new life into it, and behold its sacredness. It is magic to be an emotional being, and we need no longer apologize for it.

Emotional pain has been pathologized in our world, along with tenderness, heartbreak, grief, and any sort of state of feeling down. We doubt ourselves and question our very being, afraid to trust in the purity and integrity of our experience as it is.

But emotional pain is not pathological. Grief is not a condition to be diagnosed and treated. Feeling down and blue and a bit hopeless is not a disease that needs to be cured by consumption, whether that consumption is of material goods or new inner states. A broken heart is pure and complete on its own, filled with integrity, intelligence, and life. It need not be mended nor transformed into something else. It is the vehicle by which the poetry of your life will flow.

To stay embodied with waves of grief, confusion, rage, fear, exhaustion, hopelessness, and doubt ... to provide sanctuary and safe passage for the pieces of a broken world ... to dissolve once and for all the trance of self-abandonment ... this invitation is one that is radical and nonconventional by its nature, appearing now for your consideration.

To infuse the entire spectrum with breath, life, awareness, and holding will liberate an eruption of skillful energy and help us to find meaning, to bear the unbearable, and to truly be there for others when they are suffering. And to be warriors in the world at those times when we are needed most.

3

The Crucible of the Broken

The Invitation of the Broken

AT TIMES, A BROKEN HEART WILL APPEAR AS YOUR TEACHER AND YOU will be asked to place your raw, shaky vulnerability on the altar before you.

The invitation of the broken is rarely sweet or peaceful, but is always reorganizing and whole.

"The freedom you are longing for is found inside me," it says, "not in sending me away with spiritual process."

Your ancient companion aloneness has arrived as a clarifying wisdom-guide from beyond, along with your fellow travelers the moon and the stars.

They have come to walk with you on a blessed journey.

It's Okay to Be Sad

It's okay to be sad. Really. For just one moment, allow sadness to be here. No shame, no blame, no urgent self-improvement project … just sad. It is so holy.

The presence of sadness is not evidence that something is wrong with you. It does not mean anything about who you are or your inherent value as a person, or that you have "failed" or lost your way. *It means you are alive.*

Go ahead. Be sad. But be sad *fully*. Set aside the resistance to this movement within you and allow it to express itself, share its secrets, and bestow its gifts upon a world that has forgotten the purity of the broken. Love is full spectrum and will unleash all of its children here, including sadness, to awaken itself in form. It is an act of profound kindness to turn into the open, achy caverns of the heart and seed them with holding.

Dare to see that the presence of sadness is not evidence that something is wrong with you. It does not mean that you have done life and relationships wrong, or that you are lacking in faith, trust, or gratitude. It doesn't mean you have forgotten a "secret," need to meditate better, become more adept at staying in the present moment, or that you are unlovable or beyond redemption. It means you are human, and you are whole. Thank god for that, for your ability to feel and to have your heart be touched by others and by this life. Perhaps what this world needs is more broken-open hearts.

Sadness is not something you need to fix, cure, or transform. It need not be healed, but held. You need not shift sadness into some "higher" state or apply teachings so it will yield into something else, for it is complete and pure on its own. You need not pathologize your sadness or fall into the spell of a world that has abandoned the wisdom buried inside the broken pieces.

Stay close to your sadness and surround it with curiosity, presence, and warmth. With the fire of awareness and with the ally of your breath, descend underneath the *story* of the sadness and into the crucible of the body where the sadness essence dwells and makes its luminous home. Go on a journey into the core of the feelings, sensations, and images and into the raw, shaky life that is longing to be held.

The Traveler of Aloneness

As an alive, sensitive human being, at times you will encounter a familiar sense of loneliness as it seeps into your awareness and begins to color your world. *What is this visitor,* you wonder, *and what does it want from me?* You question whether it will ever go away, when it will yield to your deep longing for connection, and why all the work on yourself has not yet transformed the unknowing despair. The feeling of *loneliness* is a reminder of separation and has a way of cutting into the aliveness of immediate experience.

The reality of *aloneness,* on the other hand, is an expression of intelligence and is surging with life. Despite our connection with others, we are asked to make the journey alone. No one can experience life for us, love and be loved for us, embrace and feel our achy heart for us, or die for us; nor can we for them.

The traveler of aloneness is at home in this environment—and even welcomes it—knowing that organizing her reality around love will inevitably trigger the experience of tender, penetrating vulnerability. Living in the delicate field of aloneness is so fragile, so unknown, and unbearably touching; it is always uncertain, shaky, and groundless, and a piercing reminder of how open it really is here, revealing the disorienting truth that you can never really look to the known to tell you who you are or why you've come here. It is a penetrating invitation to live *your* life, for you cannot live someone else's.

Within the environment of purifying aloneness, we know that at any moment our hearts may break, that we may fall in love in the most excruciating way, and that we will likely be asked to meet deep waves of feeling and sensation. We know that as we open in this way, we will no longer be able to avoid true intimacy, the certainty of being exposed, and the reality that who we think we are may always be falling apart and reconfiguring. We realize that without our conscious knowing, we have vowed to turn *toward* the nakedness of this life, to enter directly into uncertainty, suffering, darkness, *and* light, guided by the unknown and a love from beyond. It is not easy to live in such an open and unguarded way, yet here we are.

Though related, the experience of *loneliness* is usually born out of resistance to our present experience, of turning from feelings of grief, sadness, hurt, and shame, as well as from more "positive" feelings that are too exposing, including intimate experience of all kinds. When we are unwilling to provide a home for these feelings, we feel cut off from life, lonely, and disconnected. We long, at the deepest levels, to know the *entirety* of what we are; anything short of that is never going to meet our primordial cry for wholeness. On some level, we intuit that each visitor, whether invited or otherwise, is its own unique doorway into presence, into one of the unique crystalline qualities of love, and we become lonely when we abandon those parts that only long to be allowed back home. The only way out is through; and the only way through is by love. While the mind is sure to forget this simple yet revolutionary truth, the body knows … the heart knows.

For many of us interested in the spiritual journey, this embrace of direct experience is something we have learned as a conceptual goal. As we deepen our inquiry, we may notice a hidden agenda lurking in the background. "I'll sit with this feeling of sadness, grief, shame, or fear because I've been told that's what I'm supposed to do, and when I do it right, the feeling will transform, I'll be healed and free to carry on with my life." This orientation is evidence of a subtle resistance to our experience and thus continues to support the ongoing encounter with loneliness, with that sense of cut-off-ness. When this intention is primary, we move toward our experience not out of curiosity or love of the truth but unconsciously in service to and reenactment of earlier strategies of aggression and self-abandonment. With clear awareness, we just begin to see how these dynamics might be operating in us, that's all. No shame, no blame, no self-attack. Just more awareness.

And more kindness. We can make use of even this behind-the-scenes agenda as a way to come closer to ourselves and lay down new paths of empathic attunement. Nothing is rejected on the journey of love. All is path.

It is so bittersweet, really. Being an open-hearted human being, one who is simultaneously broken *and* whole, can feel so fragile, so precarious. Our old friends sadness, grief, jealousy, hopelessness, and rage are often sent out the back door of our hearts into a lonely forest. This is sad. Please, don't go! Stay close! Let us keep the door open to them, moment by moment crafting a warm home and safe refuge for the entirety of what we are. For in doing so, the path from loneliness to aloneness will become illumined.

Aloneness is a sacred friend but its mysteries and power have been lost in a world that has forgotten. Its invitation is direct, relentless, and shattering, but also filled with deep peace, creativity, and stillness. It is a deep call from within to return to what is most important, a portal like no other into a transmuting sort of heartbreak: not the heartbreak of the mind convinced that something has been lost but the shattering reorganization that comes by way of revelation of what has finally been found.

The Gift of Melancholy

What is the role of that feeling state we call *melancholy* on the journey of re-embodiment and the path of the heart? In my experience, melancholy is a very misunderstood (and therefore often unmet) energy in our psyches, in our hearts, and in our culture at large. So much of our effort—psychologically, spiritually, and societally—is fixated upon becoming happy, feeling good, and abandoning any feelings that do not immediately conform to these states.

As with other raw feeling states such as vulnerability, embarrassment, or disappointment, we tend to disembody from melancholy, concluding its mere presence is evidence that something is wrong with us. If melancholy comes to visit, we will scramble to change, heal, or transform it, replacing it with more "spiritual" or "healthy" thoughts, feelings, or states of being. Shouldn't we be more grateful, we wonder? More "in the now"? More forgiving, joyful, in a state of oneness? Surely if we were evolving on the path we would at some point set aside lesser states such as melancholy, sorrow, and despondency. We would leave their "low vibration" behind and replace them with something much higher and more spiritually impressive.

Before we cut the experience of melancholy too quickly, however, let us take a moment to turn and face it and finally see what it has to say, to dare to consider that melancholy is an utterly valid experience that contains important information for our journey. Perhaps he or she has been with us for many years, the melancholic one, and has never felt safe enough to come forward. Or we have not been interested enough in the wisdom this one carries. The experience of melancholy contains a unique signature and fragrance, and when explored can open us and reveal a hidden connection with others, the natural world, and our own hearts.

The direct, embodied experience of melancholy has a way of shattering old hopes and dreams—who we thought we were and what we've come to think we need—illuminating the shadows of our unlived lives. As an experiment, you could look out for this visitor as it appears in your experience and invite this one into intimate communion. In this meeting you may discover that melancholy is not an obstacle on your path but is a misunderstood emissary of integration, and will come from time to time to remind you of something rich and mysterious that may have been covered over in the busyness of becoming.

You Are Not a Project to Be Solved

It is unlikely today is going to be the day when you figure your life out; when you heal your past, resolve all your wounding, get all your questions answered, or know what is coming next.

It is unlikely today will be the day you finally manifest all the great things you think will make you happy. Call in the soul mate that will complete you. Permanently wiggle into some state of high vibration, invulnerability, and freedom from confusion. Or complete some mythical journey of spiritual awakening, landing in a fabulous ongoing state of untouchability.

What a relief. A day of celebration ... of what you are. And of the end of the dream of postponement.

You need no longer delay full, embodied participation in the miracle as it surges out of the darkness, the fragility, the shakiness, and the uncertainty. The invitation is into the opposites and the contradictions, where that which is unknown and unprecedented is taking form, where the energies of separation and union co-emerge and spin out the relative world.

Yes, today may not be the day for answers but to finally let your heart break open to the vastness of the question. To stand on the rooftops and proclaim that you are not a project to be solved, but a mystery to be lived.

Buried inside the glory and the mess, right in the core of the not-knowing is pure creativity. This is what you are. Love has come into form, somehow, by some grace, as your feelings, as your imagination, as your body, and as the ragingly unique signature of the cells of your heart. There is no greater miracle than this. It is complete. You are complete.

Return into slowness and into this current breath, which contains all of the seen and unseen worlds. You are here, rippling and pregnant with life, and there is no urgency on the path of wholeness.

An Experiment in Self-Care

You may be accompanied throughout your day by subtle feelings of slight panic, anxiety, and a cosmic sort of restlessness. Perhaps you feel it as you wake, some vague sense that something is missing or just off.

Nothing specific is going wrong that you can identify; nonetheless you cannot quite rest, or fully engage the life that you know is possible. Somehow the aliveness, the creativity, the intimacy … they are so near yet so far out of reach. But you can't quite pinpoint what is going on.

At sunset, at dusk, as you listen to certain music, walk in nature, or gaze up into the sky, or as you are falling into the dream world at night. As you wander through the world, as you come in contact with an unnamable but vivid longing within you, or as you become aware of some images of the way you thought it was all going to turn out … the death of an old dream, a relationship you were sure would last forever, a career that unexpectedly fell apart, a friend who is no more.

It is tempting to try to locate the source of the unsettling feelings—to attach them to something someone said, to a way you're not being seen or understood, to the fear of an anticipated future scenario, to a loss that has occurred or is impending, or to some specific aspect of your life situation that isn't flowing the way you'd prefer. But whatever you come up with, while it seems to potentially be a *part* of what is happening, you have a deeper sense that you're still not penetrating to the source. It's as if a certain ancient existential uneasiness was wired into you and cannot be approached by conceptual process. The mind is just too slow, too dense to reach it. But something is brewing in your organs, in your cells, in your heart, and starting to emerge from out of the depths of your body, from the deepest caverns within your psyche. From even deeper than what we normally refer to as "personal." It's almost archetypal in nature, arising out of the earth itself, more of a collective shakiness and unease.

In the face of this, it can feel as if there is great urgency, that you must take some action in response, to find secure ground from which to orient and take the next step. But is something actually wrong? Or is everything okay? Is there a problem … or is there not? Is there something you must resolve? A question that must be answered … now? An underlying pressure to maintain a particular identity? To fill a raw, empty hole inside you? To figure out, finally, who you are and what you're doing here? Is there something you must do to prevent things from completely falling apart?

It is so easy to dismiss these archaic companions of uncertainty and nervousness, to conclude that their presence is clear and convincing evidence that something is wrong with you, that something must urgently be shifted, or that some sort of profound error has occurred. Further, these types of experiences are certainly not very "spiritual," are they? If you were fully "in the now," accepting everything the way it is, resting in a high vibration, and manifesting what you want and deserve, would you be feeling this way? Isn't the goal of the inner journey to do away with this primordial anxiety once and for all? What if others knew you were feeling like this? Especially your spiritual friends. Or students. Or clients. Or new partner. What would they think? Maybe they would turn from you in the discovery that you are human after all—or would they? Or would you instead become closer? Would the barrier between you and life finally fall away? The questions can be relentless.

It is an act of self-kindness to take some time to explore all of this, with as much patience, curiosity, and courage that you can muster. What conclusions do you come to in the face of uninvited waves of anxiety, panic, unease, and dissatisfaction? To what degree have you come to believe that the simple presence of these energies serves as *accurate* evidence that something is wrong with you, that you are unworthy of love, that you are just not okay as you are? It can be helpful to ask these questions and pay close attention to what you discover, allowing yourself to refrain from taking the first response that bubbles up as your deepest truth. Often (though not always) the first "answer" is a knee-jerk reaction, a function of your conditioned history and a reflection of avoidant strategies that arose at an earlier time. Be willing to sit in the intensity and contradictory energy of the question, without needing to immediately scramble into an answer. As Rainer Maria Rilke, the beloved Austrian poet and novelist, reminds us so beautifully:

Be patient toward all that is unsolved in your heart and try
to love the *questions themselves* like locked rooms and like
books that are now written in a very foreign tongue. Do not
now seek the answers, which cannot be given you because
you would not be able to live them. And the point is, to live
everything. Live the questions now. Perhaps you will then
gradually, without noticing it, live along some distant day
into the answer.[1]

While feelings of shakiness, uncertainty, and groundlessness are
conventionally viewed as obstacles and mistakes to be corrected and
cured, the invitation is to discover for yourself if this is actually true.
There is another view of this material that is much more vast, majestic,
and purposive, rooted in the observation that the psyche is always in a
movement toward wholeness. Even the most disturbing "symptoms"
are attempts at integration, ways that psyche is making sense of your
experience and pulling you toward deeper levels of meaning and purpose. As an experiment, you can hold these feelings and inner stirrings
as the possible expression of high-voltage guidance, pure information,
and sacred data. The invitation here is to make the commitment to
no longer pathologize the activity of intense, disturbing, and fierce
energies within you, instead daring to honor their workability, validity,
and the hidden wisdom that is buried in their core.

From this non-shaming and compassionate holding space, you can
inquire as to whether the disquiet, shakiness, and unsurety—though
misunderstood and dismissed in our modern world—are in reality
forerunners of breakthrough, special representatives of the sacred
death-rebirth cycle. As part of your contemplation, you can explore
whether the freedom and aliveness you are so genuinely longing for
will ever be found in transforming, replacing, or even *healing* this
tender vulnerability in the core of your being. Or whether your deepest
yearnings will be met by way of entering into relationship with it. By

---

1. Rainer Maria Rilke, *Letters to a Young Poet* (New York: Norton 2004),
13.

opening your heart to it. By daring to practicing intimacy with it. By no longer apologizing for it.

As unique, unprecedented, one-of-a-kind human beings wired to discover meaning, purpose, and depth, despite our cultural (and spiritual) fantasies to the contrary, we quite naturally experience waves of anxiety from time to time. This word "anxiety" has come to be associated with something deeply problematic, unworkable, invalid, and certainly not very "spiritual." When we meet someone who reports that they are feeling "anxious," or these feelings and sensations arise in our own experience, our initial response is often rooted in the perception that something has gone wrong, that we are ill, broken, neurotic, or worse. There is not often much curiosity or interest in exploring the nature of this experience, the life and information that is surging under the surface, or much openness to the possibility that the anxiety might actually be a messenger, an admittedly wrathful sort of guide, arising to point us into a deeper exploration of what is most important to us, to something we may have forgotten in all the busyness, schedules, and stress of our overly structured lives.

Before I go any further, I want to clarify what I mean when I use the word "anxiety" and to distinguish what we might call "existential" anxiety from a more serious and debilitating clinical condition that is the result of an injury to the brain, profound trauma, or other situations where a person's physiological and psychological symptoms have debilitated them to the point where they are unable to function in ordinary life. Without such distinction, the perspective being offered here could appear misattuned, lacking in compassion, and even dangerous.

The invitation and guidance offered in this book is intended for those with adequate ego development who are struggling with the "ordinary concerns of love and work," as Freud described it. It is meant to address what we might call *existential anxiety* that arises daily in the lives of all human beings as they face the wide open and unresolvable nature of their lives—pointing to the first noble truth of the Buddha—and to address the shaky, uncertain angst that very organically underlies the realities of birth, old age, sickness, and death. The suggestions here are not intended for those with very debilitating forms of clinical anxiety. These situations usually require a very different modality of treatment, including, in some cases, medication, regular supervised treatment, and other biologically oriented approaches.

When you are caught in cascading, ruminative thinking—and the emotions, feelings, and sensations that often accompany or underlie it—it can be helpful to return into the body and allow the word "anxiety" to fall away. This word has become inextricably associated with something horrid and unworkable, and it is a disembodied, experience-distant concept for many. As you release the word, you can become increasingly curious about what you're *actually* being asked to meet in any given here-and-now moment. What is actually here in your immediate, noninterpretive experiencing? Something alive is occurring, that is for sure, and it is requesting a moment of your care and attunement. The more these feelings are abandoned as they arise, the more the circuitry is enforced that they are unworkable, invalid, and an *accurate* representation that something is wrong with you. You can honor the truth that it *feels* as if something is wrong, while simultaneously cultivating the courage to go into your experience and see if this feeling is a true representation of reality, to explore whether it is a reliable indicator of a current threat in the here and now.

As you deepen in your inquiry and train yourself for short periods of time to stay with the feelings and sensations that are moving within you, you may discover that there is no ongoing, solid, continuous thing called "anxiety" that is happening *to* you from the outside. This may seem like such an ordinary thing to realize, but when you fully allow in the implications of this, you may be astonished at the energy that is released and the freedom you might discover. It is important to remember that the word "anxiety" is a concept, and as with all concepts is one step removed from the actuality of your lived, embodied experience. Underneath the very loaded word, in a given moment of here-and-now experience, the concept "anxiety" overlays a unique, alive, unprecedented arrangement of physical sensation, emotion/

feeling tone, and conceptual narrative, at times accompanied and fueled by mental, visual imagery as well as an impulse to take action. Becoming aware of what is actually happening at each of these levels of experience, one at a time, can help you approach what is happening in a bite-sized way rather than feeling you need to confront the anxiety all at once, as if it were an enemy you are being called to go to war with. No, what is happening now is a fluttering in your belly, some constriction in your throat, some repetitive thoughts about being unsafe, a feeling tone of restlessness and claustrophobia, and so forth. Relating to your experience this way requires kindness, courage, and curiosity, and allows you greater perspective to explore what is truly happening and the purpose or meaning these symptoms might have in your life. It provides an opportunity for you to practice new levels of awareness and self-love. In this way, your "anxiety" is not an enemy coming at you from the outside, but a mindfulness bell, an invitation coming from deep within you to come closer, to become so curious about who and what you are, and to recommit to your life, exactly as it is.

Once you connect in a very direct way with what is *actually* happening within you—instead of primarily with your *interpretation* of what is happening and the habitual conclusions you have come to about what it all means—you may sense that continuing to claim you are "suffering from anxiety" is a subtle form of self-abandonment, and even self-violence. For those who struggle with anxiety, this can be a difficult reframing to let in. But please remember: this is all just an experiment. I do not claim to know what is true or most accurate for you. I am simply inviting you into another level of inquiry, and sharing what I have discovered in my own experience as well as in my work with others. As always, please do not take my word for it, but explore deeply for yourself, testing anything shared in this book in the fire of your own direct experience. If it does not resonate, please discard it and return into what is most true for you.

Yes, the symptoms of anxiety can be disturbing and can be quite icky. It can feel as if you won't make it, that your very survival is at risk, that if you stay for another moment with the feelings coursing through you, you will fall apart. The question is this: Are these feelings *accurate* representations of the deepest truth of your situation, in the here and now? This is not an inquiry to take lightly, but one to make slowly, over time, with curiosity and an open heart, so you can see for yourself what is most true—now. Not what *was* true when you were a young child. Not what some spiritual teacher or therapist or author *said* may be true. Not what your spouse or family *believes* is true, but what is actually *most true for you,* in the fire of your own direct experience.

You can fully honor these feelings of pending dysregulation and shutdown while at the same time challenging their real-time accuracy and the historic storyline that has become wrapped around them. There is no need to judge any experience you are having, pathologize it, or question its validity. But it is an act of kindness to hold the intention to discover what is *most* true in a moment and to see if there is a deeper call from within to reauthor the narrative and bring it up to date, weaving a more integrated, present-time, nuanced story about who you are and what is happening.

Slow down and return to the "here and now" while simultaneously honoring the past movement of the "there and then." Remain committed to what is most true in present time. In so doing, you train yourself to touch, contain, and even practice a certain kind of intimate holding toward the sensations, emotions, and storylines that have previously come to be associated with overwhelm and unbearable feeling. In this, you can discover for yourself if your feelings are in fact harming you, if your survival is *actually* at risk, and if there might be a wiser, more skillful, and more compassionate way to care for yourself in the wake of what is moving within you.

It is easy to dismiss waves of anxiety, angst, and apprehension, to conclude that their presence is clear evidence that something is wrong. While it is perfectly natural to want to take some sort of action to calm the storm, we don't want to do so at the expense of our own growth and evolution. Before we rush to quell the symptoms, we can practice attuning to what is arising to be met. We can practice holding, containing, tolerating, and opening into it in a given moment of time. In this way we may come to discover that our freedom—even our "healing"—is not dependent upon making these symptoms go away, but upon befriending them, getting curious about them, and investigating our actual experience as it unfolds from moment to moment.

The project of "fixing me" is birthed and the unending war of self-improvement waged from unexamined emotional conclusions about what intense and disturbing feelings mean about who you are as a person at the deepest levels. Many have discovered how exhausting the journey of self-improvement has become and are aching for deep rest, an ancient sort of relaxing into their lives as they are, which is not dependent upon first "fixing" our emotions or replacing one experience with another. The notion that you can be free *within* the experience of anxiety can be boggling to the mind, but the body and the heart know this truth, that your freedom is not dependent upon the appearance or disappearance of any particular psychological, emotional, and somatic phenomena.

Dare to consider that you are not broken simply because waves of sensation, emotion, and narrative are surging in and out of your open psyche, your raw heart, and your tender nervous system. You are not a project to be fixed, but a mystery coming into form. This doesn't mean that you love these feelings or that it is easy or that you hope they stay forever. It simply means that you are no longer willing to abandon yourself or pathologize the movement of feeling within you. It means you are willing to explore the possibility that moving away from *what is* is the root cause of so much of your suffering and struggle. It can be astonishing to discover, in a truly embodied way, that there is no suffering inherent in waves of unease in the belly, constriction in the throat, racing in the heart, or even the ruminative thinking that passes through your mind. Rather, it is the abandonment of yourself and your experience that plants the seeds for future struggle.

Again, please do not take mine or anyone's word for this. Go into the laboratory of your own body and heart and see, finally, what is most true, now. From this place of curiosity, slowing down, and the longing to know what is *most* accurate, you can then wisely, skillfully, and compassionately explore the following questions: What if this anxiety is not an error or a mistake that I must correct, but a messenger sent by some part of me that is longing to be met? An indication and forerunner of wholeness and a fierce and often disturbing guide and invitation toward integration? What have I abandoned in myself out of unmet shame, grief, despair, and fear that now longs to be allowed back into the majesty of what I am?

What are my psyche, my heart, and my body attempting to reveal to me? What are all these symptoms saying about me and my life, about where I have been and where I want to go, about where I will discover true meaning, about how I have been living, about my purpose, about what is truly most important to me? Not what I've learned *should* be important, or what my parents or spiritual teachers or therapists have *suggested* is most important, but *what is most alive for me?* And will I have the courage to open into that journey of individuation that will allow me to discover and live from the deepest truths that I know inside?

Something is knocking at the door of your heart. What is it? While it may *appear* that it is knocking from the outside, get curious and look again. Maybe the waves of sensation, emotion, and narrative are intelligent yet nonconventional invitations into the sacred world that is always already here. Perhaps the kindest act of self-care and self-love is to finally slow down and see, to be willing to set aside everything you have concluded about who and what you are, about who and what others are, and about what this life is all about. To return to the mind and heart of the beginner and (re)enter the mystery. And to finally discover whether the feelings and sensations themselves are the cause of your struggle or whether it is the abandonment and rejection of them, bolstered by the conclusions you've come to about what these feelings mean. There is no answer here—it is really just an experiment. An experiment in radical self-care.

At the Edge of a Cliff

Why am I not changing? Why have I not healed yet? Why do I keep engaging in the same limiting habits and patterns, choosing the same type of unfulfilling partner, and still being unable to find meaning in my work and relationships?

Why am I not feeling grateful, joyful, and able to appreciate all the things I have? Isn't this what I was promised when I took up the inner journey? What about all this fear, anger, jealousy, and confusion? And why, despite having so many blessings in my life, am I feeling flat and uninspired?

As seekers, these questions can haunt us and we can spend an incredible amount of life energy consumed by them. But what is the way through? Part of us entertains the very seductive and compelling notion that we might just set aside our historic conditioning and finally just choose love over fear—or joy over despair—sort of the way we might choose one type of green smoothie over another at our favorite natural foods store. We're bombarded with all sorts of promises that this or that course or process, this or that book or method, this or that new lover, or this or that spiritual teacher will come in and finally remove it all in one cosmic stroke of unbelievably fantastic and awesome grace.

Even though we may chuckle at the absurdity of it when it's stated this way, if we look deeper we might be astonished to see how active the archetype of the savior truly is, in the personal as well as in the collective. As with all archetypes, there is nothing inherently neurotic or problematic about savior energy; the invitation is to be in conscious relationship with it.

Perhaps *you* are the savior you have been looking for.

Many of us remain quite invested in our avoidant and protective strategies, but the details of this investment tend to dance outside conscious awareness, influencing our perception and our behavior just below the surface. These ways of interacting with others and the world, which have formed the templates from which we orient, are not just random and neurotic. They were formed intelligently to help us engage a world that was so much bigger than us, that was overwhelming, one in which we needed to do whatever we could to fit in, to be seen, to be accepted, to receive some modicum of love and attunement. These things are not negotiable in the developing brain and nervous system of a little one wired for empathic connection.

One of the most important inquiries on the path of awakening and healing is an open-hearted and non-shaming exploration of the ways we may be holding on to these strategies and perceptual filters, and how they might still be serving a function. Because they mostly operate outside conscious awareness, it can take time and practice to uncover what may be going on behind the scenes. In my experience, it is very difficult to get to the depths of this material on our own; an attuned therapist, a wise and trustworthy friend, or an empathic intimate partner can all help us if this is the contract we have with them.

It can come as quite a shock to see that we are still benefiting from holding on to embedded ways of protection and avoidance that, on a conscious level, we believe we have outgrown or "transcended" through all our inner work. This realization can generate disappointment, judgment, and deflation and has a way of catalyzing profound humility if allowed in. Rather than overly identifying with the disappointment and following it down the rabbit hole of unworthiness and self-aggression, we can use it as fuel for our inquiry. For a heartfelt commitment to know the truth of our experience—even those aspects that are humiliating, embarrassing, and shameful—can help us make real-time decisions about how we will move forward. Once we acquire some insight into our current investment in the developmental strategies of an earlier time, we can make a more conscious, here-and-now, adult-level decision as to whether we're truly open to challenging these strategies, reauthor the narrative of our lives, and re-envision the way we've come to perceive ourselves and others.

In my experience, this is not something that you can choose one day and accomplish the next by way of a powerful weekend workshop. It is difficult work that unfolds over the time and never ends in some grand realization that you can list on your spiritual *résumé.* Your heart is endlessly deep, and your body is an endless temple.

To set aside the ways you have come to defend yourself against the tenderness and depth of what you are would require that you first return your conscious awareness directly to those parts you have disowned at an earlier time. All of the feelings, emotions, images, fantasies, complexes, personas, and the entirety of the shadow in all its forms: the fears of intimacy, the anxiety around death, the panic of abandonment—all of it. Most have spent their lives organizing their experience around minimizing or altogether avoiding contact with this material, a strategy that makes sense from the perspective of maintaining a kind of homeostasis and status quo. The question, however, is whether the status quo is really going to cut it for you. Or whether you are called to something else.

It is important to see that these organizing principles are not the expression of some neurotic, intrapsychic conflict but are relational strategies rooted in regulating what would otherwise be an avalanche of overwhelming anxiety. While we all may have some hope that we are ready and willing to release these strategies all at once, it doesn't really work like that. The wholesale dismantling of our defensive organization is not recommended. In fact, to do so is often more an expression of self-aggression and fear than it is of wisdom and kindness, as it is only the ego that feels the need to storm its own castle and tear itself down.

It can't be emphasized enough that our defensive organization serves a protective function. It emerged in a young brain and nervous system as a way to guard us from overwhelming emotional states that we simply could not metabolize on our own at that stage of development. We learned very quickly how to stay as far out of harm's way as possible, how to receive the affection and attention we needed, and how to survive—emotionally, psychically, and sometimes even physically. Until we are developmentally mature enough to go back into, contain, and metabolize the anxiety and existential groundlessness that wait for us on the other side, we should be mindful of what is required and tread carefully and kindly: pushing ourselves a bit, but not into overwhelm generated by impatience or by way of reenactments of unworthiness and shame.

But what to do now? Where to go from here? You aren't likely to urgently disassemble your defensive organization in a rush to transcendence. But at the same time, you can no longer ignore the call of transformation and healing that rages within you. In the wake of receiving this call, many have found themselves standing on the edge of a cliff, with the known behind and the unknown stretching before them. On the one hand, there is the lure of what has come before—familiarity, safety, security, and certainty—while on the other there is a thundering longing to dive into uncharted waters, to swim in the wholeness of the ocean of love and be transparent to its movement. Not exactly sure what will come next, but all the while sensing an opportunity that has been laid out in front of them: to turn back toward those parts they have spent their lives avoiding and provide the attunement and holding they have yet to receive.

While your strategies of protection have provided a critical level of care, the time has now come for you to consider reorganization. The invitation is to open into the unknown without demanding that same level of protection, moving at a speed that is provocative and challenging but not so quickly that you become overwhelmed and fragmented.

These realizations, these insights, this renewal of the vow of wholeness—this is not an ordinary moment. In fact, it is the heralding of a new world. To reintegrate what has fallen out of awareness is one of the most rewarding and difficult tasks you are asked to embody on the path of love. Yet it offers fruit beyond your imagination. There is a trade-off, though: you will no longer be able to go back to the way it was, not in the same way. You will no longer be able to stay on the sidelines, relying on the old ways to protect you from the wide-open, groundless, ever-changing, wildly alive, and creative dimensions of reality and your true nature. While the foreshadowing of this new reality is exhilarating, it can also be quite disorienting. It is important to recognize the immensity of this and to engage the journey with slowness, mindfulness, and compassion.

Living in this way in the unknown, while simultaneously terrifying and exciting, elicits a sense that anything is possible. It may be confusing, at least at first, but one thing is certain: only through kindness can you approach your neurotic organization and defensive strategies. There is no other way. You need to be willing to make the most radical commitment you could ever make: to the truth of your experience, exactly as it unfolds, and to receiving whatever appears in a holding field of warmth and compassion. Nothing need be discarded. Nothing is "nonspiritual." Everything is valid, everything is path, everything is God.

Yes, you may be asked to stay with some very groundless states of confusion, uncertainty, vulnerability, and the unknown, open to the possibility that the rug will be pulled out, again, with heartbreak and deflation on the other side. But heartbreak and deflation are sacred, and I think this is a trade-off you are willing to make.

A Breakdown That Is Whole

At times you may become aware of a wave of despair rising and falling within you: you're feeling down, hopeless, uninspired, and unable to find any meaning. It's as if something has been lost, or is just *off* in some unexplainable way. But you can't quite pin it down. Everyone around you seems so content and joyful, enjoying their lives. *What is wrong with me?* you ask.

There is a deeply embedded cultural fantasy that you shouldn't feel depressed, that this sort of downheartedness is a clear sign that something has gone wrong, that you have failed and are flawed in some fundamental way. Oh, and by the way, it's not very "spiritual," is it? I mean, what about staying in the now, loving what is, accepting the moment, laws of attraction, and all of that? I mean, would a "spiritual" person feel depressed? We seem to be quite confused about all this.

But what if this lowliness were a *legitimate* experience, a messenger of some sort that is trying to break through an old dream, an outdated image, a worn-out narrative about yourself and something you thought was so important? What if in the totality of what you are, a wave of "unhappiness" is just as authentic and genuine as a wave of "happiness," laying the ground for something new and unexpected to emerge? In a way that the mind might find crazy or even dangerous, what if we were to dare to see that even a moment of depression is valid and an attempt of psyche to communicate?

Love not only takes form as flow, sweetness, and so-called "positive" feelings, but at times as the activity of death and deflation, reorienting old vision so rebirth can occur. This cycle is the essence of creativity and appears to be nonnegotiable on the path of the heart and of individuation, becoming who you truly are. While we do not get to choose whether the energies of death and rebirth dance within us, we seem to have some choice as to whether we will willingly participate in this truth or not, whether we will greet it with self-aggression or kindness. Whether we will dare to see it not as a mistake but as a potential opportunity, even if we cannot at this time attune to its guidance. To open and attune in this way does not require that we *like* what is happening, love it, or even "accept" it. It means that whether we like it or not, we know firsthand that arguing with what is, is the root cause of so much of our struggle. Yes, the experience is disturbing and intense, but before we throw it out as useless, let us take a moment to turn toward it and open to the possibility that it is purposeful.

The appearance of this sort of anguish can serve as a very piercing invitation to reexamine what is most important, where you've been, where you're headed, and where you will turn to find new meaning and purpose. Have you been living your own life or someone else's? Whose choices have you been making? Whose dreams have you been dreaming? The appearance of this existential despair can signal the death of an old dream, the falling away of an outdated persona, or the realization that your current life—including a certain relationship or a way of working in the world—is no longer large enough to hold who and what you are, or what is longing to come next. The images you have been working so hard to maintain are no longer vast enough to contain the mystery of you and your life and must be sacrificed for a greater vision. While this sacrifice is often painful and disturbing, it is sacred from the perspective of wholeness. It is a holy disorientation that is not always perceivable in the midst of the chaos.

During these times of psychic transition and reorganization, what we conceive of as the purpose of our life begins to crumble and fall apart, and the rug is pulled away. What is the new reference point around which we'll organize? Where are the identities we were once able to rest in and find meaning? As if this dissolution isn't enough on its own, nothing has arrived to replace the old with something new. We are between worlds, without the past to lean into but also without any future that we can look to for solid ground and inspiration. We are in the realm of Hermes, guide of the liminal and the dead, and in the undefined space between it all. Yes, it can be disorienting and bewildering in this place, but has something gone wrong? *Is death wrong?* Must we scramble urgently to replace it with "life"? Does any of this make any sense on the path of the heart?

While it is not easy, it is possible to open to what is happening and approach the breakdown as holy, to reframe the entire process in a way that honors the radical and uncompromising nature of what it means to be an alive, sensitive human being going against the grain of a society that has turned from the darkness out of a deep fear of its wildly creative, reorganizing nature. But what if this collapse was intelligent, and a forerunner of new life? Not an expression of pathology but of a wrathful, nonconventional sort of grace?

The journey of death-rebirth is by its very nature disturbing, not in promotion of the status quo, and not supportive of our cultural and spiritual fantasies that you're not supposed to feel anxious or depressed, that these and other, "darker" feelings are evidence that somehow you're doing something wrong, lacking in faith or gratitude, lost in the ego, need to meditate more or better, ignorant of some law of attraction, or must surrender more or differently. And if you were truly waking up and healing, you would be bearing witness to a more continuous flow of happiness, high vibration, and bliss. But what if happiness is not going to meet your deepest longing? What if "happiness" is not at the deepest level what you're after, but rather meaning and a full-spectrum sort of aliveness? What if you were sent here to this place for something much more majestic and even magical than happiness? There is nothing wrong with moments of joy, periods of contentment, and surges of bliss, for these too are aspects of your true nature. But you are vast, you contain multitudes, and you may never be satisfied with only one band of the spectrum.

It's important to note that my use of the term "depression" here and throughout the book is not meant to refer to a clinical diagnosis, which is a very serious condition that can be profoundly debilitating for those suffering from it. In most cases, such depression requires ongoing professional assessment and treatment, including medication (at times) and other biologically based interventions. I want to contrast this with what I call existential depression, which all of us face from time to time as a natural result of "ordinary" human suffering—the falling away of a job or death of a loved one, chronic pain and illness, the ending of an intimate relationship, the loss of hope and meaning. This type of "depression" is a natural function of being alive, is not pathological, and is part of what makes us human.

Existential depression can also arise without any obvious cause, as a reflection of the fragile and tenuous nature of our existence, knowing that one day we will die and no longer be able to participate in this precious world or be in contact with those we love. It is this existential depression that I am referring to in this book, those times in our lives when we feel down, flat, hopeless, and despairing. While it is certainly possible that the perspective and strategies offered here may be of help to those suffering from clinical depression, this book is not intended to replace more conventional treatment, which often requires a breadth and complexity that is not possible via the poetic prescriptions that are offered here.

Similarly, while those suffering from other clinically diagnosed conditions such as obsessive-compulsive disorder, bipolar disorder, PTSD, schizophrenia, social anxiety phobia, and generalized anxiety disorder may derive some help, benefit, and relief from the words and inquiries suggested here, it is beyond the scope of this book to provide the clinically based treatment that these conditions usually require. Please keep this in mind if you, or a close friend or family member, have received such diagnosis, and care for yourself by seeking out professional help.

It is difficult but possible to befriend waves of numbness and depression as carriers of a certain kind of life, though theirs is a signature that does not conform to conventional ideas about who you are and what you're doing here. Depth, meaning, and information are often buried in these experiences, but you must open in new ways to receive this level of guidance. These visitors come not as obstacles but as invitations for you to slow down and provide safe passage to something that needs to die within you, so that you may lay the groundwork for new forms of love to emerge, be reborn, and flourish. It takes a tremendous amount of courage, curiosity, and self-care to go into this material and open to it, for it is not what is normally presented as what is required on the path of healing and inner work. But love is not only peaceful, calming, and creative. At times is wrathful, dark, and destructive.

In fact, it is *everything,* and a partial love is never going to do. For you are wired for something immense.

The Petals Are Unfolding

In each moment, the archetypal journey of crucifixion, resurrection, and transfiguration is being enacted within you. Each breath, each image, each symbol, each feeling and sensation: something unprecedented is attempting to break through, the signs are all around, and the guidance is longing to emerge. But it is easy to miss in a world that has forgotten.

While the forms love takes—relationships, life circumstances, and the way you thought it would all turn out—will inevitably be crucified and resurrected, this is the native way of form and is not evidence of error but of wholeness. Love itself, though, is beyond birth and death, and is eternally transfiguring into greater levels of integration.

On this new day, which may appear ordinary from the perspective of the conventional, the invitation is into depth. There is nothing ordinary about what you are. Your body is a temple greater than even the sun and the moon.

Buried within the inner sanctum, petals are unfolding that are filled with vision and information for the way ahead. Look carefully. Listen closely. Attune to what has been longing to be known. Provide a sanctuary for the unmet, the unheld, and the unintegrated to return home.

Honor the forms of love as they appear but allow them to depart so they may continue their journey. For it is one of cosmic creativity. Yes, your heart may break as the forms dissolve in front of your very eyes, but it is by way of this breaking that you may be resurrected once again.

Dancing Within the Opposites

Learning to suffer consciously is an art that has been lost in our times. By training yourself to enter into an intimate, curious, embodied relationship with difficult psychological and emotional experience, you reclaim your right as an alive, sensitive, empowered human being. And proclaim your willingness to practice transmutation for the benefit of life everywhere.

Each time we turn from a painful feeling, bodily sensation, or disturbing emotion, we practice self-aggression, encoding circuitry of self-abandonment, as we hope to end-run the reality of our vulnerability. As I discussed earlier, this split-off material is not healed, but placed into the shadow, where it is sure to surge in less-than-conscious ways in our relational worlds. We need only look around (and inside) with eyes wide open to see the consequences of this.

It is by way of compassionate confrontation and integration of the full spectrum that we dance within the opposites and provide sanctuary for the unconscious to come into form. Through this integrative and consecrated activity the meaning of our experience will be revealed, and its role on the journey ahead clarified.

At times, the ally will appear in a sweet, peaceful, and light form, which we can take refuge in and be grateful for. At other times, the form will be fierce, wrathful, and of the dark, oriented not in peace, but in wholeness. While not as easy, we can come to be grateful for this one as well, who has not come to harm, but to reveal.

While the mind may turn from the wisdom and the love buried inside the shadows, the heart knows. The body knows.

The Re-enchantment of Healing

There's a lot of talk about "integrating" or "healing" traumatic experience, which has led to a lot of confusion. It's important to re-envision these words as they have in large part lost their relevance, aliveness, and magic. Additionally, for many they have become further tools of shame, blame, and self-attack, reenactments of an early environment lacking in empathic attunement. We must breathe life back into these ideas in an imaginative, grounded, and creative way.

Often what is meant by "integrating" or "healing" trauma (loosely defined here as any experience characterized by unbearable or overwhelming affect) is that one day we will "get over it," "transcend" it, meditate or "manifest" it away, or otherwise purge it from what we are.

In my clinical experience (in sitting in the fire alongside many courageous men and women with the most heartbreaking histories), this view of trauma is in large part inaccurate, aggressive, misguided, and at times even dangerous and violent. There are some things that happen to us that we will never "get over," nor would this even be an appropriate goal or lens to use in approaching the sacredness of the human temple.

Let us set aside any spirituality or "healing" that is (unconsciously or subtly) rooted in self-abandonment, self-attack, and self-hatred and replace it with slowness, empathy, and a grounded, relentless compassion. We must re-enchant this entire area of inquiry with presence and with love.

But if what we mean by "integration" is discovering a place inside us where we can hold and contain our experience, make sense of what happened in new ways, and discover deeper meaning, then these concepts can come alive again. Slowly, over time, guided by new levels of kindness, clear-seeing, and multileveled awareness, we can begin to bear that which has been unbearable and provide sanctuary and safe passage for the shards of the broken world to reorganize.

As we train ourselves to re-inhabit our bodies even in the face of profoundly disturbing cognitions, feelings, and sensations, we can begin to weave a more integrated narrative of our lives, reauthoring the sacred story of who we are, our purpose here, and what is most important to us. We can gather the pieces into a coherent whole and begin to trust in the validity of our experience again.

The goal, then, is not some fixed state where we have successfully purged an aspect of our self-experience from what we are, as if it were some wretched foreign substance, but rather to find a larger home for it within us. Slowly, we can allow what has become frozen and solidified to thaw and become flexible. Ultimately, it is love, in the most resplendent sense of the word, that will soften the wounds of the body and the heart, for they will never unwind in an environment of self-aggression. It's just not safe or majestic enough there.

Over time, beyond merely holding and containing the sacred wound, we are invited to practice intimacy with it, to come even closer than we imagined possible to the lost children of the psyche and soma ... discovering that they have not come to harm us, but only to return home, to resume their instinctive place in the inner family.

In this way, perhaps we can salvage concepts such as "integration" and "healing," at least for today, re-envisioning and re-enchanting them with the force of an uncompromising and unapologetic compassion, soaked in the wisdom-essence of our true nature, as we open into the mystery together.

4

Wholeness and the Spiritual Journey

The Depths of the Shadowy Soil

As with any significant activity that offers the promise of depth and meaning, engagement with spirituality can provide a very rich pathway into the unfolding of the sacred world and the endless dimensions of the human heart. It can also be used to avoid emotional pain, to protect us from the demands of intimacy, to provide a buffer against unresolved feelings, and to keep at bay the very alive, untamed landscape of our vulnerability in all its forms. This observation is not meant to suggest that we turn from our most sacred beliefs and practices, but rather that we engage them with eyes wide open. There are an infinite number of ways ego can co-opt even the most revered teachings to fortify itself in the attempt to remedy early developmental failure, unresolved attachment wounding, the pain of chronic misattunement, and unmetabolized trauma of all kinds. Believing we are becoming more intimate with our experience, we may be surprised to discover that we are in fact unconsciously distancing ourselves from the aliveness we so deeply long for.

During the course of our journey as spiritual seekers and practitioners, many of us can come to dismiss the relational and somatic worlds altogether, believing we are manifesting some sort of pure, transcendent, and unconditioned reality that is somehow free from our own unresolved wounding. In the rush to the transpersonal, the personal and interpersonal are trampled and abandoned. As a result, what is then downloaded through us to others is simply more traumatic and unintegrated organization, and a realization that is anything but whole. As Ken Wilber, integral philosopher and pioneering theorist, once told me, "Absolute, always already enlightenment can never be properly transmitted through a broken relative vehicle." But it requires everything we have to see this, to allow the implications of it to sink all the way in, and to care enough about ourselves, our world, and others around us to respond with an open heart.

It is not that difficult to look out into the contemporary spiritual landscape and see these dynamics in full force. The spiritual path has become a commodity, bought and sold on the open market, with its endless fantastical promises of permanent happy feelings ("blissful" if we're *really* spiritual), a life completely free from surges of anxiety and depression, endless moments of "being in the now," and a reliable escape from the messy realities of intimacy, the body, money, sexuality, family dynamics, and so on. It's much more compelling (as well as less threatening and better selling) to focus on the bliss, the positive, and the high, and how we can wiggle ourselves into a safe and resolved "spiritual" state and manifest all the things we have been conditioned to believe we want.

In ways both subtle and not so subtle, the chaotic, imaginative, organic darkness becomes covered over and, as many of us discover the hard way, this does not really end that well. And in the covering we bury and disavow those jewels that are only reachable in the depths of the shadowy soil. Many are discovering that some current stream of "happiness" isn't what they are actually after anyway, but meaning, depth, intimacy, and aliveness. "Happiness" is simply not large or majestic enough to contain what they are.

Making use of spirituality to avoid certain aspects of ourselves is not "bad," pathological, or inherently problematic. Nor do we need to diminish, critique, or practice aggression toward it, making use of our inquiry to reenact early dynamics of judging and shaming our organizational strategies. We do not engage in avoidant behavior because there is something wrong with us but because we are alive, sensitive, and doing our best to take care of ourselves using the tools we have at our disposal. Like any defensive behavior, the activity serves a function and can be respected as such. And then from a clear, spacious, non-shaming seeing, these subtleties can be explored with compassion, care, and open curiosity—fueled by the longing to know what is most true. As we inquire with our hearts open, we can see what feelings and aspects of ourselves our beliefs and practices may be inadvertently helping us avoid, and investigate whether we are ready to turn back toward them and provide a home for their metabolization and integration. No shame, no blame, no self-aggression. Just more awareness, presence, and kindness. No urgency to dismantle our defensive organization or "get enlightened" overnight or resolve it all on the heels of an insightful weekend retreat. Just grounded, open-hearted curiosity and inquiry, inspired by the love of truth.

Of course, what I'm outlining here is not new. Many great siddhas, yogis, meditators, and depth-oriented psychotherapists have reported on this phenomenon for quite a while now, beginning formally with psychologist John Welwood's naming of *spiritual bypassing* several decades ago, though we can of course find underpinnings of the phenomenon in Freud himself, and back even further into antiquity. In summary, I'll leave you with a few words from Chögyam Trungpa, guidance I believe worthy of frequent reconsideration, and in his ever-poetic style:

As long as we follow a spiritual approach promising salvation, miracles, liberation, then we are bound by the "golden chain of spirituality." Such a chain might be beautiful to wear, with its inlaid jewels and intricate carvings, but nevertheless, it imprisons us. People think they can wear the golden chain for decoration without being imprisoned by it, but they are deceiving themselves. As long as one's approach to spirituality is based upon enriching ego, then it is spiritual materialism, a suicidal process rather than a creative one.

"Ego" as an Invitation into Presence

What do we mean by this word "ego" anyway? I don't use the term very much because I have come to find it to be a rather disembodied and experience-distant concept. Also, it usually carries with it an undercurrent of judgment and shame, at least in spiritual circles, often employed as a way to attack our vulnerability, our humanness, and our relative (and equally sacred) nature as separate individuals. But mostly, I have looked long and hard and have never found such an entity in my immediate experience. Or in another's.

Just to be clear, I'm referring to the term as it is used in contemporary spirituality, not in depth psychology, which is a different conversation altogether and beyond the scope of this book. From the perspective discussed here, it can be helpful to relate to this more spiritually oriented "ego" as a *process* or a *verb* rather than as a noun. Viewing it in this way can help prevent holding it up as some reified entity that exists *within us,* as some super unconscious homunculus who wreaks havoc on our deepest spiritual aspirations.

"The ego" is often spoken about as if it is some sort of self-existing *thing* that at times takes us over—some nasty, super unspiritual, ignorant little person living inside—and causes us to act in a really unevolved way, creating unending messes in our lives and getting in the way of our progress on the path. It is something to be horribly ashamed of, and the more spiritual we are, the more we will strive to "get rid of it," transcend it, or enter into imaginary spiritual wars with it. If we look carefully, we may see that if the ego is anything, it is likely those very voices that are yelling at us to get rid of it.

But how do we get rid of something that isn't there? In order to discover the deepest truths about this process of ego, we must return to the mind of the beginner, to set aside what we think we know about this topic, and approach it in a way that is both humble and fresh. For a moment, let us forget what the gurus and the "experts" say and go deeply into our own bodies and minds and see for ourselves. As with all of the inquiries in this book, we must follow the Buddha's admonition to be a lamp unto ourselves and to shine the light of our own awareness into the hidden and the subtle areas of our immediate experience to discover what is most true.

When we slow down and step outside the world of conceptual spirituality, attuning to our actual present experience, do we find an "ego" there? Or is the "ego" a disembodied concept that further entrenches us in the trance of a solid, continuous, separate self (one that is wretched and unworthy, no less)? Is "the ego" merely another concept by which we can reenact the abandonment, shaming, and dissociation that we learned as young children in response to environments lacking in empathic attunement?

One simple way of defining "ego" as a process (if we must) is any activity—conscious or otherwise—that leads us to turn from, abandon, practice aggression toward, or stay in resistance to what appears in our immediate, subjective experience. So, if in a moment of activation, we become aware of feelings of rage or grief, a constricted throat, a heavy heart, an aroused nervous system, a limiting self-narrative, or a cascade of critical, ruminative thoughts, we might see the ego as that process whereby we *move away* from and avoid that experience rather than approach and move toward it, which would be a more embodied, compassionate, or contemplative response. This movement away, which we might come to discover as the root of nearly all of our psychological suffering, usually takes place either by denying what is there or by indulging in interpretations of it, fueling it, and fusing with it as who we ultimately are. Both of these strategies (corresponding to limbic fight-flight as well as to anxious-avoidant attachment) will inevitably trigger engagement of compensatory (addictive) behavior, designed to take us as quickly as possible out of our vulnerability and the oftentimes messy and sticky world of feeling altogether. As noted previously, this activity was intelligent from the perspective of a young child lacking the developmental capacity to tolerate, contain, and metabolize intense cognitive, affective, and somatic material. The question, of course, is whether such splitting off (whether by way of repression or fusion) is necessary or in service of an adult longing for intimacy, connection, and aliveness, with developmental capacities that were simply not available at an earlier time.

In other words, ego is a process of dissociation and splitting off, to use psychological jargon, in the attempt to prevent overwhelming anxiety from pouring into conscious awareness. Or, in more spiritual terminology, it is the attempt to keep us out of the otherwise naked reality of how open, unknown, and groundless our lives truly are, where anything could happen at any time, where reality is never going to correspond to our hopes, fears, and dreams, and the way we thought it was all going to turn out. It is just too alive without a reference point of "me" to organize around, and the only possible response is to contract and return to safe ground. It is this process of contraction that we might refer to as "ego."

If we want to get to know more about how "the ego" works, we can begin by getting curious about those feeling states that we will do just about anything to avoid. Start to become really familiar with the specific strategies you employ to avoid feeling, which can include any sort of habitual, addictive behavior. Remember that the goal of this inquiry is *increased awareness,* not the cultivation of a new tool to shame yourself or beat yourself up with. From the ground of clear awareness, you can then slowly re-invite the feelings you are avoiding into your experience and begin to hold, contain, and reintegrate them, very slowly, one moment at a time.

Whenever you notice yourself complaining, blaming others, shaming, or attacking yourself, or completely lost in ruminative thinking and worry, you can inquire if there is an underlying feeling state that these activities are serving to keep you out of. Of course, there is also the more generic list that we are all familiar with, of habitual behavior that we engage in to take us as quickly as possible out of the hot, sticky, restless claustrophobia of pure feeling: overeating, excessive internet usage, mindless shopping, unconscious sexuality, unhealthy conflict avoidance, the failure to enact appropriate boundaries, hiding out from intimacy when we claim we long for it more than anything else, numbing ourselves with back to back episodes of *Game of Thrones*, slamming rapid-fire shots of tequila in the face of boredom or emptiness, and even the use of spirituality to keep us out of some really vulnerable and messy human experience. I'm not personally familiar with any of these pathways of escape, nor are you, the reader, I'm sure. But just theoretically speaking ... we all know many others who engage in this way, and we might be so kind as to help bring awareness for their sake.

Once we notice the ways we are avoiding feeling through habitual behavior, with kindness as our guide we can slow down and get curious about what might *really* be going on under the surface. What do we need to escape? What will happen if we stay with the feeling and cut into the momentum of our addictive behaviors? As we're heading to the refrigerator when we're not hungry, as we're mindlessly logging on to Facebook, as we're looping around with the same storyline about how wretched we are or how no one will ever be there for us, as we fail to stand up for ourselves when we are being taken advantage of ... what feeling state are we trying to avoid?

As you discover your particular strategies for avoiding feeling, the invitation is to slow way down, to drop into the body and renew your commitment to no longer abandon yourself. To meet this long-lost feeling companion who has been trying to reach you for so long, and provide just one moment of holding. To breathe into the feeling and surround it with warmth. Perhaps it is some grief, heartbreak, rage, or hopelessness. Despair, confusion, restlessness, or emptiness. For some it can even be intense states of joy, aliveness, or creativity that are being avoided. But for one or two seconds, to start, envelop these ones with your presence. It may appear that they have come to do harm, but they are only *you* in disguise, lost parts of yourself, little children who are longing to return home. They are filled with important data, energy, and information, but their guidance can only be released into a field of nonaggressive and non-shaming kindness. It will take practice to reunite with these lost messengers of the heart, for they have come to be associated with trauma, overwhelm, and dysregulating anxiety. The freedom we long for will never be found in their eradication, only in attunement to the wisdom they carry.

As we come to discover in a deeply embodied way that turning away from what is is the root cause of nearly all of our emotional suffering (this is referred to as "experiential avoidance" in psychological jargon), we can begin to explore a commitment to replace the abandonment with care, to end the aggression toward our experience, and to turn back toward what we have been trying to escape for so long. This is something we must be willing to practice, over and over again, realizing that it will take time, energy, and effort to rewire the pathways of dissociation that were embedded in our psychic (and neural) structure in an effort to care for ourselves at an earlier time.

In this way, we can use the surges of "ego"—whatever it is—as a summons and fiery reminder to be mindful of the potential to split off and dissociate. We can train ourselves to meet our experience instead with empathy, warmth, and compassion. And proclaim to ourselves and to the world that the *entirety* of our inner experience is valid, intelligent, and worthy of our care and holding. *In this sense, ego is an invitation into presence.* As we slow down and reaffirm our commitment to knowing ourselves at the deepest levels—no longer meeting our present experience in a field of judgment, dismissal, and aggression—we can re-craft the narrative of ego in new and more integrated ways rather than using the concept to indulge in reenactments of the shame and blame that so many of us were met with in our families of origin. In this way, we can actually use the energies of "ego" to come closer to ourselves, and as an ally on the path of deepening clear seeing and self-compassion.

Love will do anything to reach us, even create spiritual ideas like "the ego" in the hope that we will use even the most experience-distant concepts to return home. So I suppose in this way we can salvage the use of the term "ego," at least for today.

A Most Sacred Story

The goal of this work is not to "get rid of your story" but to have a more flexible relationship with it. At times you can wear it as an ornament and at other times you can set it down for a while, allowing it to rest from a long journey, picking it up again only if it is helpful in connecting with others and in opening into the mystery.

We human beings are storytellers. Go ahead: tell one. Then listen carefully as the characters, plots, subplots, and settings share their longing to be authored in more integrated forms. With openness, acceptance, and kindness, you can practice intimacy with your story, touching the beauty, the pain, the joy, and the heartbreak of your life as it is and as it has unfolded over the months and years.

Allow yourself to come close to the narrative of your life. What story are you telling? It is both wise and kind to know the stories that are surging under the surface and discover whether they are yours or belong to another. Are you living your own life or someone else's? Take a moment, and see. There's no need to be afraid. You will not be tainted, or lose your way, or fall from grace, or lose your powerful "nondual" realization. The invitation is to move *toward* the story you have been telling, to get really clear on the lens through which you organize your experience, for it is only in the knowing the story you are telling that you will be able to make a conscious decision as to whether you would like to tell a different one.

Come close, but not so close that you fuse with the story, get lost inside it, and identify it as who you are in an ultimate sense. Explore the narrative with an open heart, while remembering that *no story* is ever majestic enough to contain what you truly are, and at best can only represent a part of you. Listen carefully to what these longtime companions have to say and meet their longing to be integrated into the fullness of what you are, the wholeness that both transcends *and* includes the conceptual. The stories and ways of organizing your experience are an important aspect of your journey and they are valid and honorable as allies on the path, but they can never touch the entirety of what it means to be an alive, majestic, and complex human being.

Of course the greatest story of all is that you no longer have a story, that you have "transcended" all stories and that there is "no one here any longer" to tell a story. You are welcome to tell this story as well! But perhaps you will be willing to see that it too is only partial, like all stories. And that it will never capture the luminous essence that you are. A great tale to be told, for sure, and one that you can play with wholeheartedly as it arises and dances in and around you, only to fall away into the great space from which it came.

In this very moment, you can finally call off the war with your stories. What a relief—it is so exhausting to do battle with yourself. While it may seem that the stories are working against you, they are not obstacles to the freedom you are seeking. Like all form, they are expressions of wholeness and open awareness itself, arising to be authored over and over again. You can hold them with a light touch, resting in the unresolvable, rich middle territory between denial and fusion. In this alchemical middle, you can dance with the story as an ally, re-enchanting it from time to time and dreaming a new story when you are moved to do so. But always remembering that no story is vast enough to contain the splendor of what you are.

It is an act of kindness to update the story of your life as you learn more about yourself and journey deeper on the path of the heart. You can revise the conclusions you have come to about others and about the world, replacing outdated and outmoded perceptions as they are clarified over time. You can train yourself to hold your stories with spacious awareness rather than aggression and even violence, and like all form your stories will reveal their nature as open, flexible, and translucent.

Wholeness and the Spiritual Journey

It is all too common in contemporary spirituality to be anti-story, to devalue any sort of narrative about one's experience, as if engaging at the level of story is something to apologize for, evidence that we're missing the mark and getting caught up in "drama" and "the ego." Often when I speak with people about what is going on for them, they will preface their report with something like, "Well, I mean, not to get into my story or anything, but ..." As if it were something to be ashamed of to have a story, to have a way to organize and make meaning of their experience.

The thing is, we're all telling a story. We're all storytellers. This seems to be a unique expression of being human, of interacting with our world and exploring our inner lives, relationships, and outer life circumstances. We don't know if a rose tells a story about itself, or a deer, or the moon, or an owl. In any event, it's nothing to be embarrassed about or to think of as lesser than other modes of being and expression. Even the great "powerfully awakened" teachers have a narrative (even if it's a narrative about how they no longer have a narrative). Just get to know them a bit or, better yet, ask their spouses or their kids. Things are not always as they appear.

As long as there is any sort of identification left with the narrative of "me," it is an act of self-compassion to become as clear as you can regarding the story you are telling about yourself, others, and the world. When all is said and done, what do you think about yourself? When no one is looking or you are activated in relationship, what conclusions do you come to about your worthiness, about whether you can count on others, about whether there is safety in this world, about what you're doing here? Rather than pretend you don't have a story—or that it is meaningless, a mistake, or evidence of how unspiritual you are—you could open into it with curiosity, kindness, and care. And from this clarifying ground of acceptance, holding, and non-shame, you can then decide if you'd like to update your story, weave a more integrated or cohesive narrative, or author a version that is more accurate and more representative of what you now know to be most true.

Yes, from the perspective of the ultimate, the story of you is nonsolid, translucent, and will never touch the vastness of what you truly are. While honoring this, you can also appreciate the relative truth of the human body, psyche, brain, and nervous system, not discarding these dimensions of experience with spiritual theories and unacknowledged aggression. And with kindness you can watch and passionately participate as your narrative unfolds, changes, and shifts, flexible and responsive to the ongoing discoveries of the heart.

Even your story is pure when met with eyes wide open, a luminous and unique expression of the mystery that you are.

Love Has No Opposite

Some will tell you that fear is the opposite of love. And in this teaching the war begins. But love has no opposite, for it is whole and without division. It is the vast, open field in which all form comes and goes, including the temporary, wavelike appearance of what we call fear.

When inquiring into a psychologically and spiritually based concept such as "fear," it can be helpful to set the word aside for a moment, as it has become so charged with conditioning. It is so easy to become caught up in the word and all of the associations surrounding it, distancing ourselves from the fires of our immediate experience before we even realize it, believing we're in touch with the aliveness of the present when in fact we're orbiting around it with concept and conditioned history. If we will set aside the *word* fear, even temporarily (we can pick it back up later if we must), we can explore in a more intimate way what is *actually* unfolding in a given here-and-now moment. Not what we *think* is happening or what we've *learned* is happening, or what a particular emotion or sensation means about us as a person, but a simple, bare, open, and kind awareness of what is *actually* happening. Once we slow down in this way and connect with our natural curiosity, we can then ask: What is this life that is surging in me that I have overlaid with this word "fear"? What is erupting underneath the surface, longing to be known, emerging out of the depths for a moment of my undivided, loving, unconditioned attention?

It can be helpful, of course, to engage this inquiry during moments of emotional and psychic activation, conducting a real-time experiment in the laboratory of our own bodies and minds. Additionally, also producing insightful data, we can practice by means of visualization and imagination, recalling a recent time when we were captured by fear, worry, and anxiety, and invite these energies into our conscious experience so we may meet them and explore their qualities, in our quest to know what is most true. While they may not be quite as vivid by means of imagination, we are often able to nonetheless become intimate with the associated complexes, emotions, sensations, and organizing principles associated with the experience of what we call fear.

For example, are we aware of a constriction in the throat? A fluttering in the belly? A pounding in the heart? Images of something unsafe happening? Ruminative thoughts of worry and impending danger? Feelings of heat or cold? A speedy sensation in our chest? An urgent impulse to take some action—to get away, fight, escape, find relief? Or is it the combination of two or more of these? In this full-bodied inquiry, we might discover that there is not some solid *thing* called "fear," but rather that this word "fear" has become associated with something very unworkable and unworthy of our attention, an experience that must quickly be converted into something else. We immediately come to see the appearance of fear as an obstacle on the path rather than a hidden aspect of our experience arising out of the unconscious as a carrier of important information for the journey ahead.

Upon investigation—fueled by slowness, curiosity, and self-kindness—what is revealed is an unprecedented assembling of perception, images, emotions, sensations, and impulses that configure and come together in a totally fresh way and then falls apart as the wave merges back into the ocean from which it came. There is nothing solid that we can find that exists on its own, no entity called "fear" that we are being asked to do battle with, but some embodied experience that may in fact be quite disturbing and not easy to work with.

As our inquiry deepens, however, we may discover that there is no suffering inherent in the arising of this inner material. Yes, it might be intense, it might not be fun, it might take everything we have to stay close and to stay open. But the movement *away* from what is alive within us is the root cause of our struggle, along with the deeply embedded emotional conclusions about the *meaning* of this unprecedented assembling of emotion, rumination, and felt sense. While in most cases we do not have much control over the arising of the inner world, we do have some say, with practice, over how we respond, whether we will meet what appears in a field of openness, curiosity, and compassion. Or whether we will receive it with misattunement, self-aggression, and the strategies of self-abandonment. Training ourselves with our hearts wide open to reorganize the meaning and purpose of our symptoms and difficult emotions is a profound act of self-love, rooted in wisdom and creativity.

We will never pin down what love *is* with concepts, but one way of approaching its open limitlessness is to see it as a majestic, tender holding space into which all emotions, feelings, and sensations arise, play for a short while, and then dissolve. Just as passing clouds can never taint the purity of the sky, the temporary dance of fear can never stain the magnificence of what you are. Unlike the density of the conceptual, love appears to have no bias for the presence of courage over fear, joy over despair, or oneness over multiplicity. All experience is welcome as valid and worthy of your care. Everything is path, including the raw, immediate, somatic experience of fear, as long as it is not abandoned, rejected, and made into an enemy via spiritual process and theory. In this, a great mystery can be revealed: there is no suffering inherent in the experience of fear, but only in the moving away from it, invalidating it, and concluding that it is an error that must urgently be remedied.

Allowing in the implications of this mystery can reveal a revolutionary freedom that is always already here, not dependent on your first transforming fear into something else, including its "opposite."

These concepts simply fall away in the fire of direct experience and the spaciousness of open awareness. Is it love or is it fear that would make the statement "fear is the opposite of love"? Love is welcoming to all of its children, even the fearful one—perhaps especially this one, who is only longing to be allowed back home. Love would never claim that one of its own is its opposite.

Fear is merely a temporary wave in the nervous system, longing to be met, integrated, and metabolized in the wholeness that you are, as are all forms that appear in the mystery of the inner landscape. It is not an enemy against whom you fight imaginary spiritual battles. You can call off the war and set aside the conditioning of a spirituality of aggression once you see how much unnecessary suffering such fictional wars generate. Apprehended with an open heart, fear is revealed to be a unique form of aliveness that seeks the light of your presence, which could never, ever be blemished by the temporary movement of fear.

By abandoning fear and concluding that its presence is evidence that something has gone wrong and you have failed, you inadvertently keep alive the ancient pathways of self-abandonment and self-violence. Love is not opposed to fear but wishes to embrace it, enter into intimacy with it, and provide room for its essence to unfold and illuminate. There is no need for you to *fear fear* any longer. In this very moment, you can call off the war with your experience, holding whatever arises within your body and your heart as an invitation into wholeness.

When fear is fully met and safe passage is provided, it reveals itself, like all form, as none other than love in disguise. You need no longer practice a spirituality of exclusion and aggression. Fear is not the opposite of love, for love has no opposite.

The Sacred Invitation of Not-Knowing

There's a fantasy that we're supposed to know what to do with our lives. And if we do not then this is clear evidence that something is wrong with us, some cosmic error has occurred which must urgently be remedied. Especially if this not-knowing is accompanied by waves of uncertainty, hopelessness, and confusion … more evidence that we have failed, fueled by further fantasy that feelings such as contradiction, doubt, and deflation are not very "spiritual." What about the endless stream of "high" vibrations? The manifesting of more and more cool things for myself, that I've dreamed will make me happy? The unconscious belief that the role of my partner or my spiritual practice is to make me feel good?

Yes, at times it will appear that nothing is happening, that we are being asked to marinate in waves of the great ocean of nothing. Before we turn from the nonconventional allies of confusion and doubt, let us reimagine their purpose and holy function. In a world that is fixated with doing, with answers, and with resolving the wildness of life, we must remember that death is required for new forms of love and creativity to take form. The death-rebirth journey is one that is nonnegotiable and cuts through our preferences, hopes, and fears. While this reality is deflating to a mind seeking control and resolution, this cutting through is an emissary of wholeness, and is sacred.

As our center of gravity drops out of the density of the conditioned and into the intelligence of the body, we discover profound wisdom and creativity in the core of the not-knowing. We come to see that not-knowing is a perfectly valid, honorable, and authentic place to be, and not in need of transformation. It is a pure expression of transformation, in and of itself, exactly as it is.

As an experiment, you could say out loud, with the earth as your witness, *"I don't know."* And give yourself permission to not know, for now, without any shame, judgment, or self-aggression. You need no longer pathologize the movement of not-knowing, but embrace and explore it with curiosity and a fiery tenderness.

Sink into the raw, ripe, pregnant, muddy glory and mess of your unique, unprecedented heart … and see what you are.

Always in the Flow

We often hear how important it is to "be in the flow" and that if we could somehow consistently be in this state, we could fully show up and enjoy our lives. We could finally take the risk of leading with intimacy, share our vulnerability, feel truly connected, and step all the way into the miracle we sense is unfolding here. We could dance in relationship with that part of the spectrum that we prefer, safe and free from other, less wanted feelings and experiences. "Getting into" the flow and "staying in it" has become a goal, somewhat akin to "being in the present moment," which while being poetic and potentially inspirational, is also a tool of shame and aggression for many, as they inevitably fail to live up to the demands of a conceptual spirituality. While there may be power in "now," there seems to be very little power in the *concept* of now.

As we explore this in a way that is embodied and rooted in the actuality of the present, we may discover that it is not actually possible, at an experiential level, to be "outside" the flow. We are always in the flow of life. The *idea* that there is some "us" on one side and some *thing* called "flow" on the other that is the great trance that seems to be unique to the human experience. It is difficult to imagine a tree or the moon or a deer wondering if it is "in the flow" or not.

Usually, when we talk about being "in the flow," what we mean is that we *like* the thoughts, feelings, and sensations arising in our experience. Or, our families, societies, and even our spiritual teachers have told us that these experiences are the "right" ones. If we have more vulnerable, intense, "unspiritual," or contradictory feelings, we deem this as accurate evidence that we are "out of the flow." We have a difficult time tolerating ambiguity and in response often move quickly in the attempt to resolve it, lest we have to stay close to the paradoxical nature of reality and the fact that the emotional world is a dizzying field of alive and contradictory energies, rarely conforming to our need for control and consistency. It is from this inability to hold, contain, and tolerate the tension of the opposites that self-aggression takes root and flowers, and the dream of abandoning the "non-flow" to return to the flow as quickly as possible is born. But if what we mean by "the flow" is a natural state of freedom, aliveness, and wholeness—the uncaused and already-existing reality of our true nature as open, spacious awareness—then this process of preference and abandonment is *not* the flow. It is a prison, actually, the fantasy of "returning" to a state of flow. This dream becomes the foundation of a life of struggle and unnecessary suffering.

Perhaps it is only in the willingness to fully participate in our present experience, exactly as it is, that the always already nature of flow will be revealed. Flow is not something you will one day arrive at as some sort of acquisition when you line up all of the right experiences, successfully abandoning and replacing what is here with something else. The flow is here right now, utterly inseparable from what you are, and is revealed by way of your commitment to close, empathic self-attunement, rooted in curiosity and self-care.

When you are willing to bring warmth and presence to whatever is arising in the immediacy of now, the question of how to feel more flow ceases to arise. Or even if it does appear from time to time, it passes loosely through you, like a knife through warm butter. By the time you recognize it, it has vanished and no longer lingers as yet another self-improvement project that you must first complete before you can fully participate here. You are already fully alive, and the flow is everywhere. From this perspective, the distinction between "flow" and "non-flow" falls away, and all you are left with is what you already are, which is complete and not lacking in or "outside" anything.

The Aggression in "Letting Go"

There is a deep desire in us to "let go" of those parts of ourselves that trouble or disturb us and that we believe are keeping us from the freedom and aliveness we long for. Often accompanying this desire is a profound and exhausting sense of frustration and even shame about not being able to let go in this way. It is seen as yet something else we've failed at, and this is painful. Whether it's letting go of the past, a certain person or attachment to them, an idea about ourselves, or certain feelings and emotions that we believe are evidence that there is something fundamentally wrong or unlovable about us. The project of "letting everything go" can quickly become a tool of aggression and self-abandonment, a reenactment of an earlier time when we split off from certain aspects of ourselves in order to fit into a world that could not contain the unique fullness of our experience.

We are often admonished (and admonish others) to "get over it," as if our past traumas, surging emotions, addictive behaviors, and organizing narratives are something we can just "choose" to "get over" one sunny afternoon. If we will allow ourselves to get curious about this, we can explore whether this demand to "let go" is serving us, and if so, to what end. And as we look even deeper, we may see that in large part the demand to "let go" has its origin in early childhood, where this was often a subtle (or not so subtle) message from the attachment figures around us: "Just get over it." "Stop crying." "Stop being so sad. You should be grateful for all you've been given." "Don't you dare be angry with me."

For many of us spiritual seekers, the *ultimate* letting go, what we *really* need to let go of, is the "ego" itself. The ego has become the bad girl and boy of spirituality, hiding inside the cracks and crevices, ready to surge at any time in a way that is very nonspiritual, mucking up everything with its selfish, ignorant, and pathological activity. As we slow down and inquire with deep interest, care, and spacious awareness—with the natural and transformative qualities of beginner's mind—we can explore whether love would ever ask us to "let go" of any inner experience. Must something, truly, be "let go" of? Again, to what end?

It is important to note that I'm not talking about an external behavior that is abusive, harmful, or unskillful toward yourself or another. Yes, please let go of these. Rather, I'm speaking about the relationship with your *inner* world of beliefs, images, fantasies, meanings, hopes, fears, emotions, feelings, and bodily sensations—the entire landscape of your internal world and subjective experience. This is an interesting inquiry and one that you must enter into without any preconceived notions about what you might find. As with all of the inquiries and invitations in this book, it is important to approach these experiments with a fresh and spontaneous heart and mind. Not as the expert, but as the beginner. Dare to see as clearly as you can what is *most* true, even if it does not conform to what you'd *like* to be true, what you've been *told* is true, or what you *should* arrive at if you conduct the inquiry in the "right" way. From this open and inquisitive place you can then explore whether it is the wisest, most compassionate, or most skillful course of action to "let go," your intention for doing so, the implications of taking such an action, and what that process might actually look like in real time.

What would it mean, for example, in your actual, present experience to "let go" of fear, a limiting narrative of abandonment, a wave of nauseous anxiety in the belly, a contraction or racing in the heart, constriction in the throat—or heartbreak, confusion, grief, or rage? Is this the deepest invitation you are receiving? To "let go"? Why? Do you believe that "letting go" of parts of yourself is going to make you happy? Fulfilled? At peace? Whole? Become passionately curious and interested in knowing your motivations for this, and what is truly driving the demand to "let go." Is it coming from love? From fear? From wisdom? From avoidance? From unresolved feelings of unworthiness? From the fragmented self-narrative that something is wrong with you as you are?

These are not questions to take lightly but to spend time and care with, discovering in the fire of our own direct experience what is most true. Does "letting go" truly get rid of something or does it bury it and keep it alive in more subtle forms, and in fact lead us to organize our experience around it? Is it "letting go" that is most helpful or is it something more whole, more integrative, less aggressive that we're longing for? Is the offending material simply a cosmic error that must be eradicated through spiritual process, or is it an invitation, a form of intelligence and counsel, that carries with it hidden wisdom and guidance to be integrated? Please do not take my word for any of this. Make the embodied journey and see for yourself.

As you descend deeper in this inquiry, you may discover an unconventional sort of gateway, one that is not organized around "letting go" but comes with another invitation altogether: to finally turn *toward* what is arising within you, all the way into what has been longing to be held, without pathologizing it or needing to change, heal, or transform it, without needing even to "let it go." In this environment, you open to the possibility that whatever appears in the sacred laboratory of your body, your psyche, and your heart is pure and luminous as it is, filled with information, and not in any way an obstacle to your true heart's longing. It doesn't mean you will *like* it or it will be easy and "flow-y" to stay with, or that it will provide support to an old persona that is dying to make way for something new. Nor does it mean it will conform to your hopes, fears, fantasies, and dreams about who and what you are, who others are, what relationship is, or what the world is. But when you finally meet, hold, contain, and offer it sanctuary, it will reveal its true nature, as well as its role on the path of depth, meaning, and love.

While the "ego"—the entity that is the ultimate target of our project of letting go—may appear vivid and colorful, are we able upon investigation to find such a one lurking around somewhere in our psyches? In our bodies? Or is "ego" just another concept we've been taught, another way to disembody from present experience, and another vehicle by which to shame ourselves and move further away? From the intention to no longer abandon our experience—to in fact make contact with and hold it in curiosity and kindness—we will discover a freedom that is always already here.

By way of this inquiry we may discover that we need not "let go" of any inner experience, but that it will "let go" of us when we meet it with loving presence and the energies of non-abandonment. It will release its hold on us when infused with breath, awareness, embodiment, and life. Further, it will "let go" of us when we have received its revelation and when we are no longer in need of the function it provides. In the Dzogchen tradition of Tibetan Buddhism, it is the nature of all phenomena to "self-liberate" upon a meeting with naked awareness. When we are able to stay with what arises in the field of consciousness in an embodied way, wrapping it in a cloak of warmth and loving presence, we may become astonished to discover that it takes care of itself without any effort, striving, or struggle of our own. "Taking care of" doesn't mean that the experience we do not like will go away and be replaced by alternative experiences that we like better, or think we should be experiencing, or have been told by others are the "right" ones to be having. "Taking care of" refers to the inherent great natural perfection of things as they are, and the reality that the forms arising in awareness are no different from the ground of awareness itself; that they are in fact made of the same luminous and alchemical substance. And even that unique configuration we call "ego" comprises these same strands of awareness, radiant and vast, and will reveal its nature when we meet it in direct embrace.

If you take the risk to call off the war with yourself, love will be waiting for you, for it is what you are. And in this you will see that there are no "obstacles" on your journey, only further revelations of just how subtle, magic, and endless the path of the heart truly is.

Closer to the Wound

As a psychotherapist who works with clients committed to spiritual growth and transformation, I have discovered with my fellow travelers just how natural it is for us, at times, to use spirituality to hide from life: from intimacy, from our feelings, from our vulnerability, from unresolved emotional wounding, as well as from intense, exposing, naked experience of all kinds. Despite our noblest intentions to live a life of authenticity and integrity, we can engage with spiritual teachings and practices in a way in which we deny, stuff, shut out, and abandon real feelings of hurt, anger, disappointment, and despair as if they are "unspiritual," unacceptable, and further evidence of our own ignorance, unworthiness, and the untamed functioning of our "ego." Alternatively, in addition to denying things like depression, anxiety, and even the reality of having a need (which for some comes with tremendous shame and judgment), we may find ourselves acting out the unmetabolized material in our relationships, or "acting in" toward ourselves with aggression, shame, and blame, convinced we are making actual contact with the deeper recesses of our being, while in actuality orbiting around the surface, doing everything possible to prematurely discharge the disturbing energy that is seething underneath.

Of course, splitting off from this material, acting it out, or hastily "transcending" it, as I discussed earlier, does not remove, transform, or heal it, but only sequesters it deeper into the shadow, where it will inevitably emerge in the relational field as partly processed images and fantasies, hazy figures from the dream world, and even as physical symptoms and conditions.

Depending on the unique configuration of our core vulnerabilities, protective strategies, and ways of organizing our experience, we learned as children to shut down certain aspects of our personalities as well as particular emotional experiences to avoid disruption in our connection to early caregivers. For example, if our expression of sadness triggered anxiety or aggression, or if our need to be seen was met with shame and rage—or if our natural inclination toward being independent and caring for ourselves led to judgment and ridicule—we learned very quickly to bury these aspects as maintaining the tie to critical attachment figures was paramount to our psychic survival. To continue to assert these aspects of our personality and emotional life would require us to step into tremendous anxiety and survival-level arousal, and this was simply too volatile for a growing brain and nervous system.

As young children, it was an act of intelligence and creativity to split off, dissociate, and disconnect from material we were not developmentally capable of digesting and metabolizing on our own, including the dysregulating and traumatic feelings and narratives that arose in the face of misattunement, neglect, and empathic failure of all kinds. As infants and young children, we were wired to do everything possible to maintain the ties to those critical figures around us, even if that connection was misattuned, less than healthy, or even dangerous. A shaky, tentative, and even potentially harmful connection is more regulating than none at all in the little nervous system of a helpless infant.

As adults, we can see the remnants of this need to receive mirroring, empathy, and presence from others, even when a part of us knows that a particular relationship no longer truly serves our deepest longings. To allow ourselves to inquire into this, in a way that is non-pathologizing and non-shaming, can provide some very important data. And it is usually quite humbling as it reveals the very natural, mammalian aspect of ourselves that is so wired to connect with others and receive their attunement and validation. The goal of this inquiry is always greater freedom, which is in part reflected in a broad array of choices in how we are able to respond to our lives. In difficult life situations, such as whether to stay in or leave a relationship, we want to have access to the wide range of conscious choices that are available to an adult in the here and now rather than have to rely unconsciously on those reactions of a young child in the "there and then."

As we engage over time in these strategies of denial and acting out—both pathways being oriented toward self-abandonment and turning away from our vulnerability and the emotional landscape altogether—we might find ourselves wondering why we are not feeling alive, why our experience is flat or numb, why we aren't able to step in and take risks in our relationships or our vocation, and why things just aren't flowing the way we'd like. There may not be any specific thing we can point to that is "wrong" in our lives, but we are still quite convinced that something is off, something is missing, something important is out of place. We sense that there is something deeper, something more meaningful, some more intimate way of being, but nevertheless it remains just out of reach. Though usually occurring underneath the radar of conscious awareness, the deeply embedded sense that we are not loved or lovable as we are infuses and colors our perception and interactions with others. This coagulation of energy has a way of perpetuating itself and eating at us from the inside, sure to emerge at some point (usually at the most inopportune times) in behavior that is passive-aggressive, avoidant, critical, or anxious.

Even though all of this is seething underneath the status quo of everything being "okay," a deeper part of us senses that only in intimate and direct contact with our vulnerability and unprocessed somatic feelings will we know this aliveness firsthand. And only then will we be able to take a risk, be spontaneous, and embody new levels of wisdom, compassion, and creativity in our lives, especially in our relationships with others. As long as we use spirituality to avoid intimacy, vulnerability, and the darker depths of our own being—as long as it remains yet another means to avoid full, naked contact with our unlived lives—we will feel lonely at our core, disconnected, and split off from love. As we start to discover, with as much kindness, compassion, and curiosity as possible, the ways we are using spiritual ideas, beliefs, language, teachings, and practices to avoid relationship (with self and other), we can make a commitment to deepening our awareness, caring even more about what is most true, and going on a journey of discovery. We need not shame ourselves for what is unearthed in our inquiry, or deem it evidence that we have failed or that something is wrong with us. But we can use what we discover as an opportunity to illuminate the strategies we've brought into adulthood to keep us safe from the vastness that we are. We sense that in order to know this wholeness, we must re-embody to those aspects of ourselves that we disconnected from at an earlier time in order to fit in and receive attunement from others and from a world that was not able or willing to meet us in this undivided place. It can seem like moving a mountain to take on this work, but here we are. We have somehow come here for this, and can start exactly where we are, one small step at a time.

As I mentioned earlier, it was not insane, pathological, or a function of blind conflict to split off from this material when we did not possess the developmental structures to hold and stay with it. We were doing whatever we could to take care of ourselves and prevent states of overwhelm and dysregulation—and we can honor this caretaking. For it is from this ground of kindness, warmth, and empathy that we can discover whether we still need to be protected in this way, whether such protection is still in our best interest, and whether we might now be ready to take care of ourselves and engage the world in a radically new way. We cannot go into this inquiry convinced that we know where it will lead, what it will evoke, or the "right" way to respond. Our discovery will be unique to us. We must enter with our agendas or preconceptions held very lightly, and open to the truth of whatever we discover. And if we are so inspired, we can slowly start to allow the protective function to dissolve in the light of our awareness as we begin the journey of reclaiming responsibility for those feelings and qualities that we've lost contact with along the way.

As I stated at the beginning of this section, the spiritual journey is one of the most illuminating vehicles we have available to explore the depths, to discover who and what we are at the most profound levels. The invitation is to engage the journey with eyes wide open, vigilant and ever discerning the ways that we can co-opt even the sacred path of the spirit to keep us from the confrontation with the unconscious: an encounter that is nonnegotiable at some point on the way of the heart. While we may naturally feel fear and anxiety in the face of such confrontation, it is the doorway to the immense light that is longing to emerge here. But we must remember that this light will at times take the form of the dark and the unexpected.

The Re-enchantment of Nonduality

While it is perfectly natural to prefer silence over noise, oneness over multiplicity, and harmony over chaos, reality appears to not share this bias. A star appears to not hold this same view.

The natural world and the energies inherent in the human spirit are creative, destructive, and full spectrum. Love is equally prepared to make use of the noisy, the multiple, the dual, and the confused to seed the relative with its qualities. To come at times as uncontaminated dualistic rage, bewilderment, and disordered wildness, so that form may come into being.

The unfolding of form is not always the expression of a clean, nondual view: untainted, invincible, and safe from reorganization, deflation, and the exposure of tender human vulnerability in all its dimensions. At times, the articulation is of a messy, untamed, ragingly empowered union of ascendant and descendent currents, heaven and earth, sun and the moon.

It is common to have a dualistic understanding of "nonduality," in which it is synonymous with silence, stillness, clarity, and transcendence, in a subtle war with confusion, activity, and the chaotic purity of emotion, imagination, the body, and the heart. Implied is the unexamined belief that the formless is more pure than form, spirit is more pure than matter, and silence is more pure than noise. But this is not nonduality. This is fear. It is not possible for there to be division in that which is nondual.

Let us reclaim the essence of nonduality by seeing that it is not opposed to duality and would never be at war with it, and end the dream of a conceptual spirituality. Let us re-enchant nonduality and infuse it with life, holding it loosely in one moment and discarding it the next, staying with the magic of now as it erupts in and as our lives as they are.

As we cultivate the courage to travel inside the opposites, hold the tension in balance, and compassionately confront the entirety of what we are, the inseparability of form and formless will be laid bare. The curtain will come down behind the Wizard of separation, and the purity of the human form will be revealed.

You Are Endless

It is possible to discover that the purpose of the journey is not to solve our problems or make us happy. And by insisting that our inquiry, our practices, and even our intimate relationships function primarily in this way we vastly limit what they are truly offering. As emissaries of wholeness and depth, they have seeded an invitation within you. To proclaim once and for all with the earth, the sun, the moon, and the stars as your witness. With the roar of a lion or lioness, shouting from the rooftop that you will no longer abandon your surging immediate experience, pathologize your sensitivity, or turn from your raw achy heart. But only honor and bow to the altar of your tender not-knowing.

As you continue along the way, yes, sometimes your problems will be solved, sometimes the symptoms will go away, sometimes the feelings you like will replace the ones you'd prefer be banished into the dark wood. But your inquiry is no longer oriented around replacement. It is far too wild, unprecedented, and creative for all that. As a pure expression of your love of the truth, it is full spectrum. For your longing will never be satisfied by that which is partial.

Love has brought you to this very place that you are now, as it continues its journey to know itself, through you and as you—by way of your perception, emotions, feelings, and imagination; and by the signs and symbols that it places along your path. Not so that you can fix something that is broken, or even "heal" in any conventional sense, but so that you can connect more deeply with your longing, to more clearly hear the call of the beloved within you, and become more and more transparent the feast of the offering that has been laid out before you: To be fully alive to and to fully participate in the mystery as it makes its way into the world of time and space.

No longer oriented in how to get from "here to there," but endlessly fascinated with how it is that love wishes to infuse "here" with its qualities. The path is endless. You are endless. Your heart is endless. And love will continue to reveal this endlessness to you, in ways that are at times peaceful, sweet, and soaked in pure joy. At other times, as wrathful, disturbing, and awash with the transmutation of the dark.

Both equally grace and appearing now as vehicles of love, and as infinite doorways into who and what you are. And what is to come.

The Invitation to Re-Imagine

On the path of the heart, we will inevitably be asked to re-imagine and breathe new life into concepts that have lost their meaning along the way. Words like "growth" and "healing" must be seeded with new vision and brought alive again in the fire of direct experience.

In some ways, the journey has very little to do with "growing." But is one of shedding and deflation, of recycling and reorganization. Or, in other words, what is it that is being "grown" within us? To what degree are we willing to rest in not-knowing, realizing that we're never going to resolve or come to terms with the wildness of love as it takes form here? It's just too creative for all that. For it is within the field of not-knowing that new meaning can emerge.

For many of us, "healing" has come to refer to a condition in which we no longer have to be in direct contact with our vulnerability, our sensitivity, and only in touch with a small band of the emotional spectrum. But this is not healing. It is partiality. And this will never satisfy the longing for wholeness that has been placed inside us from beyond.

For the alchemists, the first phase of the journey requires a confrontation and exploration of the *negredo,* the embrace of the black. Here the reference points around which we have previously organized our lives are dismantled. Even our deepest realizations and discoveries are converted into darkened space. While the temptation is to spin into resolution, to find answers to questions, and to be reborn as quickly as possible, a new invitation has appeared: to rest in the dark, rich, pregnant groundlessness. While it may seem that something is missing here, it is overflowing with essence.

Yes, all that you were so clear about even a few days can dissolve and lose its meaning: who you thought you were, how you would spend your time, the relationships you were sure would always be there, what was truly going to bring you the life you envisioned. Something new is longing to emerge, but you cannot skip over the process of death in order to create the conditions for its appearance. Rebirth will come, but can only arise from a direct, embodied, and compassionate confrontation with death.

The invitation before you is into re-imagination. Sink into the muddy earth. And provide safe passage for the reorganization. There is guidance all around and inside you: your fellow journeyers, the sun, the moon, the animals, and the stars. You are being asked to re-enchant your world, and to see with new vision.

5

An Extraordinary Meeting

Orphans of the Heart

As you continue to explore the depths of what you are, renew-ing your vow to turn in to those tender aspects you had to disconnect from along the way, you are sure to meet many orphans of the heart, abandoned ones of the emotional and somatic worlds who have been turned away and denied holding in the crucible at the center. Personal and collective allies of integration, surging within and around you, seeking communion and permission to return home.

Sadness, shame, heartbreak, and rage: travelers on an old journey, tired and in need of rest. Loneliness, confusion, joy, and fear—secret messengers sent from inside to remind you of an inner family member who yearns for reunion. At an earlier time, you were unable to provide safe passage for these voyagers, an attuned sanctuary where they could join you on your passage of wholeness. But they have not given up.

Whether during a conversation with a friend, hidden in the purple of an evening sky, or buried in the unfolding crystals of newly fallen snow … as a fragrance, a vague sense of longing for home, or by way of a vivid, translucent figure of the dream world, they are always appearing and will never stop trying to reach you.

While at times they come in sweet and peaceful forms, at other times they utilize energies of deflation, ferocity, and wrath, whatever they must use to remind you of what you are. In this way they are relentless, making use of the entirety of the phenomenal world to illuminate your path and reveal how majestic it is inside you.

If a Child Were to Appear

At times, a child will appear at your door. She will be cold, scared, and tired from a long journey. Her heart may be broken, rage may be erupting from her body, and she may be confused and uncertain about who she is and what is being asked of her.

How will you respond when she comes calling?

Will you allow her entry, move toward her with love and curiosity, and provide a sanctuary for her to fall apart in your arms? Or will you first demand that her fear convert to joy, her anxiety be healed, her confusion turn to clarity, and her heart be mended?

Will you take the risk of caring deeply and listen carefully to the dreams, the stories, the feelings, and the vulnerabilities which emanate from the little one in front of you?

Or will you admonish her to "get over it," to urgently forgive even if she is not ready, quickly "transcend" her heartbreak with spiritual techniques, or require that she stay unwavering in the present moment? Demanding that she first surrender the dream of a separate self.

The "other" is always appearing, in both inner and outer forms. Look carefully and you will see. Externally as the people you are in relationship with, who provide endless opportunities for you to remember. And internally as the unmet other of the unlived life. Of the abandoned feelings, emotions, and somatic material that have been sent away into the forest of the unconscious, in the hope of protecting you from the full-spectrum nature of the path of the heart.

The tired, open, and luminous children of love will continue to appear, not to harm or as an obstacle along the way, but as alchemical allies of integration and wholeness. By way of feeling, sign, symbol, and soma, they will do anything to reach you.

Before you turn from her and demand that she be someone other than what she is, open the door and see.

Honoring the Internal Family

Look carefully and see how the split-off pieces of your body, your psyche, and your heart continue to appear as your partners, your family, your children, and your friends ... even as the colors, the trees, the sun, and the moon. They will never give up on you and will continue appearing until they are integrated and allowed back home. While their longing for reunion is profound, they are patient and will wait into eternity until you are ready.

Even though you sense an unknown world of aliveness around you, it is not possible to access it until you break the spell that you are undeserving. This trance is subtle and is deeply embedded, the result of both personal and collective misperception. The cleansing of this perception requires full-spectrum attunement and reorganization at psychic, emotional, somatic, and transpersonal levels. But the guidance is already here. It is not something that needs to be produced, for it is not caused. The signs, symbols, and information are wired into you but are often hidden and must be retrieved in nonconventional ways. In order to access the data of wholeness, you must travel into your own body, for there is no greater temple. As the great mystic Teresa of Avila revealed, there is an inner castle where the jewels of the heart have been buried, excavated through surrender, devotion, and love.

It can be a revelation to allow in the sacred truth that is found in the center: You are not broken or in need of fixing, nor is something cosmically wrong with you that must be repaired by process, seeking, and struggle. You are not a project to be solved, but it can *appear* that something resplendent has been forgotten and displaced. The new vision cannot be released into a field of self-aggression and abandonment of the fire, but only into an environment of kindness and presence, where the circuitry can be re-encoded with empathy and attunement, and flooded with new levels of creativity.

This journey will inevitably require an encounter with the darkness and we must be willing at times to set aside our demand for consistent joy, happiness, and ease. There are no quick steps, no prefabricated instructions, and no guarantees of getting everything we want. The raw material for the work of love is found in the crucible where light and dark are one, and buried inside the very core of the rage, the emptiness, the heartbreak, and the disappointment.

Through deflation and reorganization, we step into the wholeness of the sacred world, which will never conform to the way we thought it would be. It is unprecedented here, a place of wisdom. Nothing is to be discarded any longer. The path is everywhere, but it requires being willing to turn toward and integrate *all* psychic and somatic energies, including rage, fear, jealousy, and confusion. The bias toward only half of the spectrum must dissolve into the wholeness.

As a sensitive little one in a world that was unable to hold the light, you made meaning of an environment lacking in empathy and attunement by blaming yourself, by constructing the emotionally weighty narrative that something was wrong with you, that you were flawed, and that you were not worthy of resonance and consistent, loving presence. As painful as this organization was, it was much safer than allowing in the reality that those around you were limited and incapable of providing the empathic connection you so deeply longed for—to do this would be to open the gates to profound feelings of terror and overwhelm. While these conclusions once served an important function, the veil is starting to part and the call to reorganization is beginning to thunder. While the trance once served an important adaptive function, the spell has remained alive within you and is longing to be rewoven—the dream is aching to be unwound and re-imagined in a more whole, integrated, and luminous form.

Honor the role your internal family has played until now: the unlovable one, the unworthy one, the broken one, and the one who has failed. They have served as important companions, providing context and purpose and keeping you out of unworkable states of fragmentation. They represented your best efforts to care for yourself and find meaning in an environment where meaning was not immediately apprehended. You need not aggressively send them away or even "let them go." For they will let go of you when their protective function is no longer needed, when the time is right for you to return to the vulnerability, tenderness, and wide openness of your true nature.

While a battle has been raging inside, the invitation now is into surrender, to step off the battleground and call off the war. Surround these ones with your awareness and breathe warmth into their center, into the images and symbols that have danced within you for so long. The inner family never intended to harm, but only to protect you from the raw, fiery tenderness of your own innocence. While you required this protection at an earlier time, it may no longer be necessary. But you must look and see for yourself. When you are ready, while honoring the safety and ground that has been provided, you can offer safe passage for these ones to end their tired journey, and go back into the vastness where they can rest. While they have done whatever they could to care for you and keep you alive, they are longing to return to you the sacred task of tending the aliveness of your own heart.

The Fear of Being Loved

The fear of being abandoned. The shame in being rejected and not seen as you are. The terror of being alone.

The anxiety of being dependent upon another. The panic of unbearable vulnerability and exposure. The dread of the looming death of yourself and everyone around you.

These are the great fears that come as you wake and dream and wander along the path of the heart.

In your willingness to take a risk, to feel it all, to truly allow another to matter, to step all the way into this life, and to expose yourself to an eternal sort of heartbreak, you may come face to face with the most devastating fear you've ever known, one you have been unable to articulate: the fear that you *are* loved. While paradoxical and disorienting to the known and to what has come before, this fear may even be more shattering in its implications than any other. For to allow this all the way in requires the death of an ancient dream.

To come face to face with the reality that you are loved by life as you are will leave you with no familiar reference point, no solid ground from which you can orient. Things will never be the same again. You will no longer be able to pretend that you are other than radiant and whole as you are, no longer able to postpone embodied, naked, unguarded participation as you work through the dream of separation, no longer able to take refuge for another moment in the safe, protected spell of unworthiness. This is no ordinary moment.

If you are not able to claim, even in a subtle way, that you are unworthy of love, how will you navigate? Through what lens will you see you the world, others, and your relationships without the reference point of unworthiness? This revelation is dizzying in its implications.

Stay close as the unlovable one, the unworthy one, and the unseen one arise into your awareness, longing to be unwound, untangled, and released into the vast expanse of what you are. Your inner family is gathering, longing to integrate and reorganize the world as you have come to know it. But it can feel disorienting when the safety this family has provided is no longer in reach.

One world is ending so that another may begin.

Your Confusion Is Not Pathology

Your confusion is not pathology; it is path. It has something to show you that clarity could never reveal. The nature of chaos is wisdom, but you must provide sanctuary to receive its essence. For this revelation will only release into an environment of embodied, attuned kindness.

Your feeling of disconnection is not neurotic—it is intelligent. It has something to show you that oneness could never reveal. Travel inside the felt sense and into the hidden passageways and you will find the emissaries waiting.

You are neither "separate" nor "one." You are the erupting holding field in which the energies of "separate" and "one" interpenetrate and dance the relative into being. While you may be biased toward oneness over multiplicity, love does not share this bias and is ready at all times to employ either equally as its envoy.

Your loneliness, shakiness, and fear are not mistakes. Your vulnerability is not pathology; it is path. Here, there are no "obstacles," only endless invitations into the center, and into the center of the center. The freedom you are longing for will never be found in eradicating the unwanted, but only in attunement to the love and information it carries.

Surges of somatic activity contain very important information for your journey. If you will offer safe passage, you will receive the secret offering: nothing is missing, nothing is out of place, and nothing need be sent away.

Yes, the burning can be unbearable. Such is the nature of the human heart. You may burn until you are translucent, but it is by way of this burning that wholeness is revealed.

The Field of Love

It is not always clear what love is asking of us, and where we will find true refuge. The forms that love takes are by nature arising and dissolving in each moment. This is the way of form. But love itself never comes and goes.

We never know what form love will choose to take in the future, for there is no love in the future. Love is only now. We will never be able to resolve or control the movement of love—it is infinitely creative and an emissary of the unknown.

If we become too fused with a specific form we believe we need love to take, our heart will always break when love recycles that form into something new, which it always will. While we may resent love for this, it is one of its great gifts to us: the opportunity to know not only its creative aspects but its destructive nature as well. This dissolution and reorganization is a special kind of grace that the mind cannot know. But the heart knows. The body knows.

Before we seek to "heal" our heartbreak through a psychological or spiritual process, let us turn in to the tenderness and ask our heart if it truly wishes to be mended. For this breaking is sacred, sent from the unseen to dissolve old dreams so that new and more creative forms of love may emerge.

Honor the forms of love while they appear, for they are an expression of wholeness. But allow them their own organic process of death and rebirth. While we may never be able to state unequivocally what love *is*, we can participate with open hearts in the unfolding of its essence.

Seek refuge not in love's forms but in the field of love itself, that which never comes and goes. For this is what you are.

An Archaic Homesickness

You can feel the call into the transformative fires of love yet know that something will be lost there. You want love to give you something, but you already *are* everything. How to make any sense of this? What does it mean to a heart longing for connection, for union, for intimacy, and for aliveness?

This path may always ask that you meet this conundrum directly, a sacred confrontation that the mind will struggle to understand and reconcile. But the heart knows and will guide you. Honor the waves of contradictory feelings, setting aside the demand that you resolve the creative unfolding of love, which you will never do. It is just too high voltage, and the struggle *against* this reality lays the groundwork for so much of our unnecessary suffering.

The delivery of this mystery is one of the secret gifts of the beloved. Not the mirage beloved that has come to confirm your hopes, dreams, and fears. Not the beloved who has come to make it all safe and certain. But the beloved who has nothing to give you, because you already *are* everything. The beloved who will dare to see you as you are but never conform to what you thought the role of the beloved would be in your life. The beloved who will illuminate the energies of separation *and* union, connection *and* separateness, oneness *and* multiplicity. We must all ask whether this is the sort of beloved we are ready to enter into relationship with, for he or she comes with the energies of deflation and reorganization.

While the beloved may at times appear as another person—one of his or her most evocative forms—love will never limit itself to only this appearance. Look at the patterns in the clouds, the crystals in the snowflakes, and into the inner substance that forms your emotions, senses, and neural pathways. The beloved is everywhere, spinning the relative out of the absolute to reveal their oneness and ultimate inseparability.

This "nothing" that love is here to give is the fruit of embodied integration. It is a "nothing" the mind can never touch, for it is a "nothing" that is *everything*. Yes, the identities may fall away one by one, the great images and personas of who you think you are, and the ground may be removed from underneath you. But surprisingly, what is left is wholeness, the raw naked essence of what you are, which is nothing. This "nothing" is not the nothing of the mind, which is void and empty of essence, but is pregnant, full, and overflowing with qualities of warmth, aliveness, and fiery compassion.

The risk in allowing in the implications of this "nothing" is that you will end up a refugee, homeless in love without any hope of resolution or final landing place where you will remain forever safe from further revelation. But is this certainty what you are really after? Or something else, perhaps something more vast and majestic? You must discover for yourself to what degree you are ready and willing to risk the loss of the known, of all the less-than-whole ways you've come to see yourself. Are you prepared to watch the ground fall out from under all of your identities and personas—the spiritual one, the unlovable one, the special one, the lonely one, and the one who has moved beyond?

What if love came raging into your world to show you that you were no one? Would you meet this? Or would you turn quickly away, scrambling into a new identity, urgently recreating the personas of the past—the one who has it all together, the one who is "healing," who has "awakened," who has figured something out, or who has transcended heartbreak, vulnerability, and confusion once and for all.

Open to the longing to return home, to rest in your true nature as a unique expression of dark and light, unprecedented, whole, and undefinable. As naked before the moon and the stars. Give everything to know the fragrance of this archaic homesickness, to be that vessel in which pure, tender, transmutative love may come like a wildfire into this world, erupting through your body and your heart, leaving nothing behind but ashes of grace.

Infused with Color and Light

As we become curious about exploring and committing to having a relationship with our vulnerability, heartbreak, and other activating states of experience, we might begin to discern between the experiential *awareness* of our internal landscape on the one hand and the willingness to *practice intimacy* with it on the other. Being aware of surging emotion, feeling, and sensation in the body is not necessarily the same as fully *experiencing* it, traveling inside it to explore its inner terrain, which for some may be more of a heart practice than one oriented in pure awareness.

One important milestone along the path of awakening is the cultivation of what is often referred to as "witnessing awareness," where we observe with nonjudgmental attention what is appearing in our experience without becoming identified with it as who we are in an absolute sense. This is a critical capacity to develop and hone, and provides very effective skillful means to cut through much of our unnecessary suffering.

It is also possible, however, to use the practice of witnessing awareness in a defensive or avoidant manner, as a way to stay safe and at a distance, protecting ourselves from the raw, groundless nature of the emotional spectrum. In the stance as a "witness" to our experience, it is possible for us to remain on the sidelines, standing back and protected from the fires of intimacy, lest we get caught in the messiness of the relational and feeling world altogether. It's a fair concern, and there is a fine line between practicing intimacy with our inner experience and fusing with it. But I believe we can—and must—train ourselves to skillfully and wisely navigate this line on the path of the heart. In fact, learning this art and refining it over time are developmental requirements on the journey. Intimacy without fusing. More on this later …

While clarity is one pathway and a deeply important dimension of our inquiry, the way of the heart may be another. These paths are not separate in an ultimate sense, and interweave at all times, but they do involve differentiated capacities and qualities. It's not a matter of choosing one over the other, but of being willing to penetrate and fully participate in the undivided nature of our raw, naked experience as it arises. It is relatively easy to train ourselves to stand back—safe and detached—from the chaos, complexity, and unresolvability of the emotional and relational terrain, dissolving everything as it arises into empty space. But it is something different to take the risk of intimacy, to allow yourself to be touched, to move beyond the great witness of your experience and into the world of the lover.

When all is said and done, my experience has shown me that (at times) the beloved has very little interest in our safe witnessing—but more so in our burning, in communion, and in our unclothed, unprotected presence. Not all that impressed with our crystal clear awareness, his or her invitation is into the chaotic, unresolvable wildness of the heart. To travel here requires taking refuge in not-knowing and empty space, not the mind's version of "empty space" that is a vacuum and void but one that is filled with warmth and overflowing with the pregnancy of compassion and light. What we think we know and the powers of our clear awareness lose their primary importance in this crucible, which is oriented in the body, pure feeling, and in union of the opposites. The high-voltage nature of the sort of creativity found here burns away the known and uncovers essence, removes the veil and reveals the luminous, the spontaneous, and the fresh. It opens you into a field where lover and beloved were always one, interpenetrating in union and spinning the relative out of the absolute.

This field of creativity is what you are: erupting, alive, fresh, and limitless. Pregnant and overflowing with the purity of form. Here, form is no longer viewed as an obstacle but a chaotic, naked, illuminated messenger of Shiva-Shakti, the co-emergent union of yin and yang. Dancing outside the conceptual world altogether, yet ready at all times to infuse the conceptual with color and light.

Attuned to a Burning Within You

At times, you may become aware of a burning—a very unique form of longing—deep within you: as you wake in the morning, wander through the day, or fall into the dream world at night. As you feel the ache to deeper communion with yourself, with others, and with the natural world. This burning can appear as an actual sensation in the body or more energetically as the activity of reorganization within your psyche, where the known is falling away but is not yet being replaced by what is to come next. Here, you are in between worlds, in a liminal place, inside the opposites of death and rebirth, which can be simultaneously exhilarating and terrifying. Something is calling, drawing you into communion, but you can't quite locate, name, or isolate it. It's either not the right time or just not approachable by way of the known.

Perhaps the burning holds some sort of key to why you have come here, to the unfolding of your destiny, or to the unique contribution that only you can offer to the world at this time. Something to do with your vocation, your life's purpose, or the specific way you are wired to help others. Or perhaps it has nothing to do with any of this but is more cosmic and collective in nature, and not all that personal after all. While you may never resolve the source of the longing, it is nonetheless calling you into new levels of birth and creativity.

For some, this experience is associated with profound melancholy, for others an actual ache in the heart, and for others still, feelings of hopelessness, despair, joy, or bliss. You are being called back home: not to the familiar home of what has come before but into your homeless nature as a wanderer and traveler of the inner and outer worlds. For those who are attuned to this movement, it can take form as an actual substance in the physical or subtle body, a type of nectar intuited within the inner pathways, dissolving all that is outdated and partial in order to make way for the unknown and whole.

At times, in the face of this movement you can feel as if your very survival is at risk, that you might not make it through to the other side. And that even if you did, you would not recognize what you found there. You cannot return to the way things were, but the new way has not yet appeared. You are back in the liminality, where you are accompanied by an unnamable restlessness and sense of urgency, where you scramble for answers, clarity, and ground around which to orient. It feels imperative to understand something, to discover some new information, or to heal, transform, and move on. To resolve something and complete the death part of the cycle and get to rebirth as soon as humanly possible, for hanging out in the unresolvable and contradictory middle feels unsustainable for much longer. Just resting in the chaos feels untenable and even dangerous. But another part senses that there is an offering inside the spinning energy and a doorway there into what is to emerge next. Stay close. Everything has led up to this very moment. Everyone you've met and every experience you've had … you are at the threshold.

As you train yourself to stay embodied and present, befriending the alchemical fires erupting from within, you may come to conceive of the burning as a sacred ally, albeit it a wrathful one. Underneath the very colorful narrative of what is happening, an old and unmet aspect of yourself is coming into view, a shadowy figure made of light, not coming to do harm but as a harbinger of integration. Somehow, in the busyness and struggle of the inner and outer worlds, you have forgotten the guidance and vision that are represented by this ally who has come in an unexpected form. But early in the morning, late at night, and during other moments of in between, when your guard is down, there is no mistaking the invitation that comes thundering out of silence and into the periphery of your awareness. You can even perceive it at times in the natural world and the atmosphere around you, as well as seeping out of conversations you have. Something is attempting to contact you and is using the burning as its bridge to make the connection.

As the burning makes its way into conscious awareness, you can meet it in slowness, in presence, and with curiosity. Dare to allow in the possibility that nothing has gone wrong, that it is not evidence of a problem, nor is it a dragon you must battle and slay. Rather, it is a symbol of aliveness, a nonordinary doorway into the depth you have been longing for but for some reason have not been able to access on your own. It is a pure messenger that has arisen out of your psyche and body to reveal the next phase along the way. As you surround the guides of the burning with your warmth and holding, they will purify your heart and your connection with beings everywhere, so you can wisely and compassionately attune and help them in unknown, infinite ways.

Into the Jeweled Palace

We want to know so badly ...

How things will turn out, when we'll be awakened, when our heart will no longer be at risk of breaking, when we'll be healed, when our past will be resolved, when the partner who will complete us will come, when we can finally step into life and experience the miracle we sense is all around us. Before we realize it, even our spiritual lives, as they become organized around accomplishment and acquisition, become yet another expression of our own undigested emptiness, boredom, and unmetabolized pain; of our unmet addictions, chronic self-aggression, and deeply embedded conviction that we are ultimately not okay as we are. We are convinced that something is missing, and that if we just continue our search and our struggle we will find it, and finally be able to rest.

It is no secret that our culture is one of acquisitiveness: *"Please, somehow, give me more. What is here now is most definitely not enough. I know there is some divine glorious reality waiting for me where angels are singing, harps are playing, perfect soul mates are appearing, fulfilling and easy spiritual careers are presenting themselves, all of my dreams are manifesting abundantly, and above all I am experiencing only high, spiritual states of consciousness, safe from the unknown devastatingly creative aspect of love."* But love will never conform to our hopes, dreams, and worn-out images. Thank god. It is too wild, too creative, and too outrageous for that. Its refusal to conform in this way is its greatest gift, the reorganizing deflation that naturally emerges when our personas and fantasies begin to crumble, only to be replaced by... well, nothing, other than an unbearable longing for aliveness, to finally participate in the sacred world that is always already here.

The invitation is to allow in the possibility that life has no interest in your living up to some secondhand image. It doesn't want or need you to be "perfect" or "divine" or "awakened" or "healed." Or to continually try to manifest all the things you think you want and need for your fulfillment. The deflating but illumined revelation lurking behind the mind rooted in acquisition is that life is not organized at all around your hopes and fears. While this may appear to be a gift of utter disappointment, seen with eyes wide open it is the doorway into pure richness. Something vast and majestic is *already* happening here, and you are invited to participate fully in it. Not *after* you acquire the inner states and outer goods you have been taught you must first create, call in, and manifest, but *now*.

No, life is not organized around our acquisition of inner and outer experiences, but offers something infinitely more precious and fertile. It is structured around high-voltage creativity and an immense field of not-knowing. It is the realm of quantum possibility, where anything can happen and where we will never know ahead of time how it is going to all turn out. But it is out of the unprecedented and infinitely original, pregnant nature of the unknown that you will be in direct contact with the mystery and the pure aliveness that is your birthright and the purpose of your unique, individual unfolding.

I hear from so many who are exhausted from the journey of *becoming,* of becoming someone who is more healed or more awake or more accepting of the now or more invincible or more invulnerable. They are tired of chasing around a fantasy of a "spiritual" life touted by some teacher, author, or expert who has figured it all out and landed in a sustained transcendent state, untouchable and safe from the reality that the beloved could come in at *any* time and pull the rug out from under them and the states they have constructed. There is a deep longing for rest, respite from becoming, and the chance to partake in what is here now: the true miracle, the Kingdom that is already here. This does not mean, of course, that you do not plan for a future, have goals and intentions, and seek to transform your sense of self and your life circumstances, if those things are alive and meaningful for you. It is kind to take care of yourself and attempt to create the life you want. But you do these things not from a foundation of poverty but one of true abundance. You already have what you need right now, the core ingredients and raw materials required to fully be here and to live fully. If you want to improve your life, you can do that, but not because you *have to,* not because there is something fundamentally wrong with you or missing from your life now. Rather, you do so as an expression of the great dance, the play of the formless as it comes into form. You are no longer willing to postpone participation, stand on the sidelines, and engage the spell of unworthiness until you can line everything up according to your hopes and dreams.[1]

In the very center of your being, there is always an open doorway, a treasure of immeasurable value. Admittance through this doorway into the jeweled palace has nothing to do with your first transforming into some other state that transcends the one that is here now—for what is here now is complete and pure by its own nature. The Kingdom is upon you, if you will cleanse your perception and see. Neither is it dependent upon first achieving completion of some mythical spiritual journey or moving beyond the messy world of intimacy, confusion, chaos, and human vulnerability of all kinds. This door, which is none other than the essence of your own heart, wants so badly for you to walk through it and meet for the first time this unbearable longing to go home, to behold for the first time the miracle of *this* precious human body, *these* emotions, *these* feelings, *these* passing states of consciousness, exactly as they have been given, as unseen, unknown expressions grace.

For in just one moment of caring enough—of somehow resisting the call to exit *this* experience for another—what you discover is that it is all made of wisdom and the sacred, crafted out of the substance of love, all the way through, from the inside out and the outside in. And no matter what the details of your current circumstances, love has somehow configured itself as your unique life and offered itself as

---

1. Thank you to psychotherapist Bruce Tift for his insight and articulation in the area of navigating and holding the tension between the opposites of "acceptance" and "improvement."

a doorway into a palace beyond imagination … only forever waiting for you to enter and touch it, exactly as it is.

Setting Aside the Project of Self-Improvement

What would it be like if you took the day off from becoming someone or something different? Or just a few hours? Or moments?

To set aside the grand project to improve yourself, heal your past, be someone different, or to learn something new. To figure something out, to manifest new things or experiences for yourself, to replace what is here for something different. To dare to allow in the life-shattering possibility that nothing is wrong, nothing is truly missing, and that your life is not a project to be solved, but a mystery to be lived.

To take a walk on this new day knowing that you are already fully connected. That there is nothing you must first learn or solve or understand or even heal in any conventional sense. To allow in the implications that you might not need to improve this moment. For these implications are revolutionary.

To allow in for just a moment the possibility that you have everything you need to fully participate here, in the sacred word that is all around you, with all of its glory, confusion, excruciating hopelessness, pure hope, causeless joy, and shattering heartbreak.

It can be exhilarating to allow this in, to give yourself to this, for just a few moments. And also quite disorienting. The mind will scramble to find the reference point of a problem to orient around and to defend against the utter spaciousness of being. It's so open here, but the mind contracts in response to so much space. Wait a minute, there's something wrong, isn't there? I could have sworn something is wrong? There must be something that needs to be fixed, healed, shifted, or transformed; some more growth, understanding, insight, more realization which must first occur before I can fully show up here, fall to the ground in awe and gratitude, and commit to this life.

It's just an experiment. Just for a few moments. Don't worry. You can return to the life of there being a problem later on today, if you'd like. And attend to what must be attended to. But for now, look up into the sky, rest on the muddy earth, touch the water, feel your heart beating. You are alive. You are here. Everything that has ever happened, everyone you have ever met has brought you to this moment. By some miracle of grace, love has come into the world of time and space as you, as your life, exactly as it is, as an expression of the great mystery.

The breath is coming in and out now, whether you believe that you deserve it or not. The earth is unconditionally supporting you; you are not falling through space. But the breath will be gone at some point, usually much sooner than we'd all like. Breathe deeply now. And attune to the miracle. You need not postpone your participation here any longer. We never know if we will be given another opportunity tomorrow.

6

The Sacred Middle

Intimacy Without Fusing

WHEN A FEELING OR EMOTION SURGES WITHIN YOU, IT DOES SO LONG-ing for two responses.

First, to be met with your presence. To be received and held as valid, worthy of your curiosity, openness, and attention. You don't have to pretend to "like" the feeling, or even to "accept" it, but you honor it as the way reality is appearing in this moment because you know that arguing with what is, is the root essence of your emotional suffering. Even if the feeling is one of utter *nonacceptance* or a sense of being closed, you can open even to these experiences, allowing them to permeate the field around you. They are not obstacles on your journey but portals into empathy, attunement, and compassion. In ways the mind may never be able to come to terms with, it is possible to *accept your nonacceptance* and to *open to your closedness*. This is an art that you can learn.

The goal in this work is not to always be accepting, open, or loving, but rather to be in direct, embodied, and compassionate contact with whatever is appearing as valid and worthy of inquiry. You can call off the war with nonacceptance, nonforgiving, and a closed heart. Open to your closed heart and allow it safe passage and it will reveal its essence as pure life itself. The mind may struggle with this as an *idea*, but at the level of direct perception, it is something you can discover inside by way of intuition and nonconceptual revelation.

The despairing one, the raging one, the unworthy one, and the abandoned one—though they can be quite intense and even disturbing, they are not obstacles on your path. They are not working against you, intending to lead you astray, though of course it can *feel* like that at times. You must go inside your own body and discover the deepest truth around this. Rather than coming as enemies to foil your unfolding, they just want to be heard, felt, and re-parented, and finally allowed back inside the palace, which until now they have not felt safe enough to enter. But there is intelligence in the chaos, wisdom in the mess, and raw life in the disturbance. These are emissaries of the destructive and reorganizing aspect of the journey, equal in power and beauty to the sweetness and creativity that you generally welcome.

In a moment of activation, the invitation is to deep listening: not just with your ears but the entirety of your senses, not from the lens of your hopes and fears, but a listening that is born of the radical commitment and intention to know what is true more than *anything*, even if it contradicts or challenges your most deeply cherished beliefs. This is an intention you can cultivate day by day and moment by moment; it is not something you must perfect or shame yourself for failing at, as we will all inevitably do.

Each of the visitors is a carrier of sacred data, but their revelation is released only into a field of kindness, and it is the abandonment of them that reinforces their centrality in your inner circuitry. While you may gain some relief from turning away and sequestering them in the underworld and outside conscious awareness, they will continue to appear, often in unexpected and less-than-ideal ways. If you do not take care of them consciously, they have no other recourse than to communicate by way of the unconscious, including through symptoms, emotional and physical challenges, dreams, images, fantasies, and the unfolding of the shadow in interpersonal relationships.

In addition to the meeting in presence, the invitation is to see that the feeling is not who you are in an ultimate sense. It is not fused with you and does not carry any information about your *worth as a person*. As a young child, you did not have the developmental capacity to discern between *feeling* bad and *being* bad. Observe carefully how this leftover association continues to color your current perceptual landscape, often subtly, in the form of the conclusion I *feel* bad = I *am* bad. It can be a very useful inquiry to see the ways in which this old conclusion might be alive for you. When you feel sad or depressed or anxious or physically ill, what meaning do you automatically associate with these experiences? What do they mean about you? What secondary judgments, evaluations, shaming, or interpretations become added to your raw experience of emotional or physical feelings and sensations? Just because a negative thought or image, or a painful feeling or emotion appears, that does not mean this is who you are. Slow way down and discover if and how this might be true in your own experience. This must be a deeply embodied realization as a merely conceptual understanding is not enough to lay down a new neural pathway and write over the deeply grooved associations and organizing principles of the past.

Pull back slightly and enter into *relationship* with your feelings. Separate a bit from them, but not so much that you dissociate and disembody. You may discover that there is so much space around your experience. Commune with your inner world without being engulfed by it. Practicing intimacy while not fusing is a holy art that you can learn. You are the warm, open field of awareness where all feelings and emotions can come into being for a short while, dance within you, and then dissolve back into the vast, spacious ground from which they arose. Find the sacred middle and rest there, between the old, worn pathways of denial and fusion. This is where the great process of metabolization by love will unfold.

The old way is that of a provoked and aroused limbic system, spinning out its (at times very helpful) strategies of numbing, denying, indulging, and acting out in order to remove you as quickly as possible from the vulnerability and aliveness that is surging in you. It's just ... not ... safe. These strategies saved your life as a little one and were the best ways you knew to care for yourself at the time. You can honor them for the service they provided. But something else is calling now. Listen carefully and you will hear the invitation—early in the morning, late at night, and as you wander through the day. As you allow another to matter to you and mingle your awareness with a sunrise or the moon in her fullness. Come closer. Open into. Breathe with.

The new way is alive now and rippling inside you. The pathways are revealing their flexibility and their longing to be reorganized. Soothe the fire with your presence and a fiery compassion. Open your heart to your vulnerability and meet it with just one moment of awareness and warmth. And then slow way, way down, and see what you are.

A Pathway of Attuned Aliveness

When you are triggered and emotion is surging, you stand at the precipice of a new world. On one side is the old pathway of self-aggression, shame, blame, complaining, numbing, denying, and acting out. Of disembodying and returning into the storyline of what happened as a way to take you out of the raging, sacred data that is alive in your torso. For it is much safer to tell a story about rage, heartbreak, and fear than to descend into the body and into communion with alive, rippling, unknown energy.

But emerging along with the protective strategies of fight, flight, and freeze are the new pathways of attuned aliveness: neural grooves of presence, warmth, kindness, and self-care. To descend with your awareness out of the looping narrative and into the somatic landscape is a radical act of compassion and inner and outer revolution.

Right in the core of the very hot, panicky, and claustrophobic sensations that are erupting through your belly, your heart, and your throat, the unmet ones have come again. They will never give up on you; they are unrelenting emissaries of love, coming in wrathful form to remind you of wholeness and of how full spectrum the heart's journey truly is. They are not here to be understood, transformed, shifted, or healed but have come as part of the sacred return, seeing the light of holding. In the crucible of awareness, their energies are purified and metabolized so they can be used as fuel for the journey ahead.

Use your breath to direct attention into the center of whatever feeling is arising. Send awareness *inside* your emotions and saturate them with warmth. It is possible to surround the arising material with your presence, as a parent would surround their little one with a warm blanket on a winter night. For just a moment, replace the urgent need to find relief with curiosity. A visitor has arrived and is longing for care.

Dare to practice intimacy with this one, close enough to receive the transmission of its nature but not so close that you fuse with it as who you are or become engulfed by its energy. The visitor is not in need of healing, but holding. Even for one second, two seconds, three seconds, and then rest. Set aside the requirement to understand, resolve, or even heal the feelings, just for a few moments.

As you go deeper with this inquiry, in a way that is real time and embodied, you may discover a measureless space around your sadness, rage, disappointment, and hopelessness. When you feel into these emotions and sensations, you also come into direct contact with the space in which they are appearing. They are inseparable from this space, which is not a vacuum or a deadened emptiness but is filled with qualities of light, warmth, intimacy, and possibility. While your emotions have such a vivid, intense, colorful, and at times disturbing appearance, they are made of this space; they arise from it, play in it, and then dissolve back into it. What you are and what they are … these are not two things. The forms that appear in awareness are of the nature of awareness itself. Pure. Untainted. Translucent. Spacious. Workable. Trustable.

As you practice relational intimacy with the display of the somatic world, you will naturally attune to the breath as it passes in and out of your lungs. Take a moment to behold the miracle that this truly is, to be given even one more breath on this new day. The implications of that alone are enough to take you to the ground and cut through the trance that you are unworthy of love.

As holy as the breath is, there is another substance passing through you. It is flowing in and out of your heart, is subtle, and is apprehended only through one of your nonordinary senses. It is wild and creative and keeps the stars from falling out of the sky. It is the substance of reorganizing and transmuting love.

Oxygenate your entire being with this sacred material, and allow it to wash and nourish you, cell by cell by cell.

Into the Sacred Middle

Falling apart, holding it all together. Then falling apart, then holding it all together again. Cycles of integration and disintegration. Chaos and cohesion. Stillness and activity. Sanity and confusion. As flows the natural world, the unfolding of the heart is alive and of the unknown.

In ways the mind may never resolve, guidance is pouring through you, washing away that which is less than whole, preparing you for what is next. But what is next is always of the nameless and will never be approached ahead of time by means of the conceptual. Stay close, and attune to the creativity as it emerges out of the here and now.

While the narrative that you are "falling apart" is rich and multilayered, look carefully and see if you were ever "together" to begin with. You are the vast space in which "together" and "apart" dance in union, and you will never be limited to either of these narratives.

Rest for a moment and honor the unprecedented nature of what is moving within you.

If you remain too identified with "falling apart," you cut into the natural aliveness that is the essence of pure, immediate experience. You lose contact with the radiance within and become misattuned to the wisdom of your unfolding experience, exactly as it is. You disconnect from the power of embodied presence, from the intelligence of the earth, and from the realization that nothing has ever been wrong with you. You forget that the darkness, when provided sanctuary, is brighter than a thousand suns.

But if you remain too identified with "holding it all together," you disconnect from your natural vulnerability and the spontaneous mystery as it appears, turning from the surging reality that your heart could break at any moment. It is true that raw, tender sadness could approach at any time, requesting safe passage inside you. But it is through this broken aliveness that the poetry of your life will flow.

Right in the middle of "falling apart" and "holding it together" is the secret place. Stay there. For it is the greatest, most radical act of kindness to provide the gift of pure rest. This is where the light and dark are in union, where integration and disintegration emerge as one in love, and where lunar and solar weave together particles of the sacred world.

An Alchemical Art

When you are activated and burning up inside, behold the ancient pathways of fight and flight as they present themselves. In the face of a dysregulating narrative, anxious feelings, and seemingly survival-level sensations, memories of an earlier time are brought alive within you. You have stepped into a time machine, with the "there and then" masquerading itself as the "here and now," clouding clear perception of your current, real-time experience.

While it may seem otherwise, you no longer need to deny or flee from what is here, nor urgently act it out in the hope of purging the material in order to find relief. In a moment of caring attune-ment and self-love, you can train yourself to contain and hold what is appearing, and meet it with your presence. And in the thundering silence of the here and now, you can chart a new course. Yes, it takes practice as well as courage, vigilance, and the willingness to befriend your experience in ways you may never have thought were possible. But the good news is that you can start *right now,* wherever you are and however you are feeling. For there are no prerequisites other than the longing that has already been placed within you. The first step is to slow down, pause, and flood your experience with awareness. What beliefs are shaping your perception? What do you think about yourself, others, and the world? What conclusions have you come to? Who do you think you are? What is the fundamental perceptual lens through which you see yourself?

Next, what emotions and feelings are present? What does it feel like, right now, to be you? What is happening in your body, especially in your torso? In your heart? Your throat? Your shoulders? Your belly? How is your breathing? Are you feeling calm or speedy? Hot or cold? Expanded or contracted? As you make contact with what is most alive, you can train yourself to stay with it for very short periods of time. Touch it, then let it go. While it may feel as if your survival is at risk if you stay another second, stay for one-half of a second, or one-quarter. Then rest. And then later another second. And then rest. Over time, you will build tolerance for the intensity as it surges. But it takes practice and training to stay with those feelings, emotions, and sensations that you associate with danger, risk, and impending overwhelm and shutdown. Yes, it may *feel* as if you are on the edge of disintegration and breakdown, but is this feeling an accurate description of the reality of here and now? Or is this conclusion left over from an earlier time, a painful remnant of the "there and then"? You must go slowly and discover this for yourself. Please do not take anyone else's word for it, including the words I am sharing here.

As you deepen the experiential discovery that you can in fact stay with the surging feelings and emotions, you can begin *opening* to them. Once it is clear they are not going to actually overwhelm you, you can continue the journey of intimacy with them. Using your breath and the fire of your own presence, open into the intensity and fear, breathe with the panic, and send warmth into your belly, heart, and throat. Perhaps your immediate experience—heartbreak, loneliness, shakiness, fear of abandonment, terror of being engulfed—has not come in order to be "healed" but to be held. And it has never in fact been "unhealed" but always alive and whole, always on your side. This can be challenging to let in with the mind, for it goes against the grain of so much of what you've been taught. But the heart knows. The body knows. You can trust that.

It is an alchemical art to rest your awareness *inside* the intense thoughts, emotions, and sensations as they appear in moments of activation. And to discover that your freedom is not dependent upon their eradication or transformation. Rather, the aliveness, the connection, and the intimacy that you long for will be found in the very center of what is here now, by way of your empathic, attuned awareness, and out of the deep, penetrating commitment to no longer abandon yourself.

Each of us must discover for ourselves what it is like to make contact with the space that is around our experience and with the truth that there is no suffering inherent in the feelings and emotions that arise in waves within us. Understanding this at a conceptual level can be insightful and provide inspiration to go deeper, but experiential engagement with our true nature will serve as the ultimate medicine.

Slow way down and open into the life that is flowing through you. Place your awareness in the core of tenderness and breathe with it. Oxygenate it, not only with the clarity of an outside witness but by way of intimacy, flooding it with the heart qualities of kindness, compassion, and warmth. No matter what is happening in your life right now, you can choose to provide a holding space for the unmet and abandoned material within you. This material is not an error and is not evidence that something has gone wrong, but is an invitation to integration and to reunion with the peaceful and wrathful allies of the soma and psyche.

Just as you are longing for your own presence, these waves of feeling are only longing to be re-parented and allowed to return home once again, as new forms of love and creativity within you.

An Untamed Fire of Presence

Just below the compelling storyline, beneath the colorful emotional landscape, there exists a rich, mysterious world of sensations: a somatically organized field of intelligence, creativity, and aliveness. It is dizzying here, awash with particles of the unknown. Something is pulling you, but it can be disorienting to a mind longing for resolution. The urge to return to the known, to get hold of "my life," and to renew the dream of control can appear as overwhelm in the nervous system. Without pathologizing the movement back to ground, allow the mind to rest, even for just a moment. Dare to consider that nothing has gone wrong, nothing need urgently be resolved, and that no answers are coming ... for now. Open instead to the sacredness of the question and the mystery that you are, that which will never be touched by an answer.

You are in the nonordinary world of presence: strangely familiar but dreamlike and highly creative. While the mind will continue its search for what is wrong—based on a lifetime of momentum and habitual orientation—here there are no "problems," no complaints, no shame, no blame, nothing lacking that must be manifested, and no spell of unworthiness in which to get tangled. There is nothing to be fixed, cured, transformed, or shifted and no evidence of whether you are healed or awakened, or not. These questions simply do not arise in this realm. There is no "spirituality" here or any movement to replace one experience with another. Just pure life—unprecedented, spontaneous, and unobscured. There is no possibility of creating a new persona here, no bias for joy over despair, and no journey to make from multiplicity to oneness. Only an untamed fire of presence.

In any moment, you can participate in this open expanse, which is none other than your own true nature. It is not something you must create, manifest, or otherwise add to your experience by way of process, accomplishment, acquisition, or new understanding. Whatever arises in your present experience is at once apprehended as trustable, intelligent, valid, and utterly workable. It is pure and complete on its own and need not be converted into something "higher" or more spiritual in order to emanate its purity. In this dimension of essence and being, every inner experience is apprehended as it is—naked, fresh, and unprecedented—arising, dwelling, and dissolving outside the confines of the conceptual altogether.

Descending into the body, into this wide-open, undefined space can be terrifying. The shaky uncertainty you feel can be honored and allowed safe passage, and not seen as evidence that you are doing it wrong or have fallen off course. You are right on track. It is perfectly natural for feelings such as fear, disorientation, and confusion to arise in the wake of so much openness—they are only invitations into further creativity and depth. It is not required that you heal or transform the fear, or covert it into any other experience, in order to participate fully in the journey of the heart. In ways the mind may never understand, fear and love are not opposites but arise together in the vast spaciousness that you are. Allow yourself to rest in the middle of the apparent contradiction, where a union is possible that will reveal new vision.

Yes, it can be a bit confounding here because in this field of open awareness there is no "known" around which to orient and secure a sense of sure footing. There is no safe landing place or fantasy of a life of invulnerability and invincibility where you remain free from the reality that love could spin new forms, breaking your heart, dissolving your life as you have known it, and pulling the rug out from under what you assumed was some "permanent" realization.

Here, you will only find yourself, as you are, and the unique arrangement of love and awareness that have come together to assemble your one, wild, unprecedented life; there is nothing like it and never will be again. Love is calling you to know yourself, finally, all the way through, because there will only be one of you, ever. It has chosen to take shape as your very heart, in this radiant here and now moment, and there is no greater miracle than this. Within the wisdom-field of what you are, there is no longer any "transformation" or "healing" as you have come to think of these terms. Nothing is "unhealed" or in need of transformation. Just raw, naked, experience, free from the idea that there is something to shift. Tender, open, and warm. Rippling with intelligence.

What you are is the erupting union of inner and outer space. Your body is an invitation, an entryway, a threshold into the activity of this union. Out of the shimmering, pregnant aliveness of pure awareness flow the qualities of compassion, attunement, and presence.

Please don't forget what you are.

Stay in the Secret Place

At times you may find yourself between worlds, wandering in the liminal, unsure about anything and with no idea what is being asked of you. It is clear some sort of death has occurred and that things will never be the same. But where is the rebirth? The new life purpose? The promised healing, intimacy, clarity, and direction? What about the assurance of new life on the other side? You've surrendered so much already, suffered and sacrificed over and over again, worked through so much … but nothing has yet emerged from the womb of Now. No direction for the journey ahead. Or so it seems.

While the uncertainty can be disorienting, in a sense you are home. But not "home" as a conventional landing place where you have the unwavering, solid knowing of who you are, or what relationships are, or what you're supposed to be doing here. It is the home of the lover whose heart is always at risk of breaking and whose mind is forever a beginner, never an expert. It is the humbling home of deflation and reorganization, where the beloved is arranging things and preparing you for new birth. But what that birth is will never be known ahead of time, and you are left back in the *bardo,* the in-between place, subject to the inner timeline of the heart, which is always of the unknown.

Really, is that the fruit of all this!? In this realm, terror and exhilaration co-arise and weave in and out of one another. How could you simultaneously be so alive and not know anything? While at other times, the groundlessness, the uncertainty, the shakiness: somehow these realities have become your refuge. What is going on?

Yes, the longing can be excruciating at times ... for healing, for transcendence, for understanding, for an attuned "other" to come and reflect back to you your worthiness, to see you as you are, and for the groundlessness to yield to ground. You feel a cosmic ache for clarity, for security, and for a resolution to the contradictions. You yearn for just a moment of rest and respite from the relentless creativity of the unknown.

Perhaps the greatest act of kindness at this point is to turn toward the death and *into* the reorganization, setting aside the idea that you are supposed to resolve something or transform it into something else. Rather than spin to locate answers, you can rest inside the question, knowing that your life is not a project to solve but a mystery to be lived. This is one of those times when no answers are coming and you are being asked to be patient, to allow yourself to be marinated in love's ways and to trust in your immediate experience. To live the question and surrender the demand of resolution by way of an answer.

It is difficult to move toward the empty and the unnamable, for our modern world has forgotten the mysteries and purity of the death-rebirth journey. We are not going to resolve death and rebirth by way of the conceptual, by planning, dreams of control, and the dictates of our hopes and fears. For this journey is archetypal in nature and is wired into the fabric of this particular star and into the cells of the human heart. We can rest in this mystery, in the core of the contradiction, and in a paradoxical way come to take refuge in the tension between the opposites.

The Path Is Everywhere

Right in between death and rebirth is the secret place. Stay there and listen. Open to the guidance as it comes in unexpected ways.

The Galaxy of Your Own Body

In a moment of activation, there is an urgent sense that we must find relief. And if we do not, that we will be overwhelmed, decompensate, fall apart, and lose ourselves in an avalanche of the emotional world. The ancient pathways of fight and flight come alive, and we move into action.

Let us honor this sense and perceptual organization, for it has been with us since our early moments in the holy womb. It was the accurate, embodied reality of a little brain and nervous system, wired for empathic attunement, and for the holding and mirroring of its erupting subjectivity.

But here we are now, as adults with capacities we once did not have, longing to enter into the mystery, into pure aliveness, and to know love as the organizing principle of this Milky Way home we have somehow found ourselves in. While there are billions of stars in billions of galaxies spread throughout infinite time and space, perhaps there is only one star of love.

The invitation is into intimate communion: to move closer, and even closer still, into the feelings, the emotions, and the sensations as they emerge. To surround the surging material with curiosity, warmth, and most importantly with kindness, as an inner explorer of the galaxy of your own body, of which there is no temple more sacred.

While prioritizing relief was critical at an earlier time—and represented the best way you knew to care for yourself—another pathway is emerging, as the trance of self-abandonment is dissolved in open awareness. Listen carefully to the invitation as it makes itself known, through sensation, image, symbol, and guidance from inner and outer nature.

Yours is the path of direct revelation, and a secondhand life will never, ever satisfy the longing wired into you. Your appearance here is unprecedented, and love will never appear in the same way again.

Into the Shaky Middle Ground

Many of us are familiar with the various strategies we employ to repress or act out feelings we do not want to experience and aspects of ourselves with which we do not wish to be in conscious relationship. Overeating, mindless shopping, surfing the internet, unconsciously watching television, becoming lost in social media ... as we've discussed, we can even make use of spiritual beliefs and practices to unwittingly move *further away* from unwanted states of feeling and emotion. In fact, we can use just about *any* activity to distract ourselves from uncomfortable and disturbing experience.

If only these strategies worked in the long run, everything would be so much simpler. Wouldn't it? From a place of deep care and love of what is true, let us take a moment to see what is going on here, to become increasingly aware of what we're doing and what we're trying to avoid. No judgment, no shaming, no apology—just curiosity. One moment of self-care. Just see.

As we inquire in this way, we might discover that the most effective strategy of escape, one that we've all mastered, is to remove attention from our bodies, feelings, and emotions, and shift it into thinking. We are all experts in this area, and the ability to abandon the emotional world for the conceptual has an adaptive function. It is not some fluke of nature, horribly unspiritual, a function of "falling into the ego" and so forth. Without needing to shame ourselves or build up a big drama around it, we go deeper into discernment and fuel our inquiry into what is most true, not because we are broken and require fixing but because we love what is true more than anything.

As the exploration unfolds and expands, we might discover that we have become masters at thinking *about* our experience instead of actually *having* it. In seconds, we can vacate what is happening in real time and immerse ourselves in our conditioned histories, falling into the deeply embedded grooves of our limited narratives, spells of unlovability, and unkind stories of our flaws and failures. All to avoid what is actually alive in the radiant here and now.

Again, let there be no judgment, no shame, no apology, no beating ourselves up for how "unspiritual" we are and all the rest of it. Just curiosity. Just a moment of self-care. Just an instant to begin to lay down a new groove, one oriented in empathy, attunement, and compassion.

As I've discussed, our old strategies were unavoidable and critical as young children in our families of origin, in order to keep alive the often very precarious ties with our caregivers and to ensure our own psychic and emotional survival. They were intelligent at the time, and quite creative. They are not inherently bad; they just need an upgrade. This may sound like a simple task, but most of us have an unconscious investment in maintaining these strategies, for to let them go would require that we come face to face with the underlying anxiety they were put in place to protect us from.[1] For this reason, they will not yield easily and the new ways will require practice and behavior change over time. We can't just *think* about responding in a new way but have to take real-time *action,* especially with respect to those actions we take in the face of emotional activation: new pathways are encoded when we act in new and different ways, working through difficult experience rather than denying it by way of habitual, addictive behavior. Many times each day and week we will be provided opportunities to attend and attune to the inner world, and respond to it in ways that are likely to reduce unnecessary suffering for ourselves and others. Rather than turn from difficult feelings, reenacting the well-grooved escape routes and exit strategies of the past, we are invited into a new world. It is the work of a lifetime and will not be mastered in a few weeks or

---

1. I want to thank both Caroline Myss and Bruce Tift for helping me to explore the unconscious processes involved in the maintenance of defensive organization, and how the healing journey itself is deeply counterinstinctual.

months—or likely even years—as the path of the heart is endless in its depth. No hurry, no urgency, just moment-by-moment awareness, attunement, and kindness.

The next time you feel triggered, agitated, hurt, or annoyed, you could remember to pause, feel your feet on the ground, breathe deeply from your lower belly, and become curious about the journey of your attention. Where is it now? Where is it headed? Where is it being pulled? Where was it just before you became activated? If you allow yourself to stay on automatic pilot, what would usually happen next? What sort of behavior might you engage in to get away from an unwanted feeling? No shame, no blame, no judgment. No fantasy that you should be doing it differently or that you are failing or that something is wrong with you in some fundamental, wretched way. To engage this sort of inquiry for even one moment is a true act of love.

Offer a holding environment for yourself, your thoughts, your emotions, and your bodily sensations. Inquire with open, loving attention into exactly what is going on in your immediate experience. As you notice yourself moving into habitual action, first note what underlying feeling state you're seeking relief from. See if you can pinpoint the precise moment when the impulse to escape gets so powerful that it feels as if you may explode. And in that moment, make the commitment to stay, even for just a few seconds. Inquire and see if you *must* exit your immediate experience in this moment. Before you follow the impulse to act, notice it and allow it to be there for a moment without moving into the established pathways of fight or flight. Explore this shaky middle territory between the awareness of a feeling and the moment of taking action. Get really curious about these impulses to act and what it might be like to instead stay with the groundless, claustrophobic, hot, and sticky energy before you move.

Perhaps you need not exit your experience as you once did. While these feelings may carry survival-level energy, you must discover for yourself whether your survival is *actually* at risk and whether you will become overwhelmed, engulfed, or retraumatized in a moment of staying. Or in one more. Or one more.

You're okay. Go slow. It is very likely that you can hold and contain more than you imagine. Perhaps these feelings are not even what you have come to imagine they are and it has only been the resistance to them and the conclusions about what they mean about you that have been the cause of so much of your suffering and struggle. Maybe you do not need to heal, understand, or change your present experience after all but rather enter into relationship with. Perhaps it is fine as it is and will take care of itself if you will call off the war. For just a few seconds, stay close. No judgment. No shaming. No beating yourself up for not doing it "right." Just a genuine curiosity, radical self-care, and newfound kindness for yourself. You may notice that by doing this, over and over, the tangles and the knots of the body, heart, and psyche and will start to unwind.

What you are is a vast field of awareness, warmth, and creativity. Rest there.

Intimacy with the Contradictions

From the perspective of exhaustion and confusion, it is intelligent to seek relief from the uncertainty and replace the groundlessness with something more stable. Honor the call to safe passage and something to hold on to. You need not pathologize the longing for solid ground from which to take your next step. It is an act of kindness to care for yourself in whatever ways you can.

From the perspective of raw, reorganizing love, groundlessness and aliveness are one. For there is no intimacy without embodiment to your vulnerability in all its forms. Here, there is nothing to hold on to, nothing to "heal," and nothing to transform. The urgent requirement for an "improved" moment has fallen away into the vastness.

While the mind may spin trying to resolve the mystery, this conundrum is holy and has been placed inside you not to be solved with an answer but to be lived as a question. The relief and the rest you are longing for may never be found within the field of conceptual resolution but only by way of embodiment of the contradictions as they appear.

Though the activity of love is infinitely tender and holding, in its essence it is everything. At times it will employ the energy of deflation, to end one world so that another may begin. This deflation is nonordinary and sacred, and is a secret doorway that you can enter.

How Well Did I Love?

It is so easy to take for granted that tomorrow will come, that another opportunity will be given to witness a sunrise, take a walk, gaze in awe at the crystals in newly fallen snow, share a moment of attuned connection with the one in front of us. But another part of us knows it is so fragile here, so tenuous, and that this opening into life will not be here for much longer.

Recognizing this, let us surrender the dream of postponement by doing whatever we can to help others, by taking a risk to fully show up here, never forgetting what is most important, no longer apologizing for our uniqueness, our sensitivity, and the gifts of our vulnerability. By being willing to dissolve the shadow of our unlived lives, one holy moment at a time, and step into the crucible with one another, where we're never really sure what is going to unfold.

At the end of this life—which is sure to come much sooner than we'd like—it is unlikely we'll be all that concerned with whether or not we accomplished all the tasks on our to-do lists, completed some mythical spiritual journey, perfected ourselves, healed our past, called in one or more magical soul mates to complete us, played it safe, got all of our needs met, made it big, or manifested all the outer objects and internal states we wanted and dreamed would fulfill us. Inside these hearts there may be only one burning question: how well did I love?

Did I pause each day to behold the wonder of just one unfolding here-and-now moment? Was I willing to take a risk, to feel more, to care deeply about this life, to let another matter, and to honor this very experience, exactly as it has been given?

Was I willing to behold the sacred offering of the natural world—the sky, the snowflakes, the mountains, the sun, the mud, the deer, and the offering of the moon above as she floods my heart with her secrets?

Was I willing to stay close to the mysterious movement of sweet and fierce grace as it took form as the others in my life, and as the wisdom flow of feeling, emotion, and sensation in this body? As my dreams, as vision, and as the way I am attempting to make meaning of this precious, excruciating, unbelievable, astonishing, and heartbreaking human opportunity?

Was I willing to fall in love, to truly fall in love with this life, exactly as it is? Was I willing to provide a home, a sanctuary, and safe passage for all of me, an environment of wholeness and integration to dance, rest, and play in?

Was I willing to set aside the unending need to make this moment different?

What is it that remains unlived ... for you? How have you been holding back? What are you waiting for? What is your heart asking of you? What is most important? What are you unwilling to compromise any longer? In what ways are you not living your own life but someone else's? Or living out the fantasies of a society or culture that has forgotten about love and what matters most ... for you? The bounty and harvest of this world are upon you. They are always already here, erupting in each moment. They are not waiting.

One day we will no longer be able to look at, touch, or share a simple moment with those we love. When we turn to them, they will be gone. One moment will be our last to witness the immensity of just one more breath, to truly see and travel inside a color, to enter into union with the vastness of the ocean. It will be our last chance to feel the presence of a tree, to have a moment of communion with a friend, or to weep as the light yields to the night sky. One last moment to have a thought, to feel an emotion, to fall in love, to smell a flower, to taste something sweet, and to know heartbreak, joy, and peace: to behold the awe of what it really means to be a sensitive, alive, tender human being.

What if today is that last day? Or tomorrow? Or later this week?

Knowing that death will come to complete the cycle of the beloved in the world of time and space, how will you respond to the breath that is moving within you right now, to the feelings washing through you, and to the opportunity to know and to be the activity of love here?

What would it be like to fully allow in the reality that today may be your last? Will you open your heart to the gift of life before it is too late?

Perhaps your "life's purpose" has nothing to do with what job you find or what new cool thing you manifest or what awesome soul mate you attract or what mythical awakening journey you complete. But that the purpose of your life is to fully live, finally, to touch each here-and-now moment with your presence and the gift of your one, wild heart. And to do whatever you can to help others remember this and know how precious and unique they are. Perhaps this is the most radical gift that we can all give.

Please don't forget how rare and precious it is here. And please don't forget what really matters to you.

Today May Not Be a Day for Answers

There are times when the ground has fallen away and there are no longer any reference points from which to make sense of what is happening. The rug has been pulled from under the life you were counting on to provide depth, solidity, and meaning. The narratives are conflicting, the feelings are contradictory, and the path forward is hazy. It's as if you can't access what was so clear from even a few days ago. All of the work you've done—the surrendering, the healing, the insights, the discoveries, the realizations … for some reason, it's no longer in reach. It's as if you're being asked to start over.

You have a sense that some sort of veil is parting, but what is coming next has not yet been given. At times it feels so alive in the unknown, but at other times it is disorienting and even irritating and there is a subtle (or not so subtle) burning for resolution. Rather than struggle against the uncertainty, give yourself permission to enter it. There is a refuge here, though it is hidden and may not be accessible via ordinary means. We don't live in a world that honors the wisdom in confusion and doubt, but it is up to you to bring this revelation into the collective, not only for your benefit, but for the benefit of all sentient life.

Stay close to what is here now, even if what is here is flat, numb, confused, and devoid of hope. For these are special allies of the path and operate outside conventional awareness. The unseen is always alive around you, taking form as signs, symbols, and guidance for the journey ahead. But the timeline is not of the known, and is crafted of the stars.

Your disappointment, your despair, and the ones representing the death of old dreams: the uncommon helpers have arrived, along with the more conventional aides of joy, clarity, contentment, and hope to midwife the mystery and reveal that you are right on track.

Listen carefully to the invitation as it arrives in a thundering silence: today may not be a day for answers but to let your heart break open to the vastness of the question.

Love Is Not Synonymous with Feelings of Safety

We want love to feel safe, but love is not oriented around any particular feeling. It is just too wild for that. As a field of immense creativity, love will make use of any feeling state, including that of "unsafe," to introduce us to the full spectrum of what it means to be an awake, alive, unprecedented human being, with a heart that is sometimes open, sometimes closed, sometimes in one piece, and sometimes shattered.

As the rich ground in which all feelings come and go, it is the way of love to transform everything it comes in contact with, for this is its nature. This activity is not oriented in the preservation of the status quo or maintenance of the conventional, but in bringing forth new forms of itself into the world of time and space. At times, this can be disorienting.

Perhaps our deepest longing is not for consistent feelings of safety, security, and certainty, but to live from wholeness, in intimate communion with the full-spectrum nature of what it means to be an attuned, sensitive human being. To live in and as the totality of what we are, which very organically contains, infuses, and transmutes the opposites of safe and unsafe, self and other, known and unknown.

Rather than approaching this as mere philosophical inquiry, the invitation is into the intimacy of immediate, embodied experience, and to discover for ourselves what is most true. As we open into the reorganizing energies of love, we will simultaneously be attracted and terrified, as we sense the ending of one world so that another may begin. We can count on the contradictory nature of the journey of the heart, turn into the core of the contradiction, and attune to the wisdom that is found there.

The Ancient Longing to Be Someone

So much has fallen away over these last weeks and months: the identities that once seemed so important, the dream of a relationship that was never going to accompany you into the future, outdated ideas about where you were going to discover meaning and how you were going to spend your time. What you knew just a few days ago is being replaced in the here and now as updated revelation. The truth is that you are no longer sure of anything ... except that an old dream has died. Yes, the known has been removed, but what will arise from the ashes of the way you thought it was all going to turn out?

In these moments, the temptation is to spin quickly to recover the lost ground, to replace the confusion with clarity, to find a new identity to merge with, and to surface unscathed from the cosmic birth canal and back into the known. Yet something is different this time ... you are increasingly aware of another voice emerging out of the thundering silence.

Honor the death that is occurring, the jewels buried within the darkness, and the implications of just how purifying the movement of love truly is. It is rewiring synapses and laying down new grooves within you, and rearranging the cells and organs in preparation for what is to come. While this activity is exhilarating, the level of creativity and reorganization will simultaneously be a little bewildering to that part of yourself that needs to hold on to your identity as "someone."

But for the short term, consider the possibility that you need not establish another identity or replace the confusion with clarity; that nothing has gone wrong, you have not failed, and nothing need be shifted, transformed, or even "healed" ... for now. For the next moments, you are being asked to provide a sanctuary in which you can rest in the center of the fires of groundlessness, where you can offer safe passage for the stormy waves of complexity, confusion, and contradiction.

See that love is always near, taking form as the "other" in all of its disguises, in ways the mind may never understand. Love will always be close, walking side by side with you into the secret caverns of your psyche, your body, and your holy nervous system. But it will never, ever protect you from the unfolding and illumination of your raw, beating heart. For you are loved too much for that.

Rest now. You are right on track.

The Downward Journey

Let us not forget the downward journey into the lower chakras, the darkness, the body, sexuality, relationship, family, and into the earth itself. In subtle and unconscious ways, the spiritual journey can become overly identified with the upward, the light, and the transcendent. We want to ascend in a rush to leave behind the very alive, untamed, and untidy out-of-control world of feelings, emotions, intimacy, and vulnerability of all kinds. It is easy to disconnect from this current, as we long to soar above our present experience, especially if it is messy or unresolvable, or too confronting and emotionally activating.

In doing so, however, we turn from the waters of life and lose touch with the wholeness that is always already here, with the signs, symbols, and guidance that are found in the core of the chaotic dark. We can start to hear the cry of the heart, out of a thundering silence: Wait. Slow down. Look carefully. The freedom we are longing for is not *from* the chaos and the contradictory, but buried *inside* it. Ultimately, of course, our skillful engagement with both ascendant *and* descendant energies and dimensions of the spectrum will allow us to touch the depths and be of most help to others.

As we make the journey with our fellow travelers, let us not disavow the lunar current flowing into the unlit places, out of the lower worlds, and through the dark caverns of the psyche. This current is of the moon and a secret emissary of wholeness. The invitation here is one of embodiment: into vulnerability, chaos, and reorganization: each unique expressions of high-voltage creativity as transpersonal love seeds our embodied human experience with its qualities.

No, it was never going to turn out the way we thought it would— the relationships, the work, the family, our bodies, our paths of awakening and healing. But the reordering of the heart is always of the unknown and will never conform to the dictates of the conventional world. By way of disappointment, deflation, and the revelation that we are all beginners on the path of love, the heart is polished and our wild uniqueness is revealed.

Yes, something is illuminating the way, but just what it is cannot often be apprehended by ordinary means. There is no external map we can rely on, only the one that is written inside us. While at times we sense the presence of this inner guidance, it often comes by hidden and symbolic means. We must learn to listen for it in a nonordinary manner, not just with our ears but with the wisdom of the body, the cells of the heart.

While it is natural to have a bias for one current over another, let us not do so at the expense of fragmentation. In ways the mind may never understand, there is a luminous middle place where the currents intertwine. It is found in a secret chamber inside your own heart. Go there. Send your awareness inside the palace and surround it with your presence. There, you can live and move from the center.

Historically, many (but of course not all) of our systems of transformation have organized the inner journey around how to get from "here" to "there," from a less pure to a more pure state. From the profane to the sacred, the low to the high, the human to the divine. While we can honor the wisdom in transcending what is less than whole within us, let us not do so at the expense of abandoning and losing intimate contact with the brilliance of what is here now, shining out of our imperfectly perfect humanness, and in no need of transformation. What we discover here is not in need of healing as this term is conventionally understood. As we inquire into the essence of our immediate, arising experience we may discover that it is pure and complete on its own.

Many of the world's great tantric and nondual traditions have recognized this truth and made its unfolding revelation a cornerstone of their approaches and practices. From this perspective, the journey is less about traveling from "here" to "there" than it is about being fully Here, committed to participate in Here, in all of its mess and glory. For it is within the core of all form that freedom is discovered, and its ultimate nonseparation with pure awareness is realized and transmitted through us.

As we continue to discover the openness, luminosity, and validity of all of our inner experience—regardless of whether we "like" it or deem it "spiritual" or an error or obstacle along the way—we may notice ourselves becoming less interested in traveling from "lower" to "higher," from "human" to "divine," or even from chaos to clarity.

From a more tantric viewpoint, our neurosis is wisdom in a yet to be unfolded form. Buried inside the very rich, disturbing energies of colorful emotion and burning sensation, the sacred world awaits, not by means of transcendence but by way of penetrating awareness and compassion.

As we deepen in our inquiry, we may notice we are less and less interested in ways we can exit one particular state of experience for another. Rather than focusing on how to transcend difficult emotions, we might find ourselves curious about them, fascinated with their color, fragrance, and texture, called to enter into relationship with them, captivated with how we might make use of their underlying energy to open to life and to those around us. We may discover that the freedom we have been longing for is not waiting around the corner ready to emerge as soon as we are able to "move beyond" or shift our vulnerable feelings, messy emotions, and chaotic relational dynamics … but is here now. Inside and around the core of the emotional and somatic material. It does not need to be transformed, from this perspective, as it is complete and whole on its own, a pure expression of life awaiting an encounter with your intimate, loving awareness.

The invitation of this downward call is to offer *this* muddy body, *these* feelings, *these* emotions, *this* imagination, *this* erupting creativity that is the human being as a vessel through which love can come down out of the absolute and pour through our conventional human experience, seeding it with its qualities. The primary mode of inquiry then shifts from "How do I transcend the relative to get to the absolute?" to "How do I become transparent to the always, already revelations of the absolute in the embodied world of time and space?" Here. Now. Not at some point in the future after the mess and glory of our humanness has been transcended, resolved, clarified, and cleaned up, but in every arising here-and-now moment. Each moment of experience then becomes an invitation into wholeness, a clarion call to integration, and yet another opportunity to commune with one of the mysterious qualities of love as it comes alive here.

We discover in our own direct, firsthand, unmediated experience that there is no state of consciousness other than this one right here, right now. While this may be obvious to those of us engaged with inner work, the actual lived implications of this realization are revolutionary in their impact. From this realization arises the most radical invitation: to honor *this* state of consciousness, *this* one that has been given, as a pure and complete expression of reality, rippling with presence and aliveness, not in need of transcendence or transformation. In the very core of this invitation is the deeply embodied realization, on all levels of being, that there is no "better" or more spiritual state coming tomorrow. There is no Kingdom of heaven arriving soon, no love waiting around the corner, no grace arriving in the future.

The only grace that could ever be is taking form right now as the eruption of the sensual world in front of your very own eyes: as the sun, the moon, and the stars; as your arms when you hold another; as your words when you speak kindness; and as the wisdom-field of your immediate experience, exactly as it is. The miracle has already occurred. Gaze into the mirror of your own heart and you will see.

Sweet and Fierce Grace

I'm sure there are times when you wake up in the morning and feel at peace, as we all do sometimes. It really is a good life. Despite the challenges, you've been given so much. Things are simple and clear, and you are full of gratitude. You have friends who really care about you, you're enjoying your work for the most part, you're feeling less anxious lately, and the looming sense of depression has lifted. You know there is great opportunity here, you have so much to give, and you are in the exact right place.

Grace has appeared, this time coming in disguise as alignment, flow, and connection. It has colored things with a subtle yet purifying sweetness.

The Sacred Middle

In the next moment you notice you aren't feeling so well. You don't have much energy, you are depleted, and your heart is beginning to ache. It feels like too much again. The depression has returned a bit; you're not sure if you're actually okay any longer. You are becoming convinced again that there might be something fundamentally wrong with you after all. While you have heard you are a perfect, radiant expression of Pure Spirit, you are unable to find the evidence. You feel that familiar sense of despair returning, joined by your old companions panic and anxiety. Here we go again.

Grace has appeared, this time coming in disguise as confusion, hopelessness, uncertainty, and despair.

Grace has many faces and will come in infinite forms in order to show you a forgotten piece of yourself. Despite the appearances, these pieces—sweet pieces, fierce pieces, peaceful pieces, wrathful pieces—are not working against you. In ways the mind may never quite understand, the darkness is yet another way for grace to hold you. For it is not limited to the light.

Intimacy with Our Neurosis

Buried inside even our deepest neuroses are the raw materials of love. In the tantric and alchemical traditions, those less-than-awakened thoughts, feelings, emotions, impulses, and raw sensations are the *prima materia* for us to work with. The shit, the piss, the dirt, the darkness, the failures, the disappointment, the deflation: this is the sacred material we have to work with as alchemists of our own lives.

Rather than becoming consumed with some mythical journey in order to get from "here" to "there," where we get rid of the darkness, we turn it all upside down and travel inside it with courage, compassion, and creativity. No longer organized around "here to there," but how will "there" erupt into form, how is it that we will become a transparent vessel in which love can come pouring in here to the world of time and space?

Yes, it will often be quite messy, utterly contradictory, and unbearably confusing at times … and so very human. But the invitation is to enter into intimacy with our neurosis, explore its color, texture, fragrance, and underlying energy, because we care so much, and want to know what is most true.

And what we discover is something quite luminous: that this material we have come to identify as "my life" is pure and sacred as it is, and inseparable from love itself. It is love in disguise, appearing in whatever form it must in order to reach you.

A Cosmic Permission

It is natural at some point along the way to become aware of a profound wish to share your joy, happiness, and peace with those around you. It is so innate to want to uplift others, inspire them, and offer to them your deepest realizations and heartfelt discoveries. This aspiration can be honored and held near.

But perhaps the greatest gift you can provide to the other is sanctuary and safe passage for the unmet within you. For it is out of profound self-attunement that the most skillful action and blessings will flow. When you are in intimate, direct contact with your own grief, loneliness, heartbreak, and confusion, a holding field emerges in the space between you and your suffering friend. Some unknown, "third" presence appears, transcending the sum of the parts and offering an invitation into something new. By way of empathic mirroring, the other is granted cosmic permission to contain, integrate, and practice compassion toward those unresolved qualities in themselves. As the unwanted is metabolized somatically, emotionally, and at the level of felt sense, you can make meaning, together, of the journey of an open, sensitive human being.

As this inquiry unfolds and deepens, the actions you take in relationship with others will no longer be organized solely around providing relief from confrontation with the emotional world. Instead, you will respond in a way that is rooted in empathy, mindfulness, and clear seeing, from the slowness and spaciousness of the "here and now" instead of the more urgent, implicit time machine of the "there and then." Because you are willing to take care of the inner family as it arises—the split-off feelings, images, hopes, fears, and vulnerabilities of all kinds—you will no longer need to look to the other to do this for you. You will allow them to love you enough to return this task to you, for it is sacred and yours to hold. You can craft a new relationship to your inner experience, where even difficulty becomes a fellow traveler and ally on the journey rather than an obstacle, obscuration, or enemy you must oppose or resist.

And in this work, you may remember, even if only vaguely, an old vow you once took to not pathologize your sensitivity, to not abandon your emotional experience, and to no longer practice misattunement and self-aggression toward your vulnerability and the ways you are striving to make meaning of your life. In the miracle of the here and now, you can choose whether to renew this vow or update it according to new vision and revelation.

A Wandering Emissary of Wholeness

For many, their greatest fear, the source of their most primordial anxiety, is that they are not truly loved or lovable as they are. This deeply embedded organization—with its attendant emotions, feelings, and physiological sensations—arose in part in response to an early environment lacking in empathic attunement, mirroring, and genuine interest in a little one's unfolding, subjective experience. To let this traumatic belief all the way in has a way of opening the floodgates to the most ancient confrontation with hopelessness and despair. It is an act of kindness on the path of the heart to become as aware as we can of this belief, how it colors our perception (especially as it plays out in intimate relationships), and what might be required to untangle and reauthor the limited story of the unlovable one.

As powerful as this fear may be, as I suggested earlier, perhaps there is one even greater that is counterintuitive and even bewildering and paradoxical to the mind: to allow in the reality that you *are* in fact fully loved exactly as you are. To give permission for this radical truth to penetrate you at the deepest level is the beginning of the end of your world as you know it. When the trance of unlove falls away, nothing will ever be the same again. You will no longer be able to stay on the sidelines, holding back from life, unable or unwilling to share your unique gifts, and safe from the risk that embodied love will always require. You will never again be able to rely on the narrative of unworthiness to protect you from full immersion in the reality that at any moment your heart could break, you could fall in love in the most excruciating way, and that the beloved—in whatever form he or she might choose to take—can and will pull the rug out from under you, leaving you naked and exposed in love's transformative embrace.

As the implications of this realization unfold, it may become clear that you can no longer avoid intimacy as well as you once could, using old escape routes or demanding that you first heal your past, feel safe all the time, or feel clear before you will be asked to fully show up. Nor will you have the option to embody only half the full spectrum of feeling and emotion that is available to an entire and complete human being. The only option left is that of a wandering emissary of wholeness, a luminous vessel in which all of love's qualities may find safe passage.

As you explore the fears that wake you early in the morning, travel by your side during the day, and accompany you as you drift into the dream world at night, the invitation appears. Watch as the spell of postponement is broken. Sink into the muddy earth and look up at the moon and the stars. Feel the raw warmth of your heart as it beats and softens. Stay attuned with your senses as they open to receive. The narrative of unworthiness is fading, dissolving back into the vastness from which it came.

When it is impossible to claim for even one more moment that you are unworthy of the wild, untamed love that is your birthright, your perception will be cleansed and you will realize you are home, in the sacred world that has always been here and is already the holy ground on which you stand.

7

Encoding New Circuitry

The Power of the Relational Field

OUR EXPECTATIONS IN RELATIONSHIP—OUR WILLINGNESS TO ALLOW another to matter, whether it is safe to assert a boundary or need, fears around being loved as we are, the excitement and terror in leading with our vulnerability—originated in a young nervous system longing for mirroring and connection. The strategies we developed to protect us from inevitable failures in empathic attunement arose creatively to prevent overwhelm and fragmentation in a developing little heart and brain.

As we inquire into these early relational templates with curiosity and an open heart, we can discover to what degree the protective strategies are still serving us, or whether they are in fact preventing us from stepping into a life of more intimacy and aliveness. While these defensive styles of organization have historical roots—originating in relational configurations with important attachment figures in

153

our early lives—they are reenacted in the here and now and require maintenance for their survival. Seen from this perspective, the limiting organization is not happening *to us* from the outside—and is not actually a matter of the *past* at all—but is something we keep alive in the present. This is a very hopeful realization, as we cannot change the past. The reality that we might be able to rewire and reauthor these lenses of perception is earth shattering in its implications. To dissolve the dream of unworthiness is a radical act that will change everything, and can prove a bit disorienting at first, requiring that we commit to being very honest with ourselves about what we truly want. As with all transformative change, it is risky to upend the status quo, for on the other side is the shimmering unknown. While we very naturally have reservations about the true implications of healing and setting aside our strategies of protection, there is a deep part of us that senses we will never feel fully alive if we do not assume this risk and set out for uncharted psychic lands.

Our neural pathways are tender, open, and responsive, lighting up as we seek attuned, right-brain-to-right-brain resonance with those around us. We want to *feel felt,* to have our subjective experience held and mirrored, and to have the space to explore unstructured states of being. We long to rest in the mystery of what we are without having to worry about being abandoned or neglected in the midst of the adventure of self-discovery. While the encoding of shame, unworthiness, and abandonment is deeply embedded, it *can* be reorganized. It may feel incredibly entrenched but it is not as solid as it appears. Even if your early environment was one of consistent empathic failure, developmental trauma, and insecure attachment, it is never too late. The wild realities of neuroplasticity and the courage of the human heart are unstoppable, erupting forces of restructuring and creativity.

Through new relational experiences—with a therapist, a lover, a friend, or a baby; with a star, a tree, a sunset, or the moon—it may be revealed that love is the basis of all neural circuitry. But let us see for ourselves. With poetic eyes and an open heart, see that this primordial love is the substance that forms the neurons and their synapses and lights up the cells in your heart in an unprecedented moment of warmth, presence, and kindness. Each time you meet and attune to another, receive their love, and return it with your presence, simultaneously staying close with the "other" within you, a new world is born. A new pathway is formed. New circuitry is encoded.

Of course there are times in our lives when such a relational container is not immediately available, or is inconsistently so. Can we do this work on our own or can we not? Is self-regulation possible or is it a myth? Can we enter into the imaginal realm and commune with an unseen "other?" Can God, Goddess, angel, or another divine being serve as an effective attachment figure? How does all this work, anyway? These are the great mysteries at the intersection of modern developmental neuroscience and the contemplative way. Let us not rush to any conclusions, but go slowly, rooted in the radical ground of beginner's mind, as exploring psychonauts on an uncharted adventure in consciousness, and see what we discover in the further reaches of our own bodies and psyches. Yes, it is true that, relatively, we are wired to rest in a relational field; however, the qualities of empathy, presence, and attunement are wild and alive within us, embedded organically into what we are, and can be accessed, uncovered, and embodied. In many ways, this is what the spiritual journey is about, to fully and experientially participate in what we are as pure, limitless awareness itself. In fact, our true nature is the *ultimate* holding environment and with training, practice, and the bravery of the warrior's heart, we can begin to rest in this awareness as our psychic center of gravity. It is here where we move beyond conventional psychological (or neurobiological) understanding and into a more subtle realm of experience.

As we engage the power of the relational field, it can be helpful to conceive of relationship as consisting of both inner *and* outer dimensions. At times, the encoding of new pathways takes place in connection with *another person* in the form of a lover, a friend, a therapist, a family member, a coach, a counselor, a coworker, and so forth. At other times, relational work is undertaken in a dance with the "inner other," that more alchemical "other" comprising those unmet and orphaned parts of ourselves that arise into conscious awareness in the form of feelings, intuitions, imagination, bodily sensations, and "symptoms" of all kinds. Manifesting even as depression, anxiety, psychosomatic disturbance, confusion, hopelessness, joy, and bliss, this material is full spectrum in nature. Whether we are working with the inner other or with an external person, the relational field is alive, accessible, and at all times all around and inside us. It is always already here and awaits our discovery, but it takes practice and the cleansing of perception in order to attune to its high-voltage, transformative potentialities.

As long as there is breath moving in and out, you can update the narrative. You can encode new circuitry and engage the power of the relational field to help you chart a new course. You can make new meaning of your life, explore the depths of the heart in a fresh way, make a new commitment to the miracle of the here and now, and learn to flood your immediate experience with new levels of compassion and acceptance. Slowly, over time, you can embed the pathways with the new substrates of holding awareness.

No matter what is happening in your life, you can start right now. In *this* moment. There is only ever *this* moment. The opportunity for reorganization is always here and wired within you. Don't give up. Love will never give up on you.

Encoding New Circuitry

When you are triggered and the feelings are just too much, it is very likely that your core narrative—what you believe about yourself, others, and the world—is nearby. It is circling around you, not to harm or work against you but as an invitation to inquiry, and to new levels of integration. This archaic patterning is yearning to be reauthored but first needs to hear that you no longer need its protection and are ready to meet those parts of yourself that have heretofore remained outside awareness. In ways that seem counterintuitive, the old, restricting narratives are and have always been trying to help you and, in their own limited ways, keep you out of dysregulation, disintegration, and emotional flooding. But a deeper call is emerging, one that is no longer oriented in mere protection and safety but into the sacred, into that world of aliveness that you sense is so near.

In a moment of intensity and disturbance, become curious about the story you are telling, about the perceptual lens through which you are seeing yourself and the world. This narrative arose when you were a young child, long ago, in the attempt to make sense of an environment lacking in empathic, attuned, right-brain-to-right-brain connection. Step back just a bit and communicate to the narrative that you are calling off the war. It's over. You are stepping off the battlefield and putting down your sword. As a warrior of the heart, you are choosing to join forces as an act of self-love. Ask the narrative to reveal and clarify itself, not in a way that throws you off center into emotional overwhelm but in a way you can stay with and understand: how it is trying to protect you, why it has come, and what it needs from you. Hold it near and honor it for all it has done, and with a boundaried kindness let it know that it is time for an update.

Then, with capacities you did not have as the narrative was formed, you can begin the journey of encoding new circuitry, of laying down a new pathway. With presence, compassion, and all the wisdom you have gathered until now, you can begin to weave a new story, one that is more current, accurate, integrated, and whole: one that represents your real-time, here-and-now, adult-level capacities rather than a reenactment of a little one longing for connection that was never quite enough. This new story will arise out of the slow, spacious, wisdom-filled domain of the prefrontal cortex, replacing the urgent, restless reactivity of an overactive amygdala, which, after all, was only trying to protect you according to its own nature and abilities.

It is very natural to be unsure about the whole thing, about whether it is possible to update the core story that has been your companion for so long and that has formed the lens through which you navigate this life. It makes sense that in some ways you have no idea how to unravel, metabolize, work through, and re-encode this deeply embedded self-narrative and the associated states of anxiety and emotional intensity that underlie it. Yes, you do not *know* how to do this, in some rational, logical way. But with this not knowing you are right on track, for the process of re-encoding is one that comes *from the unknown,* requiring that you step into new territory and allow the intuitive wisdom of your true nature to light the way ahead.

If in a moment of activation the storyline is looping and habitual—and not fresh, spontaneous, and creative with new information—it is usually serving some sort of defensive purpose. Meaning that our identification with it is serving the function of keeping us out of some very messy, vulnerable, and disturbing feeling states. As we've discussed, this was a critical function at an earlier time. The questions now are whether we are still in need of this sort of protection and what the side effects are of continuing to split off from energetically alive aspects of ourselves. By shifting our attention out of the eruption of somatic material and back into the conditioned narrative, we can to some degree, at least for a short time, effectively avoid, repress, or dissociate from the vulnerable, shaky, raw material we have deemed unworkable and unsafe. Each time a painful emotion, disturbing feeling, or uncomfortable sensation arises, if we turn from the body and place our awareness back into the storyline, we keep the circuitry of self-aggression and abandonment alive, reinforcing the very young idea that this material is invalid, a harbinger of fragmentation, and working against us. But is it the material itself that is so threatening, or is it the avoidance of it and the abandoning of ourselves that is responsible for so much of our suffering and struggle? We must experiment, over and over again, and discover what is most true in the here and now.

It is important to remember that these protective mechanisms were put in place for a good reason: to keep us out of states of anxiety that, if released into conscious awareness before we had the capacity to digest them, would push us outside our window of tolerance and into a variety of states of disintegration. In order to contain, tolerate, and eventually open into this previously sequestered material, we must re-embody and metabolize the underlying anxiety that will be there guarding the gates, which can take quite a bit of training, curiosity, courage, and self-compassion. The belief that moving *toward* this material will expose us to overwhelming and unworkable panic is deeply embedded and takes *lived experience* (not simply cognitive insight), over time, to reorganize. This fear of overwhelm was a very reasonable assessment from the perspective of a young child lacking in developmental capacity, but we must discover whether it is still accurate, *now*. We do this *slowly*, in very small doses, each time we choose to stay with the underlying intensity, even for only one second at a time. One second, then rest. Another second, return to the senses. Take a break, soothe yourself in whatever ways are resonant for you, then rest. And then next time, for one and a half seconds. Then rest.

Become committed to seeing exactly *how* you leave the fire of emotion and return to the conditioned narrative, the unique ways you seek relief from the somatic aliveness by way of fueling the old storyline or engaging in unconscious behavior. How does this process work for you? What is it like? What is usually happening just before you disembody? What feelings are there that you have deemed totally invalid and unworkable, as harbingers of overwhelm and danger? In this realization of how this dissociation works *for you*, rather than falling into the archaic loop of shame and blame and self-attack, recognize this as a moment of pure grace, as an invitation from beyond to come home. With your breath and sacred life energy, come back into your body for a second or two; you can always return to the storyline in a few moments, for it too is holy in its own way and is best approached from a soothed, calm place, after you have attended to the disturbing feelings that have been longing for just one moment of your loving attention for so long.

The storyline is our best attempt to make sense of a difficult situation that involves unbearable feeling states and can be honored as such. In my experience, it is not possible to work through, reauthor, or reorganize that narrative until the underlying material is first allowed in to conscious awareness for very short periods of time, tolerated, and contained. It is only then that the next phase of the journey is possible, where we can begin to *open into it* with acceptance, kindness, warmth, and ultimately love. But we cannot do that—we cannot "skip steps"—until we have trained ourselves to tolerate the dysregulating feelings and discover in an embodied way (again, cognitive insight, while helpful, is not enough) that our survival is not *actually* at risk when we turn toward disturbing emotional experience. We have to discover whether this is true for ourselves and honor where we are on our individual journeys. Pushing ourselves into overwhelm or re-traumatizing ourselves in the name of "healing" is not kind, but simply another manifestation of the shame, blame, and self-aggression that were encoded at an earlier time.

While the storyline is in large part conceptual and a function of cognitively oriented perception, in my experience it is the underlying emotional and somatic states that are most primary in this process. The most skillful (and compassionate) intervention, the way I have come to see it, is usually at the level of feeling, not merely via cognitive restructuring. But there are many views on this. For some, beginning with cognitive work is incredibly necessary and helpful, and in the long run an approach that integrates all aspects of the spectrum (cognitive, affective, somatic, and behavioral) can be honored and explored. Both bottom-up (starting in the body) and top-down (starting at the level of cognition and belief) strategies are worthy of experimentation and each may be effective at different times.

This is very subtle (and demanding) work that is unique to each nervous system, and it is difficult to adequately summarize in a short section of a book. In my experience, for most of us it is challenging to do this type of work alone, to self-regulate, *at least in the beginning*, and is often best approached via an empathic, attuned relational field, where it can be co-regulated, in very small doses, titrating and pendulating the overwhelming feeling states by way of the relational container itself. To "borrow" another's soothed, calm nervous system as you enter into the uncharted territory of the body and psyche can be profoundly helpful and supportive as you engage in this process.

One simple formula is that the more deeply embedded the trauma or dissociative organization, the more primary co-regulation becomes and the more important relationship is in the healing process. As nearly all of our emotional, cognitive, and somatic wounding arose in interpersonal contexts, many (including myself) believe it is often (but not always) best contained, untangled, and metabolized within a relational field.

Finding a somatically informed therapist, counselor, teacher, or practitioner with experience in this area whom you trust and experience as deeply attuned—especially in the mirroring and holding of very intense and disturbing emotional material—is often required. But I can say with firsthand experience that it is possible to work through even the most traumatically based self-narratives by way of the underlying somatic disturbance, slowly, over time. Perhaps it goes without saying, but the goal is not to become dependent upon another to regulate this material for you, but to learn the art of self-regulation and be able to shift wisely, skillfully, and compassionately between the two. You don't need to get into any sort of solidified or polarized position that one is "better" or "more spiritual" than the other; both are wise, creative, and loving skillful means at different times along the way, and can be utilized together in an integrated approach to awakening and healing.

Wherever you are on your journey, when you embark on the path of wholeness and reintegration, you can ask a guide to bear witness as you move into unknown territory, honoring the truth that this reorganization requires an immense outpouring of courage and support. Find a therapist, a lover, a friend, or a mentor; a tree, a bird, a mountain, a dog; the sky, the sun, the stars, or the moon. A God or Goddess, teacher, or being of light. Allow them to hold you as you open, to stand with you as you turn inward. To step into the holding field with you, to keep you close, and to trust in your process, while not interfering with what you are called to confront and integrate at this time. In whatever way is natural and resonant for you, call on the seen and unseen ones to help you to engage in the great task of sacred return. See, once and for all, whether you still need to be protected in the way you once did, and if you are ready now to break open into a new life, one beyond imagination.

Look carefully, and see. You can contain so much.

Love Will Never Give Up on You

Suffering and chronic states of struggle are not "caused" *solely* by what happened to us in the past. Some research suggests our *perception* of what happened is even more impactful, along with how we have come to organize the experience in our brains and nervous systems. There is so much hope in these recent revelations from the field of neuroscience. Even though we cannot change the past, we *can* reorganize our relationship to it and engage the world in a new way, one rooted in self-compassion and clear, loving awareness.

In the nearly miraculous discoveries in the area of neuroplasticity, we are seeing that we can transform the context in which we hold, organize, and make meaning of what happened to us in the past. Even if our early environment was mired in disruptive attachment, chronic empathic failure, abuse, and neglect, it is possible to create new neural pathways and give birth to more cohesive, flexible, and integrated narratives. Your brain is luminous; your nervous system is holy; the cells of your heart are consecrated with sacred life energy. With new levels of self-attunement, self-kindness, and clear seeing, these discoveries can come alive within you.

While the work of integration and encoding new circuitry is not easy, and requires just about everything we have, there is hope. While it can seem like moving a mountain, the pathways are open, translucent, and not as solid as they appear. In their own way, they are longing to be reorganized into more integrated and cohesive forms. They are hopeful that they will be restructured.

I do not speak all that often about hope, as I am a great fan of hopelessness as a wrathful and transformative companion on the path. There is a certain magic in the core of hopelessness, but the art of mining that gold has been lost in our modern world. You can still find it; it is buried inside your heart. It is not some disembodied, theoretical, philosophical hope that is offered here. It is embodied, untamed, creative, and alive. It is not a hope that things will turn out the way we want or believe we need them to, or that our most cherished dreams will not be shattered. It is much more radical than that. It is a hope that is a wild sort of confidence in your true nature, which has never been unhealed. It is the kind of hope that you shout out in the four directions from the rooftop, and embody with the sun, the moon, and the stars as your witness. It is the hope of wholeness, and the utter workability and sacredness of your emotions, your feelings, and the temple that is your own body. It is the hope that your vulnerability, your tender heart, and your ripe being are gifts here, without which the planets may fall out of orbit. It is the kind of hope that is not passive but is the material of revolution.

Navigating this hopelessness is tricky territory as the mind is wired to find relief from and to resolve contradictions rather than rest inside them and mine the creativity and magic that are found only there. If we're not careful, we can easily fall down the rabbit hole of desperation and despair, and lose our way. Reaching out to others who can help provide a home for these energies to unfold and transform within us is so very important. It is very natural to at times make the commitment to deeply explore these energies in an embodied, direct way, while at other times it most intelligent and kind to return to safer ground. The loss of hope is usually deemed a very bad thing in our world, a profound cosmic error and a dark place that serves as an obstacle or obscuration on the path. There is another view of this, embodied by other cultures and peoples and seekers who have come to discover the loss of hope as a very creative, rich, alchemical place. But we must honor our own experience and trust it to guide us either *through* the hopelessness or *into* it, as we deem in our own best interest. There is no right path for everyone. For many, it is often a matter of shifting back and forth between the various approaches.

I have been honored to witness this unfolding, illumination, and transformation in many men and women over the years who have been kind enough to allow me to accompany them into the wild internal landscape where there is no map, no guidebook, and no clear assurance that it will all turn out according to their plans, wishes, and dreams. While the unprecedented activity of love will never conform to our preferences—for it is far too creative for that—it comes offering aliveness and wholeness, which may be what you have been longing for all along anyway.

Don't let anyone tell you that you cannot allow love to reorganize your life. It's simply not true. Don't ever give up. Love will never, ever give up on you.

An Invitation to Reorganize

When feelings of shame and unworthiness appear, they come not as obstacles to harm but as invitations to reorganize. Holocaust survivor and pioneering psychiatrist Victor Frankl is widely quoted as having said that our freedom is found in the space between stimulus and response:

> *Between every thought and action, there is a space. In that space is our power to choose our response. In our response lies our potential for growth and freedom.*

Just as the anger is surging, the emptiness is looming, and the feeling of abandonment is arising, in the moment of embodied meeting, there is a choice. While we may not have much say as to *what* presents itself in a moment of activation, we *do* have a choice (and can train ourselves to have *greater* choice) as to what behavior we engage in response. Will we act urgently to turn from our immediate experience, exiting the aliveness of the here and now, strengthening the neural groove of self-abandonment and denial? Or will we take the path of self-compassion, turning toward ourselves in times of difficulty, and commit to a new way, one that is rooted in loving awareness and the willingness to be our own best friend? Will we dare to practice kindness, to practice peace, and to step off the battlefield of self-aggression, shame, and blame?

The next time you are triggered and caught in a looping narrative about what is wrong with you, how wretched you are, or how life has failed you, slow down and make contact with the felt sense in your body. Drop under the very compelling storyline for just a moment and locate the burning in your heart, your belly, and your throat. Train yourself, with kindness and gentle friendliness, to notice that holy moment that opens between your *awareness* of the feeling and the *impulse to act,* the habitual tendency to either deny what is there or to urgently seek relief from it through fueling a storyline or engaging addictive behavior. It is hot and sticky here, claustrophobic and restless, and filled with opportunity and even magic. Becoming familiar with this space that Frankl describes is one of the most significant and life-changing realizations on the journey of wholeness. There is so much power and freedom in this middle place if you will take the time to familiarize yourself with it and explore the implications of its invitation. But it does take practice. And courage. And the deep commitment to care for yourself in new ways.

As the visitors surge in a sensitive nervous system, they appear alongside a doorway. While the doorway may appear to flash open and closed, it is actually always open, though at times it can seem hidden. On one side of the door is the old circuitry of self-aggression and abandonment. It is the path well traveled, and the grooves here are deep. By denying or dissociating from what has appeared—or acting out toward others or in toward yourself with shame and judgment—you reenact the ways your vulnerability was met as a young child in your family of origin. While of course there were moments of attunement and responsiveness, our culture does not have an inspiring track record when it comes to holding intensity and energies that cannot easily be controlled. The spin is back to numbness and safety as quickly as possible, regardless of the consequences of closing down to the majesty of what we are as sensitive and embodied human beings.

Depending on the ways you came to organize the experience of empathic failure, you will be guided into unique configurations of fight, flight, or freeze as the spontaneous creativity of "here and now" is replaced with the early circuitry of "there and then." Though these strategies were once intelligent, creative, and adaptive, many are discovering that they no longer support their vision for a life of intimacy, connection, aliveness, and meaning.

On the other side is the new pathway of slowness, empathy, attunement, and kindness. Of meeting, containing, and metaboliz-ing the dysregulating narrative, emotional intensity, and body-based raw sensation using capacities you once did not have. Not as a goal to further shame yourself for not perfecting, but as an intention, an aspiration, a lifelong practice to open into. And to return to over and over again.

No matter how things are flowing for you at the time you read this, you can start exactly where you are, afresh in this moment. There is only this moment.

In my experience, we open into the sticky, pregnant, raw vulner-ability in stages; we can't just go straight to "loving" our fear, rage, grief, sadness, and hopelessness. Many hear that they must accept and love everything that arises in their experience and end up using this teaching as a way to attack themselves when they inevitably "fail" yet again, not devoted or pure or spiritual enough to do the right thing. But in the attempt to end run our humanity and get to safe ground as quickly as possible, we end up bypassing some of the very rich, messy, holy material along the way, which is filled with life and sacred data.

As we learn to recognize and tolerate the very difficult and disturb-ing feelings and sensations, for very short periods of time at first, we can slowly continue our journey with them. From tolerating to containing them within the self field, and discovering in a deeply embodied way that we can hold a lot more than we originally thought, we realize that this material is not attacking us from the outside; it is not arising to harm us but to reveal the path of integration. As we deepen in our inquiry, we can slowly begin to say "yes" to even the most disturbing feelings, to accept that they are here and that the most loving, wise, and kind approach is to allow them to be here, to call off the war and acknowledge that *this* is the way reality is appearing in a given moment. Not a "yes" that we "like" the feelings or hope they will stay, but a "yes" that is grounded in the deep knowing that arguing with reality is the root cause of nearly all of our emotional struggle.

This is when the work becomes profoundly transformative. Beyond mere recognition, toleration, containment, and even "acceptance" is the radical practice of opening our hearts to our pain, to our fear, to our sadness, to our rage, to our hopelessness, to our despair, and to our grief. This is madness to the mind! Why would we do this—what would it even mean to open in this way, to move toward our vulnerability and surround it with presence and warmth, not just "tolerating" it but entering into loving communion with it? Yes, this is bewildering to the mind, but the heart knows ... the body knows. In this deeper level of inquiry, we may come to discover that clear, cognitively oriented insight is not enough to penetrate the most subtle levels of our being, but that this journey is ultimately oriented in the activity of the heart. Here, we can explore what it would mean to love ourselves and our experience as it is at the most profound levels, to hold it as we would our little baby who is cold, scared, and feeling lonely in a crazy world.

On this journey from recognition through unconditional love, we must remember that we cannot skip steps—and we do so at our own peril, as well as to the peril of those around us. We must start slowly, with a non-urgent kindness, rather than needing to come in and storm the castle and "heal" ourselves in a couple of hours. It is this urgent need to "heal" that is often yet another hidden expression of self-aggression and self-violence—of encoded shame, blame, and self-hatred—and the remnants of an early environment lacking in empathic attunement. But we can recognize this now ... and choose another way.[1]

The New Circuitry Is Forming

"What I'm experiencing right now should not be happening."

This simple thought is the ground of nearly all unnecessary psychological suffering. As an experiment, rooted in the curiosity to know yourself at deeper and deeper levels, inquire into the unique ways that this belief becomes wrapped around your raw, naked experience. See how subtle you can get in your observation. In a conversation with a friend, during stressful times at work, when you are alone in an unguarded moment, during an argument with a lover, and even when everything is going fine and is relatively calm. In what ways have you come to conclude that there must be something wrong with this moment? That somehow you are not okay, that something is missing, that there is some problem that must be attended to?

As you become aware of an existential sort of boredom, restlessness, melancholy, or despair ... slow way down and get curious. These particular states (where nothing overtly is going wrong that you can point to) are ones that have been rejected from our world and often carry secret invitations into the inner landscape. As you sit with them and create a sanctuary where they can unfold their unique (though often misunderstood) signatures, allow the questions to bubble up: "Is everything okay?" "Am *I* okay?" "Is something missing in this moment?" "Isn't there a problem or issue I should be attending to?" If you look carefully, you may discover how deeply embedded this belief is—that something is wrong—and how an

---

1. I would like to acknowledge the work of Tara Brach as well as that of Bruce Tift in deepening my understanding of the unfolding stages in the metabolization process, and the importance of an integral approach that spans cognitive, emotional, *and* somatic process.

unconscious relationship with it keeps you from fully participating in the sacredness of life as it is. When we are caught in the seduction of "improving" our lives as a lens through which we navigate the world, we so easily miss the natural great perfection that is unfolding in a leaf, the sky, a feeling, an image, a car driving by, the eyes of the cashier at the grocery store.

Of course, the greatest improvement project of all, the most solid and embedded item on our cosmic to-do lists is the incredibly serious project of improving "me." While there is nothing wrong with the intention to improve your sense of self and life circumstances, it can be very revealing to discover how this insistence on improvement may be cutting into the direct, embodied experience of a natural completeness that is available *now*, the pure, miraculous flow of life that is here *now*, which is not dependent upon first improving yourself. We spend so much of our sacred life energy intent on bettering ourselves and our lives that we lose touch with our native wholeness and completeness, which is always already here, if we will take the time to see.

To slow down and consider that nothing is wrong, that this old belief is a remnant from another time and place, can catalyze a whole new way of being. Each time we find ourselves caught in the looping narrative that we are not okay, that there is some problem we must solve, and that we are fundamentally problematic at our core, we can make the intention to return into the aliveness of the present, ground ourselves in our bodies and our senses, and cut into this ancient thought form, slowing way down, touching the earth, breathing deeply, and relaxing into the wholeness of now.

The Compassionate Art of Doing Nothing

As you become aware of how the belief in incompleteness colors your world and your perception, as you touch in on these existential feelings of restlessness, claustrophobia, despair, and agitation, the invitation is to make the radical commitment to *do nothing* about it.

For this nothing is the activity of revolution, and the direct path to the wholeness of now.

Wait a minute. Nothing? Do *nothing* when I become aware of the feeling that there is something wrong? But don't I need to shift it? Transform it? Transmute it? Affirm its opposite? Accept it? Forgive it? Transcend it? There must be something, some action to take! I am not sure about this "nothing." What would happen if I did nothing? What would that mean about me as a person? Wouldn't that be giving up? Wouldn't that keep me trapped and stuck in the "negative" energy of the emotion? Isn't there something I should be focusing on, manifesting, and transforming? Isn't there a higher vibration I can shift into it, and quickly? What if I get swallowed up by the emptiness? Or fall down the rabbit hole of despair, flatness, melancholy, and depression?

It can provoke quite a bit of anxiety to allow yourself to do nothing in response to surges of feeling and emotion within you. There is a lot of data here if you will just try this as an experiment: sit for twenty or thirty minutes and do nothing. Not meditate or follow your breath or subtly start to do yoga or qigong or visualizations and prayers. Just nothing. What would happen? Perhaps you could see it as an experiment in self-love, to dare to love yourself so much that you will spend some time completely alone, undistracted by any practices or techniques or any way whatsoever of manipulating your raw, naked, immediate experience. To befriend yourself in a totally new way. The invitation here is not to give up your practices, techniques, and approaches forever but just for a few minutes. You can return to them later.

What does it bring up in you to step in this direction in response to your awareness of anger, grief, despair, and confusion? Or in the face of joy, bliss, and peace? Or flatness, boredom, and depression? No shame, no judgment, no trying to figure anything out. Just a few moments of direct, unmediated contact. Because you love yourself. And you want to know.

This "nothing," incidentally, is a very unique though often unrecognized representative of the path. It is not a cold, detached, resigned, deadened nothing—which is the mind's interpretation of "nothing"—but a warm, open, caring nothing that is rooted in wanting to know what is true more than *anything*. A fiery willingness and passion to stay close with your experience, grounded in openness and compassion. Curious about whether this moment is incomplete, whether there is something missing, and whether you must urgently scramble toward a remedy. This "nothing" is not passive but volcanic in its implications. It is a nothing that gives birth to stars. It is the Big Bang that resides deep within your own heart.

There is such a deeply rooted belief that we must *do something* with intense surges of feeling and emotion as they wash through: understand them, determine their cause, link them to some life circumstance or person, transform them, transmute them, accept them, love them, heal them. The pathways of abandonment are many and were weaved into our sensitive nervous systems when we were young children who did not have the capacity to metabolize the intensity in an environment of attuned presence. Out of the very intelligent need to escape, we unfolded unique strategies of fight-flight-freeze to take us out of dysregulating states of intense anxiety and vulnerability and away from the aliveness and uncontrollable nature of the somatic and emotional landscape.

But what if for just one moment you did *absolutely nothing* in response to the arising of emotional intensity? If you neither repressed nor denied it, nor acted it out nor sought to discharge the energy as it surges? What if the most wise, loving, attuned response was to take no action? Not some sort of cold, detached, uncaring, resigned "nothing" but one that was filled with warmth, holding, and a relentless sort of self-care? To make a commitment to no longer abandon the uninvited ones as they erupt and seek holding? But to become deeply curious and interested in the actual nature of your experience, *as it is*—to dare to consider that it is intelligent and valid and that its direct embrace may in fact be a portal into life. To see what is there when you do not interfere with your experience in any way. To dare to see "nothing" as a radical act of self-compassion.

In this willingness to meet your experience in the spirit of openness and receptivity, regardless of whether you *like* it or not, you might finally discover, in a really embodied way, whether your heartbreak requires mending, your sadness must be transformed into happiness, your fear must be sent away, and your anger must be abandoned. In this way, this "doing nothing" is the doorway into the sacred world, into reuniting with the orphaned ones of your inner family—not by fueling a story about what happened, who is to blame, and what the presence of these ones mean about your worth as a person. But through encoding the new circuitry of presence, guided by slowness, empathy, kindness, and curiosity.

There is a time, of course, to go back and attempt to make sense of the feelings, emotions, and sensations, to organize them and engage with them conceptually, integrating them at the level of belief and narrative. This, too, is holy work. The invitation here is not *in opposition* to that but *in addition* to it. If, in a moment of trigger and activation, you first take care of the feelings, meet them directly, and provide safe passage, you will not need to continue to engage in habitual, addictive behavior designed to take you out of your experience. Through your empathic self-attunement you can provide a home for them and listen carefully, and thus will more naturally be able to stay close. Once the fire has calmed a bit, you can go back in and engage with what happened at a more conceptual level, once you are back online, present, and in a much slower, grounded, and less reactive place. You can make meaning of what happened, connect the dots, use your prefrontal cortex to help organize your experience with the tools of wisdom, perspective, and clear seeing. In this way, your inquiry will be more fruitful and can go deeper than if you attempted to engage conceptually while the fire was still raging.

If you attempt to participate *only* at the conceptual level, it is too easy to get lost in your historic conditioning, to employ the demand for resolution and relief as a way to distance yourself from what is happening in your body, and thereby uphold the circuitry of fight-flight and self-abandonment. Yes, it is a full-spectrum inquiry we are interested in: we're not by way of some solid belief or theory claiming that sensations are more important than emotions, which are more important than cognitive insight. However, you might notice that what is being most asked in a moment of activation is an embodied, bottom-up touching and holding of the feelings, prior to engaging with the situation conceptually. From the compassionate ground of open, accepting, experiential contact with the emotions that are surging within you, you can enter into a conceptual analysis that is rooted in curiosity and truth rather than in escape. Of course, this is an art and not a science and something you must experiment with many times to come into the alchemical middle of what is right for you. But slowness, kindness, and self-compassion are always the best guides.

Your feelings and emotions are full of intelligence and guidance. They are not enemies or obstacles on your path but are *the very path itself.* They have not come to harm you but to be allowed back into the majestic vastness that you are. They are none other than Life itself, taking a more fierce and disturbing form perhaps, longing to get your attention and remind you of something you've forgotten. They appear as love's children lining up at the door of your heart, yearning for a moment of your presence, your care, and your holding and to reveal that it is only in their abandonment, not in their embrace, that suffering can take root and flower.

In between the ancient responses of denial and seeking relief is a very alive, intimate, and creative place. There is not a lot of solidity here, however, and there are not many reference points around which you can orient and chart a path forward. It is a liminal, in-between sort of place that is not all that deeply understood in the modern world, as it requires capacities that are not ordinarily honored in the busyness of life and incessant demand to be in control and to know what is coming next. While it may be exhilarating to explore this territory on the one hand—for we sense there is tremendous richness here—it may also be a bit disorienting to a mind seeking stability, certainty, and resolution. There is nothing wrong with longing for clarity and for solid ground from which to take the next step. You can honor the call to the steady and secure while at the same time opening, and opening more, and even more, into the unknown that is calling you. Holding the tension between these opposites is one of the great developmental tasks on the journey of the heart.

The threshold of this new life is available to you at all times. In each moment, the archetypal journey of death and rebirth presents itself, beckoning you to enter inside to receive the mysteries within the fire of your direct, embodied experience. Paradoxically, it is both empty and full in this place: empty of concepts but full and pregnant with possibility and creativity. Empty not in the sense of deadness or flatness but in the sense of translucence, utterly flexible, an echo of something to come, though this something has yet to take form. A new pathway has dawned. You can almost feel the new circuitry forming. It is from this ground that all skillful action is born.

In this "no-place" where your experience is allowed to be exactly as it is—without too much interference and interpretation—the knots and tangles of the heart will begin to loosen. And even the deeply rooted urge to escape your experience can be used as fuel for the path home. Each time you become aware of yourself engaging in self-abandonment, it is a moment of revelation, a mindfulness bell of love ringing inside you: Ah, come closer. Please don't leave. It can be a revolution to discover that you need not do anything with these old limiting beliefs or conditioned emotional responses, for they will liberate on their own. They will reveal their luminous nature when met with the warmth of your being.

In the heart, there is no obstacle. Only more path. And more. And more. And more.

Dancing in the Contradictions

Anxiety and groundlessness are such difficult experiences to work with. From a psychodynamic perspective, anxiety can be seen as an indication that unconscious material is threatening to be released into conscious awareness. Or that some unresolved aspect of ourselves is wanting to be reintegrated. For those interested in spiritual growth and awakening, this cosmic sort of restlessness can arise as we begin to discover just what is required on the journey of the heart: namely, to surrender the existing image we have of ourselves so something more whole can emerge; to explore with an open heart the personas we have developed and look carefully at the shadow that has been created as a result. It requires a tremendous amount of energy to maintain the identities we have worked so hard to establish because these images have served to protect us and keep us from our underlying vulnerability and those parts of ourselves that we believe do not fit in to our constructed self-image. As we begin to relinquish our hold on the personas, allowing ourselves to come face to face with the vulnerability and nakedness at the core, unmetabolized anxiety is sure to be there to greet us.

This experience of coming to terms with the unraveling of the images we have defensively created is not usually all that pleasant, but we can practice opening into and holding the resulting feelings in an environment of compassionate awareness. The habit, of course, is to view the shakiness as evidence that something has gone wrong and we must correct course, do whatever it takes to return to safe ground. Rather than enter into present, intimate relationship with this vulnerable material, we shift our awareness from the raw life that is coursing through us—which is naked, creative, of the unknown, and not easy to sit with—and reposition it into interpretation, where we turn from our bodies and hearts, and focus instead on thinking *about* what is happening, all the while staying one step removed from the action. We scatter our precious attention and life energy in an effort to understand, change, get away from, and "cure." It is natural to wish for relief and do what we can to care for ourselves. The point here isn't to shame or judge these efforts but to clarify what we are doing and why we are doing it, and to inquire deeply to see if taking this particular course of action is most skillfully in service of the deepest aspirations within us.

In each and every moment, we are in immediate contact with the world in an utterly naked and direct way. But this much openness can be a little overwhelming, especially as we come to discover that life is not really organized around us, our hopes, our fears, our fantasies, and our most cherished beliefs. Ultimately, there is nothing to hold on to, no confirmation of who we think we are, and no resolution to the mystery: just pure, naked, raw unfolding experience. While this reality, so spacious and without limitation, can be thrilling to step into, it can also be quite terrifying and disorienting to a mind that longs for control and something to hold on to. In the wake of such vastness, we (very reasonably) choose to re-clothe, armor up, and retreat back to familiar ground. It's similar to the choice Cypher made to re-enter the Matrix. Sometimes, the raw, vast, spacious truth can be too much, and we long to return to the status quo where we can forget again. Even if it feels claustrophobic and limited, we decide that it is preferable to such groundless, naked exposure. And the sacred dance of hide and seek continues ...

On the one hand, there is a genuine part of us that longs for something new and unknown, and for more integrated and unstructured ways to engage the world around us; we know on some level that when our center of gravity is grounded in the mystery, we will feel most spontaneous, creative, and alive. On the other, we sense that if we enter fully in this way there will no longer be any excuses to not show up, take a risk, and dare to be who we truly are. We will no longer be able to take refuge in the trance that we are unworthy of love or a life beyond our imagination. We won't be able to play it safe on the sidelines as we have done in the past, hiding out from the reality of death and heartbreak and messy confusion when it comes to intimacy and relationships, unwilling to meet the call of our creative potential, confidently asserting that we'll step all the way in once we "fully heal" or become "awakened" or clear up our past, or when it feels safe or we are otherwise "ready." To truly let go of our dramas of postponement, limiting beliefs, and complaints about life, we know at an intuitive level that we will be left face to face with all of those parts of ourselves we've been able to avoid for so long. All of that messy, human, sticky, gooey vulnerability. Icky. That doesn't sound so pleasant.

We're just not sure. The problems are so compelling and have become such a fundamental aspect of who we see ourselves to be, how we see others, and our views about the nature of the world we live in. Do I really want to know who and what I am without the reference point of my limited narratives, my persona, and the conditioned ways I have come to see others? What would it be like to truly live without reference to the story of the one who has become victimized, the hurt one, the one who needs healing, or the one unworthy of love? Who would be left? Who am I if I cannot organize my experience around these restrictive beliefs any longer? Would I even recognize my life if I were no longer investing so much of my precious life energy in maintaining *any* image of myself? On some level we long to see through these conditioned identities and personas, as we have come to see how limiting they truly are. On another, there may always be a bit of unconscious anxiety about it all, for they have been dependable companions for decades, in fact the lenses through which we have engaged with the world, with work, with our families, and in our intimate relationships. Do we want to hang on, or do we want to let go? Or both simultaneously?

Let us hold this sacred contradiction close, without any idea that we will at some point resolve it or wrap it all up into a tidy conceptual formula. The mysteries of the heart are not subject to that sort of analysis. In the honoring of the entirety of what we are—no longer willing to discard or abandon the aspects we do not like and have sequestered into the shadow—let us hold both parts with equal curiosity, care, and courage. The one that longs for love, for healing, for breaking all the way open into this life, with no more excuses or hesitation. *And* the other that seeks safety, the known, and the surety of what has come before. May we learn to trust in our experience to reveal the mysteries of this paradox in a timeframe that is written into a place deep within our hearts, which is not always accessible by way of conceptual understanding and planning. We can count on never really understanding, and take refuge in that, willing to dance in the contradiction in any case, awed by the pull to wholeness that has been placed within us.

You can learn to rest in the groundless ground and to relax deeply into its core, for it is the truth of your own nature and resonant with the unknown movement of love as it comes into form here. While it may feel disorienting at times, it is so open in this universe, where anything could happen at any moment. In this way, your life is like that of a star's, wide open and vast, grounded in not knowing and open to the mystery. This is an environment of pure creativity, overflowing with qualities of compassion, warmth, and presence. It is out of this tender openness that we are able to touch and attune to beings everywhere and can give our hearts for their benefit. We are willing to not know, at times to feel broken and at other times whole, to hold it all, and to use the *entirety* of our experience as skillful means to connect with others and be a vessel for love to do its work here.

The Wisdom-Field of the Awakened Heart

In a moment of activation, the emissaries arrive. When you find yourself overwhelmed by repetitive, habitual, ruminative thinking; when the thoughts are looping; when you are attacking yourself and falling down the rabbit hole of self-aggression ... just stop.

With the power and fierceness of the warrior's sword of compassion, cut the storyline. Slow way down and feel your feet on the ground. Breathe deeply into your lower belly and activate your senses. See what is around you with clear vision; enter into pure listening. Shift your sacred life energy out of the spinning and into the aliveness of the body.

It is an act of kindness to not fuel the dysregulating narrative, and takes practice, courage, curiosity, and imagination. Something is erupting under the surface, longing to be met and integrated, but it is raw, naked, and nonconceptual. Rather than turn in to the center of the restless, claustrophobic, and sticky somatic aliveness, we default back into conditioned history—to the shame, the blame, the attack, and the aggression, anything to keep us out of the fire and the tender surging tingling core of the vulnerability at the center.

The invitation in these moments is into the shaky interior. Use your breath as your guide into the inner landscape. You are being asked to care for yourself in a new way. See what feeling state the very vivid and colorful storyline is attempting to take you out of, and slowly, with kindness, drop underneath the conditioned history and into the hot, seething, pregnant life that is surging to be held.

In order to make this journey, that of the sacred return, we must set aside our agenda to understand, to change, to transform, even to heal ... for a moment. We can return to transformation at a later time. For now, replace it with a fiery curiosity. To become more interested in our original primal experience than in our interpretations of it, turning our bodies into a crucible of open awareness, filled with the qualities of warmth, attunement, and revolutionary kindness.

And in doing this we call off the war. We dare to practice peace. To step off the battlefield and into the unknown mystery of the body and the wisdom-field of the always blooming, awakened heart.

The Death of an Old Dream

It is inevitable at times that the rug will be pulled out from underneath us and we will come face to face with the naked, tender, glory, and mess of what it means to be an alive, sensitive human being. Things will fall apart, old dreams will die, relationships will end, and the allies of deflation and disappointment will dance in our hearts. Before we spin into the trance of shame, blame, unworthiness, and defeat, let us turn in to the brokenness where the particles of aliveness await.

It is tempting to become convinced that something has gone wrong, that we have failed, this time as a good spiritual person. "Spiritual" people don't experience anxiety, depression, rage, jealousy, fear, and hopelessness ... right? What about staying in the now? Stuffing the rage and forgiving everyone before you've digested the deep pain that was caused? Accepting and loving everything that appears without first confronting the heartbreak? Repressing the grief and replacing it with a consistent, flowing gratitude for all that is. Clearly something has gone wrong … hasn't it?

Inside the deflation is a hidden truth that the path of the heart is not oriented in how we can manufacture a life where this does not happen, where we can remain safe and untouchable on the sidelines, in some transcended (dissociated?) state, for periodic eruptions of reorganization are wired into this particular star. The rippling encounter with the tender and the groundless is not an indication that something is wrong with you but is high-voltage evidence that you are alive. For this disenchantment is the *prima materia* you have to work with. These are no ordinary moments. This world needs alive women and men, now more than ever. Please stay awake.

Rather, the question to ask yourself during these times is: am I going to use these reorganizing and shattering experiences as vehicles though which to befriend myself, to attune to the unprecedented flow of feeling within, and to weave a sanctuary for the wisdom pieces of the broken world to be held and illuminated? Or, will I fall back into my habitual, conditioned history, attack myself, my tenderness, and my sacred vulnerability, spinning into the habitual fight-flight urgency of shame, blame, resentment, and self-aggression?

It is not pleasant when the rug is pulled out and old dreams collapse, as this activity seeds the experiential field with the radical, fierce envoys of deflation and disappointment, who are here to reorganize, not to maintain the status quo. But it was never the status quo you were after any way. You're just too wild for all that.

Seen with an open heart and perception that is cleansed, you will apprehend this reorganization as a wrathful form of grace, filled with a light that is only found in the core of the dark—preparing, marinating, and opening you into something beyond what you're currently able to imagine … arranging the particles so that the mystery of what you are may fully come alive here.

Opening into the Middle

Co-emerging with a disturbing emotion or feeling state is an invitation into the center, into the alchemical middle territory between the opposites of repression and fusion. While the ways of self-abandonment are infinite, the most reliable is to disembody and begin thinking, to shift our awareness out of the surging, pregnant aliveness in the belly and the heart and back into the numbing flatness of the conditioned storyline. It is believed to be safer here, more sure, and more certain, but there is nothing safe about disembodiment.

Yes, the voices can be relentless—sticky, loud, seductive, and claustrophobic. "Something is wrong." "You are not enough." "You have failed." "You must escape." "There is a horrible problem that must urgently be handled." "You must improve yourself ... and quickly."

These are the voices of the orphaned one who is longing to finally be seen, met, heard, felt. Spinning and scrambling to make sense of a misattuned world, she will do what she must to reach you. She wants you out of the fire and back into safety, for this is all she knows, an earlier version of you without the capacity to turn in to the somatic aliveness and offer the healing rains of loving presence. She is trying to care for you in the only ways she knows ... but a new level of care is erupting underneath the surface.

When you find yourself pulled into the extremes of denying or repressing what has come on the one hand or fusing with it on the other, fueling the ancient story that something is wrong with you ... the invitation is into slowness, into rest, into a primordial sort of opening into the middle. Nothing need be understood, shifted, transformed, or healed ... for now. The invitation is into *holding,* not healing ... for it is from the ground of this embodied, intimate, naked embrace with what you are that all healing will organically emerge.

Wired for Love

We can be so hard on ourselves in so many ways: why did I choose the same kind of partner *again,* one who isn't able to meet me, why am I not able to find more meaningful work, why am I acting just like my mother, why have I not become awakened yet, why do I keep making the same mistakes, why do I care so much about what others think about me, why haven't I gotten over my trauma, why haven't I forgiven him, why have I not healed yet, when am I going to ever be at peace? In other words, *what is wrong with me?*

Research and clinical reports in the fields of attachment and interpersonal neurobiology have suggested that the way we've come to see ourselves was formed in the extended nervous system prior to the acquisition of language. As little ones, we lived in a nonverbal world, shaping our models of self and other according to our deeply wired need to survive, to be met and validated, and for our experience to be empathically held and mirrored back to us. When we received these things, we were able to rest in unstructured states of being, to create an integrated, cohesive self-narrative, and to allow ourselves to depend on others in a healthy way while being able to care deeply for ourselves when that was indicated.

Fortunately, the revelations of neuroplasticity have indicated that it is possible to reorganize the way we see ourselves, re-establish trust in the inherent goodness of the world, and find profound meaning in our close relationships. By some unknown grace, it appears that we are wired for love. Despite the traumas of the past and the difficulties many have suffered in abusive and neglectful relational configurations, somehow love is still there, underlying it all, never giving up on us, always ready to support us in restructuring the way we've come to organize our experience. While the journey of the heart is quite simple, on the ground and in real time it is anything but easy. We are hardwired to turn from our pain, to abandon dysregulating feelings and sensations in our bodies, and to reenact the misattuned responses that many were met with so frequently in their families of origin. To encode new circuitry is the work of a lifetime, but unfolds moment to moment and can *only* ever be activated in the here and now. We cannot do this work in the past or in the future. Only *now.*

Whenever you turn toward yourself in a time of distress, hold your experience with awareness and kindness, stay close and infuse your experience with presence, you make a new linkage. Yes, it may demand everything you have, and more, and this can be scary. But through compassionate self-inquiry, authentic contemplative practice, empathic psychotherapy, and especially through attuned, intimate relationship of all kinds, the opportunity is there to give yourself fully to this life and receive the fruits of a wide-open heart and a wise, intuitively guided mind.

One thing is required though, perhaps more than anything else. Not additional information, more advanced techniques, or steps for how to think ourselves into a new state of being. There are no gimmicks, quick weekend workshops, or shortcuts to the mysteries of your heart. No guarantees of "high" vibrations, sweet happy feelings, and dreamy happy endings. Thank god. The path of love is much more wild than all that. It is the willingness to dare to be kind to our vulnerability, to commit to no longer attacking or practicing aggression toward ourselves, and falling into the habitual conclusion that there is something wrong with us. To have the courage to be unconditionally friendly to our experience, whatever it is. While this sounds simple, for many this is a revolution: the idea that we could practice kindness toward our unfolding experience, that we could turn toward our difficult emotions and other unwanted aspects of ourselves and cut into a lifetime of shame, blame, and self-hatred. To do so requires the vigilance to notice and respond empathically to the habitual tendency to abandon ourselves and practice aggression toward our psychic, emotional, and physical bodies, and the willingness to be our own best friend, even if no one around us can see who we truly are and mirror our innate self-worth back to us. We will come to realize that it is a difficult path that we are on and yet one that bears fruit beyond our wildest imagination. Knowing that the habitual, wired-in response is often toward judgment, attack, and aggression, it can take everything we have to gradually shift this and replace it with empathy, slowness, compassion, and warmth.

May we nurture and hold ourselves in kindness today, and in every day and moment to come, as a commitment and a practice (no, it does not just happen on its own), appreciating that the journey will not always feel safe or warm or peaceful or hopeful. And when these inevitable difficult feelings emerge, may we commit to not concluding that they are evidence that we've failed but that an inner family member has appeared for integration. We can even learn to be grateful for this opportunity. Let us set aside the spiritual superego, our desperate need to be something other than what we are, and allow the grace that is always and already here to wash down throughout this sacred body, pouring through these holy senses and consecrated heart. And let us behold the miracle of this life as it is, seeing how lucky most of us truly are, and how we could only ever be in exactly the right place to take the perfectly designed next step into love.

Beyond Broken and Whole

Is it a problem that sadness has come, that we are feeling intense fear or anxiety in the face of an argument with our partner, or that we are feeling rage, confusion, loneliness, or despair? Do we need to take immediate action? Have we checked to see if these are actually problems we need to fix?

What would our lives be like if we were unconditionally committed to the truth of our experience, whatever it is? If in the face of such challenges we became increasingly present, and most of all, curious?

The habit, of course, in response to unwanted feelings of abandonment, panic, rejection, and so forth, is to quickly become convinced that our actual survival is at risk, that the very integrity of our being is compromised at the most fundamental level. That unless we take urgent action, something irreparable will occur and we will completely disintegrate. There is a place deep within us that feels quite sure that if we allow in our immediate experience we may in fact not make it, that we might actually completely break down and fall apart in a way that could be irreversible and permanent. And then what would happen? What about our jobs? The kids? The mortgage? Our spouses? Our physical health? Our friends? The bills? Our sanity? Our identity as a spiritual person, as one who has healed, who has awakened, and who is consistently grateful, loving, and forgiving?

If you are familiar with research in attachment theory, you know that when we were infants there were times when life was so overwhelming that we were unable to cohesively organize and metabolize our experience with any sort of consistency. In order to survive—psychologically, emotionally, and sometimes even physically—we had to make a critical choice: to disconnect and move away from the inner fire or to anxiously move out toward others in the hope we might find some relief, get our needs met, regulate the surging vulnerability, and return to security and safe ground. Adult attachment researchers call these two primary responses *deactivation* and *hyperactivation,* respectively. If you're interested, you could learn more about these responses and get curious as to how they may be coloring your perception and your behaviors, especially in the context of close interpersonal relationships.

Take a moment to inquire into the unique ways you react in the face of arising emotional intensity. When confronted with an emotion that feels overwhelming, or an avalanche of ruminative thoughts and dysregulating memories, or sensations in your body that appear to be forerunners of total shutdown and fragmentation, pay careful attention to the impulses to take action that arise. What are your primary strategies for seeking relief? Do you shut others out, convinced that you cannot depend on them anyway? Proclaim to the world that you will just "do it yourself?" Do you quickly move toward another to regulate the intensity for you, desperately reaching out to them, raging, shaming, and blaming them for the eruption within yourself? Make a phone call, have a drink, send a passive-aggressive text, surf the Internet, have some food (when you're not hungry), or engage in complaint or self-attack? No shame, no blame, no judgment. Just curiosity. And a genuine interest to know the truth of your experience.

When we were young children in our families of origin, these (and related) strategies very often saved our lives. They were expressions of intelligence and creativity that helped us disconnect and split off from overwhelming and dysregulating experiences so we could move forward, fit in, and do whatever it took to receive even a small amount of mirroring and attention. But as adults, might there another way?

Well, yes: the way of love.

In this context, *love* does not refer to a sweet warm feeling (though of course it could include that), but to the often fiery, uncompromising, and relentless willingness to turn *toward* whatever is arising, to not dissociate from it, and to cultivate friendliness toward ourselves and our experience. This is what we mean here by love. This sort of love is not passive but is on fire. The willingness to stand on and shout out from the rooftops, with the sun and the moon and the stars as our witnesses, that we will no longer abandon what is happening within us and that we will no longer pathologize pain, sensitivity, feeling, and vulnerability. With these and other seen and unseen forces by our side, we grant ourselves a cosmic sort of permission to stop trying to hold it all together, to maintain a particular image of ourselves, and to reject our immediate experience, as we likely had to do in our early environments to ensure our own survival.

We make the commitment to lay down a new pathway, one organized around turning *toward* ourselves—and staying close—during times when we need ourselves more than ever. Underneath what appears as a longing for relief is often a much more primordial and sacred longing: for the warmth of our own presence. This is the true gift that only we can give to ourselves. We are the giver and the recipient of this most sacred offering. It is this we miss and need more than anything during times of activation. We will never be able to fulfill this longing until we turn back, reclaiming all that we are with no more apology, no more shame, and no more judgment. Our emotions are sacred, our psyches are sacred, and our bodies and vulnerability are sacred.

We commit to entering into the fire of our immediate experience not because we *like* it or it *feels good,* or even so that it will change, heal, and transform into some other experience that we would prefer to have or have been told we *should* have if we were more grateful, forgiving, faithful, attuned to the present moment, manifesting properly, or meditating and praying better. Rather, we do so because of our love of the truth, and by way of a deep vow to no longer abandon ourselves.

And then when we sit with a loved one, a child, a colleague, a client, a stranger, a dear friend who is facing difficulty and challenge, we are able to naturally offer a holding space for the entirety of what they are, like an attuned mother expanding to contain the emotion and pain of her little one. In this open, empathic, yet often quite provocative environment, the other is granted this same permission to meet whatever experience is arising for her, to spin if needed into the groundless, uncertain dimension of being, knowing that we will be there for her if (and only if) she needs us, to bear witness to her containment and holding of confusion and intensity and to the ways she is making meaning of her suffering and her life. This work is sacred and ragingly pure.

It is never easy to watch our loved ones suffer, but during difficult times what they need most from us is our presence and our close attunement to their unfolding experience—and simultaneously, our own—honoring the reality that who they are and what they are experiencing is authentic and true for them, subjectively real for them, and that they need not have a different experience or be other than what they are in order for us to stay close and keep our hearts open. When in touch with their unfolding experience as it is—as well as with our own, which is very likely to be challenged in these moments—we enter into the alchemical environment of the relational field, where anything can happen, where we are no longer limited only to guidance and help from conscious sources. Here we are in touch with the unknown, the unseen, and the unconscious allies of the psyche, the heart, and beyond, with the deepest levels of the transpersonal Self and the healing potential of the full spectrum.

When we commit ourselves fully to our experience in the here and now, whatever it is, a portal opens to connect our hearts with the infinite, and we yet again become transparent to the play of love in this world. And then whatever Life sends to us—whatever sweet or fierce grace comes our way—we somehow remain committed to staying close to our experience, allowing everyone and everything to deeply matter, knowing that the path of the heart is endless and will always reveal greater depth. In this deepening intimacy with life as it is, we touch a profound willingness for this heart to be broken again and again, revealing that dimension of ourselves that exists beyond the concepts of "broken" and "whole" altogether. We are asked, yet again, to dance and play and explore within the contradictions, without any hope that they will ever be resolved. For it is in the core of this cosmic hopelessness that the sacred overflows and something much more magical can come through.

8

The Mystery of Self and Other

Love Doesn't Mean Becoming
an Emotional Doormat

It is important to realize that the path of opening the heart is not that of becoming the receptacle for the unloading of others' unconscious, unresolved beliefs, unprocessed feelings, and unintegrated behaviors. As we've been discussing, it is to the degree that we are attuned to the alchemical "inner other" within that we will be able to skillfully respond to the projections of the external other upon us.

As our perception is cleansed, we more deeply attune not only to the "other" as it takes form as those persons who appear in our lives, but equally to the "inner other" that we have lost contact with along the way: the unmetabolized guests of the somatic landscape that we have turned from and sent into a dark, shadowy forest. These ones will always and into eternity surge to be allowed back into the inner family, forever appearing as our intimate partners, children, and friends; as the colors, the moon, the sun, and the stars, taking infinite form to reach us. The sensual world is rich with hidden emissaries of wholeness and the heart. Slow way down, and see.

The only way to care for and integrate the "other" in whatever form it appears is by way of profound levels of self-compassion. For many, this holding does not come naturally as it was not encoded into the nervous system of a little one in an environment lacking in empathic attunement to the brilliance of the unfolding emotional world. But despite the early relational trauma, the developmental wounding, and the disorganized narratives of attachment, you can learn and practice this *now*. You can start right where you are, wherever you are, whatever your current life circumstances. The pathways are fluid and are awaiting reorientation. It is never too late. As long as there is breath moving in and out, the power of love is available, for it is wired and seeded inside you. It is not something you'll discover one day through a frenetic search. It will not be added to you once you complete a certain process or spiritual achievement, or heal your past or find your soul mate. It is here now and expecting you.

The qualities of empathy, attunement, and kindness are not passive and yielding, nor are they consistently sweet and peaceful. At times they take on wrathful forms. But they always remain grounded in compassion: not a weak and compliant compassion but one that is on fire, burning with the virtues of skillful action, ready and willing to implement yin *and* yang, feminine *and* masculine energies as needed. The attributes of empathic resonance are hardwired in us, even if they are obscured by misattuned relational experiences and our subsequent ways of organizing those experiences in a tender, developing nervous system. Despite these obscurations, the qualities of our true nature are available at all times, although they are not always reachable by conventional means.

In the tantric tradition, there are four pathways for relating to unresolved energy: pacifying, enriching, magnetizing, and destroying.[1] Pure, transformative compassion will make use of *each* of these energies at different times in order to unfold and express potent configurations of wisdom, compassion, and skillful means. In this way, love—or what you *are* as pure, luminous awareness itself—does not have a bias; it is ready to employ each of these energies equally in order to accomplish its vision. True compassion is not always soft, capitulating, and surrendering; at times it is ferocious, wild, and untamed. But this ferocity emerges from a wide-open heart and a longing to dissolve suffering in all its forms, for both self and other.

While perhaps appearing "compassionate" on the outside, being an emotional doormat usually involves reenacting early, unconscious dynamics. We learned that devaluing ourselves, often in very subtle ways, was the best route to get our needs met, to fit in, and to maintain an often precarious tie to an inconsistently available attachment figure. When we were young children, this was intelligent and served to keep us connected to the source of the only love we knew. These strategies are not errors or mistakes but are simply out of date and no longer fully in service to an adult longing for mature intimacy, connection, and aliveness.

Because the pathways are illuminated—neither solid nor fixed—it is possible to establish new circuitry that is organized around empathy, kindness, and presence. But this realization occurs only by way of self-compassion, not through old strategies of being a doormat. Look carefully and see the ways you habitually place others' needs over your own, *not out of true compassion for them* but as a reenactment of an early environment of shame and unworthiness. This can be a profound realization, one that is simultaneously deflating *and* empowering. It has a way of loosening the tangles within the heart and revealing essence.

This inquiry is best engaged slowly, from a very spacious place. As with the other invitations we have been exploring, you must allow yourself to become profoundly curious in order to see beyond the veil.

---

1. Trungpa, C. *The Myth of Freedom and the Way of Meditation* (Boston, MA: Shambhala Publications, 2002), 97.

You must enter this territory by way of your love of the truth, not as compensation for the spell of unworthiness. Pay careful attention as you descend into your experience that you do not slip into a rampage of self-aggression, shame, and blame, raging against yourself in response to what you discover. Slow way down. Be curious. And open.

Anchor yourself in the wish to know what is true more than *anything*. Feel the support of the seen and unseen worlds around you. And then open more. If you feel closed, that is fine; open even to that. Paradoxically, the goal is not to be "open" but to be in touch with what is here. In ways the mind cannot understand, you can "open" to being closed. From this place, even "closed" is grace when met and held in open awareness. It is in this clear seeing that the seeds are planted for new fruit, true heart nourishment that is encoded with attunement, creativity, and an active sort of kindness. This kindness is not passive, but is full spectrum, willing at times to integrate and make use of even anger, rage, fear, jealousy, and confusion—in fact any emotional energy—recycling their raw material for the work of love. Nothing is discarded any longer. All is path. All is grace.

It is from this revolution of embodied, skillful kindness that the seemingly solid distinction between self and other will reveal itself to be quite translucent, like a rainbow. You can actually play inside this translucence, where taking care of self and taking care of other co-arise and dance in union. It is a secret alchemy of our time.

With wise, loving presence as your guide, pour your awareness into the beliefs, emotions, sensations, and behaviors that are now arising for update and integration. Surround your immediate experience with spacious warmth and holding, surrender the habitual abandonment of yourself once and for all, and watch as a new Earth is born.

The Gold in the Chaotic Center

When speaking with a friend who is hopeless, confused, depressed, or enraged, before we realize it we can conclude that something has gone horribly wrong and we must act quickly to remedy it. We move into action, explaining to them that everything is okay, that they will be better soon, giving them affirmations or meditations to do, or reciting spiritual philosophies or explanations. A sense of urgency can fill the space between us and we lose touch with our precious friend and their unfolding experience. We find ourselves spinning, not so much in service of our friend but in the hope of cutting into our own anxiety and sense of despair. Additionally, to the degree that we have not met, held, and integrated our own hopelessness, confusion, depression, and rage, we will be reminded of these (usually all too vividly) as they appear and dance in the "other."

In situations such as these, a very rich opportunity for inquiry is presented. What is being asked to be met within us? And how can we participate in the relational field and stay attuned to not only what is arising in our friend but to the messages of the "internal other" within us, those previously unmetabolized feelings, emotions, bodily sensations, images, hopes, and fears? How can we truly be there for another—*and* for ourselves—without projecting our unlived life upon them and collapsing into a state of self-absorption? For in the scramble to put them back together, we remain misattuned to their actual, real-time, subjective experience and lose contact with their deep longing to be seen, heard, and met as they are.

Of course, it is natural to want to help a friend who is suffering, to do what we can to reduce their struggle and sorrow. But underneath this genuine wish often lurks our own disavowal of the internal darkness and the impending confrontation with our unlived lives and shadow material that the other person's anxiety can catalyze. The more we have allowed them to matter to us, the more powerful the confrontation tends to be. Our society is not well versed in the art of sitting in complexity, contradiction, and confusion, holding these experiences as valid and worthy, though often misunderstood, aspects of the psyche. To be clear, the invitation here is not to some romantic notion where we're asked to "love" and "accept" painful and disturbing feeling states just because the teaching says to do so. In what can be a very provocative, volatile situation, it often takes patience, courage, and the willingness to tolerate very contradictory and painful experience. But over time we might discover the healing potential buried within these states of consciousness and the gold that is found only within the chaotic center.

As we train ourselves to stay with the anxiety underlying our own and another's suffering—with curiosity, care, and holding—we may encounter a previously disavowed feeling or emotional state or an aspect of ourselves we've lost contact with: one that now presents itself in an attempt to be reintegrated into conscious awareness. Or we may discover an invitation to reconsider the way we've been living our lives, the psyche's attempt to suggest a course correction or change or a reassessment of what we previously believed was so important.

This material, which is often activated in interpersonal situations where one of the parties is struggling with uncertainty, hopelessness, and despair, is not a mistake or an error that we need to correct in ourselves and others but can be explored with an open heart, as a doorway into depth and new meaning. It might even come to be seen as sacred, a long lost friend that we split from at an earlier time as we sought protection from a part of ourselves we weren't ready to confront. These feelings and symptoms contain important information for the journey but are not conventional helpers, and they are often misunderstood in a world that has lost contact with the healing potential of the shadow.

Perhaps the kindest thing you can offer your friend in these situations is to sit with them in the unresolvable complexity and hopelessness, doing whatever you can so they know you will not abandon them if they do not conform to the cultural fantasy that they be happy, joyful, and full of hope all the time. They too are vast and contain multitudes, and will never be pinned down in one band of the emotional spectrum. Trust in the intelligence of their unfolding experience and stand with them as you make the commitment together to no longer pathologize their feelings, their emotions, and the uncertainty of their inner world. With the entirety of your presence, make it clear that they need not transform, heal, or be happy in order for you to hold their experience and remain near. And vow to stay close with whatever their uncertainty and struggle triggers within you. Remove the burden that they must change or "get better" so *you* can avoid the confrontation with your own unmet feelings and aspects.

Love is the totality. It is whole. It is transmitting in the light but is also raging and alive in the darkness, shining brightly in ways the conventional world may never understand. Within the confusion, sadness, despair, and grief, something very real is attempting to break through the images and identities that are no longer large enough to contain you. Something is dying and making an attempt at rebirth.

Here, in the very core of your friend's experience—which is utterly inseparable from your own—everything is alive, everything is path, and everything is holy. The divine is not only joy and sweetness but comes at times as darkness, as a force of reorder and reorganization. Step out of the trance and into the fire with your friend, listen carefully to their experience, hold them in your heart, and keep them near. You can then turn toward the darkness together, co-creating a sanctuary in which the wrathful wisdom-essence can unfold, and finally seeing what it has to say.

Your Heart Is Not a Technique

I am often asked about this or that technique, powerful new method, or approach: does it work, should I try it, will it help transform limited beliefs, deeply embedded trauma, unbearable emotions? Will it eliminate my vulnerability, increase my sense of self-worth, relieve the despair, soothe the anxiety?

In my experience, techniques do not heal. Relationship heals.

As nearly all of our somatic and emotional wounding arose in interpersonal contexts, it is best unwound, untangled, and metabolized within an attuned, empathic, relational container. This container is nonordinary, alchemical, and sacred, and weaved of strands of the heart.

The "technique" the therapist, coach, counselor, or friend employs is much less important. There is nothing wrong, of course, with learning new techniques, but there are no activities that are more creative, wild, and revolutionary than attunement, presence, and love. These are not *techniques* but are aspects of your true nature, luminous and longing to erupt and come alive here. They are already wired into the fabric and substance of what you are, uncaused and unproduced, and await cultivation.

What you are is infinitely more powerful than any technique. *You are the technique* ... each time you listen deeply, look at another with love in your eyes, speak words of kindness, allow them to matter to you, nourish and hold their experience, and attune to their inner world as it is ... as you allow yourself to care about how they are making meaning of their lives, making sense of a crazy world ... as you dare to see them not as an "object" arising in your experience—who might or might not be able to meet your needs or confirm your hopes and fears—but as an outrageously unique "subject" in their own right. And as you mirror back essence, offering cosmic permission for the ultimate discovery that who and what they are was never "unhealed."

Based on their theoretical lens, different approaches will look to intervene at different levels of the spectrum; i.e., cognitive, affective, somatic, and behavioral. Each practitioner is going to have their bias. But when it's all said and done, developmental trauma and other wounding arising out of an environment lacking in holding, mirroring, and empathic attunement is reorganized within an intersubjective field. Research in interpersonal neurobiology[2] has consistently shown us that neural circuitry is re-encoded within the context of such relational attunement.

While it is natural to become enamored with the latest "powerful" method, technique, and newly discovered strategy to catalyze healing, we can easily lose the forest for the trees, and forget that it is love that heals. *Love is not a technique.* What this "love" is must be uncovered

---

2. See the *Norton Series on Interpersonal Neurobiology* for groundbreaking work by Schore, Siegel, Badenoch, Cozolino, Van der Kolk, and others.

within your own embodied field of presence, and inside the cells of your heart. It is unprecedented, unique, and relentlessly creative … just like you.

Your heart is not a technique. And love is the ultimate medicine.

Midwives of Integration

There may be times when you are asked to sit with another who has been touched by the darkness. To allow them to fall apart in your arms, unravel, be worried, and feel lost. You may sense there is some sort of wisdom unfolding but it is chaotic, groundless, and not easy to stay with. While it is natural to want to do whatever you can to help them feel better, listen carefully to what they are truly asking for—and then listen some more before taking action. What do they long for in this moment? To be "fixed"? To be "healed"? To be "cured"? Or for something else? Where is their heart? Can you feel it in the space between? Can you let go of all of your known and unknown agendas—even to "heal" them—and stay close?

You may be burning with the need to talk them out of their experience, overflowing with answers, techniques, and processes. But before you offer "solutions," return to the field that is emerging between you. Infuse the environment with pause, rest, and resonance. With the slow circuits of empathy and presence, walk with them into the aliveness of now. Join them and be by their side as you proclaim together that *pain is not pathology.*[3] That heartbreak, grief, anxiety, confusion, and fear are utterly valid as experiences and are not evidence that they have failed or lost their way.

This may not be the moment for you to give them an answer but rather to hold them as you confront the vastness of the question together. Give them the gift of a regulated, soothed nervous system and meet them right brain to right brain so they can truly *feel felt.*

---

3. Stolorow, R. *Trauma and Human Existence: Autobiographical, Psychoanalytic, and Philosophical Reflections* (London, UK: Routledge, 2007), 10.

While this may not take them out of their pain, it will provide a holding environment in which together you can validate what they are experiencing and honor it as the way reality is appearing now, opening the hidden doorways to the temple of their heart, psyche, and body. For it is holy and unprecedented here, and not fully knowable by means of conceptual analysis. As you weave a sacred container with them, whatever is arising can finally be met, touched, received in the warmth of a relational home,[4] and explored with an open heart. Together you can create a permission field where they can be exactly as they are, not needing to be or become someone different in order for you to stay close. Together you will be midwives of integration, a holding space for the unfolding of what is longing to be met within them and for the guidance that is seeking to emerge into a field of safety and attunement.

To step into such a charged environment with another, you must first offer safe passage for the unmetabolized in yourself: unmet sadness, abandoned shame, discarded grief, disavowed hopelessness, and cast-off aloneness. If you cannot provide this internal holding, you will likely find yourself rushing to talk the other out of their experience, urgently acting to relieve them of their feelings as a way to cut into your own anxiety and discomfort, all the while disavowing the intelligence buried within the darkness. As you explore the relational holding field together, you can both make the commitment to no longer pathologize the companions of shame, grief, jealousy, rage, and heartbreak. You can shout out to the universe together and declare: *pain is not pathology.* Hopelessness is not pathology. Grief is not pathology. Shame is not pathology but is a pure expression of the path itself. The psyche is endlessly creative and will use whatever it must to reach you and point you toward wholeness.

As you attune to the "other" before you—as well as to the emerging disowned "other" within—you may become aware of an unfolding intelligence that fills the space between, taking form as a vessel of sanctuary for the pieces of the broken world, for the shards of confu-

---

4. Ibid.

sion, and for the hopes and dreams that have crumbled in front of you. Yes, something is disintegrating and falling apart, and such dissolution can be grieved with honor. To do so is to prepare the field for the forms of love to reconfigure, this time in more integrated and cohesive ways. Within the aliveness of the relational field—despite the pain of the present, the traumas of the past, and the fragmented dreams of the future—an opportunity has presented itself to reclaim the aspects of yourself that you have turned from and open to the mystery that is calling you to something greater, something that was never dependent upon what happened in the past.

Never, ever underestimate the power of love. Even one moment of empathic, attuned, contact can change a person forever. Please don't forget that many have never actually known this—or have known it in only very small amounts. For it is rare here.

As you wander on this new day, look into the eyes of those you meet so that they feel seen. Receive them not as just another object in your awareness, someone who may be able to meet one of your needs, but as a subject in their own right. Just like you, longing for love, intimacy, aliveness, connection, and meaning in a world that has gone a bit mad. Listen to what they have to say and hold their experience with your presence, ensuring that they feel your warm contact. Offer a home for their pain, their confusion, their fragility, their joy, and their fear … validate their feelings as you simultaneously invite them into their true nature as love itself. They are not broken and have never been unhealed.

You have tremendous power to help another to see this and travel with them as they reauthor the story of their lives, dissolve the dream of unworthiness, and return home. Please do what you can to help others in whatever way you are able: attune to them, honor their feelings, and listen carefully to what they are saying and how they are making meaning of their lives. Care enough to enter their subjective experience as deeply as you can without requiring that it shift to prevent confrontation with your own disowned "other." Feed them, hold them, and speak words of kindness. Allow them be what they are. In this way, you will remind them that love is here and is alive. And then stand back in awe of what unfolds from there ...

Is It "Unspiritual" to Have a Need?

Many I speak with have come to the conclusion that it is not okay for them to have a need. Or that having a need is a reflection of weakness, or that they've failed or haven't grown enough spiritually. "Shouldn't I be able to take care of myself?" "If I were healed or fully awakened, I wouldn't need anything from anyone, would I?" "My guru doesn't have any needs ... does he?" "Needs are bad, right?" "I can just do it myself." "If I don't really 'have' a self, I shouldn't have any needs ... right?" "If I was fully able to stay in the present moment, I'd be free of needs ... right?" And so forth. When we dig in under the surface, we may discover a fair amount of confusion in this area. It can be subtle, though, and requires that we look carefully and stay committed to whatever we find in our inquiry, whether it conforms to our ideas and images of ourselves ... or not.

It is really pretty understandable. For many of us as young children in our families of origin, expressing a need was usually not very safe, often met with painful neglect, rejection, or even aggression and abuse. We learned that having a need was the fast path to feelings of hopelessness and disappointment, watching helplessly as attunement, contact, and affection were removed from the field around us. Because it was unsafe to allow for the reality of any sort of limitation in our caregivers, we defaulted to the conclusion that there must be something wrong with us: "Oh, I get it now. That is the reason my needs aren't being met. I'm just not worthy of them." While this conclusion and way of organizing our early experience was quite painful, we could temporarily rest, knowing those in charge of taking care of us were good, safe, and without limitation. The blame had to go to someone, however, and it turned inward, laying the foundation for the deep shame that so many experience throughout their lives.

To adults interested in spirituality and the inner life, this core belief finds validation in teachings that (overtly or otherwise) support the notion that having a need means lack of progress on the path, evidence of not enough faith or trust, too much attachment, being caught in a "low vibration," not understanding the teachings on "no-self," and so forth. The shame and blame continue, but with flowery spiritual language replacing the voices of the "bad other" (yet all the while sounding surprisingly just like Mom and Dad). The teachings on selflessness that form the core of the certain contemplative teachings, for example (and are commonly misunderstood, in my opinion), represent a very pure expression of our absolute nature and are powerful medicine. But for those not ready for their radical implications—and especially those struggling with complexes rooted in shame and unworthiness—even these most subtle and precious teachings may inadvertently promote this limiting organization and not be the most effective skillful means for specific practitioners at specific times.

Let's just cut right to the chase: *there is nothing wrong with having a need.* It's not a sign that something is wrong with you, that you are neurotically dependent or that you have failed to understand the more subtle teachings of the path. It's so human, really, to have some yearning in the heart, some longing for connection, to be met, to be seen, to be heard, to be touched, to be held. We are relational mammals and will not override millions of years of evolution anytime soon, after learning some new meditations or in the wake of a powerful weekend workshop. We can honor the reality that we are both independent *and* dependent and that we are both separate *and* connected simultaneously. We can learn to tolerate these paradoxes and contradictions without needing to resolve them, and allow ourselves to fully be what we are … which is a mystery. At times we will feel complete, resting in what we are, and not in contact with any particular emotional needs or desires. At other times we will likely be drawn to assert a need, to ask for help, to enact a firm boundary, to state very clearly what we want. We can stay committed to *both* of these experiences as perfectly valid and worthy of our exploration, willing to be fully human in the face of either, without apology.

While having a need is perfectly natural, it is very unlikely that all of your needs are ever going to be fully met, especially by another. This is not evidence that having a need is neurotic, wrong, or bad, but simply a reflection of the truth of the relational world. With your heart open, make requests of your lovers, your friends, your fellow journeyers, and your family, knowing that sometimes they will be able to meet you, see you as you are, and provide what you are asking for. When they do, you can rejoice in this and give thanks. And when they do not, you can rejoice in that and give thanks as well for the clear reflection of relational truth and the opportunity to see how you might be able to care for yourself in a new way.

It can be difficult to let in the reality that it is not the responsibility of another to remedy the pain of your unlived life for you. Or to meet, hold, and metabolize your anxiety, depression, rage, jealousy, and disappointment (unless of course you are an infant or a young child). Not only is it not their role, but it is not actually possible for them to do so. In our culture, we often confuse the other's attempt to take care our emotional world for us as a sign of love. But let us look deeper. Let us open to the possibility that one of the greatest gifts of the others in your life is to return to you the sacred task of tending to your own soul and attending to your unlived life. For many of us, it is not easy to allow others to take care of themselves. So much of our sense of self, meaning, and purpose has become organized around taking care of others—and what doing so means about *us*—that allowing another to work through their own emotional and psychic development can trigger tremendous anxiety within us.

If you look carefully, you may start to see the ways you are asking others to do this work for you: to provide a parenting and holding function for the psychic, emotional, and somatic material that you have disavowed and lost contact with, perhaps a function that was not available to you at an earlier time. This is very natural and has been wired into you since you were in the womb. It is not something you need to judge, shame, or meet with aggression. You only need to see it, with a wide open and curious heart, and from that clear seeing to make a conscious choice as to how you will move forward.

Of course others can walk side by side with you and can support you in so many ways, holding and loving and keeping you in their hearts, vowing to stay near as you walk into the shadowy fire of your own being. But ultimately, because they love you so much, they will not make the journey for you. They remain committed to trusting your process even when you cannot, and even when it is a raging expression of anxiety, jealousy, anger, and profound shame. Even when you are quite convinced you cannot do it, that you cannot befriend yourself and reorganize the relationship with who you are and with the emotions, feelings, and sensations that are surging within you. As you remove the burden from others to metabolize your emotional world for you, you open into the field of completeness that is always already here, regardless of whether or not all your needs are met. And when some are not, which is inevitable, this is in no way an accurate indication of your worth or essential goodness.

As you learn to rest in this discovery, you may see that you are complete and, from a certain perspective, always have been. Here, "complete" does not mean you get everything you want or everything you think you need or are told you can "manifest." It doesn't mean that life or love will conform to all of your hopes and dreams and that it will flow in exactly the way you believe it must in order for you to be happy and fulfilled. But that is no longer the foundation from which you are organizing your experience. Rather, what is being revealed is something much more majestic than that: the erupting reality of your being and true nature, exactly as it is now—alive, luminous, and magical. It is not dependent on any inner or outer circumstances but is self-existing and alive, rippling with energy and creativity.

Please continue to make requests of your lovers, in all of the forms they may take, but remain committed in every moment to taking care of yourself, to the seeding of a new pathway of uncompromising, unapologetic self-compassion. For it is by way of this pathway that the very translucent boundary between self and other will be revealed and the seemingly solid line between self-care and other-care will dissolve into the vastness.

Into the Fire

It is so natural to want to help others, especially when they are suffering, hurt, confused, or experiencing profound sadness. But in order to most skillfully be present for another, we may be asked to set aside the very deeply rooted tendencies to fix, change, or "heal" them, at least for a moment, and attune to whether something else is being asked of us. The invitation at these times is to walk into the fire that is their present reality, exactly as it has been given, and remain close to their experience as it unfolds, staying open to the intelligence of their process even if it activates our own inner family of previously abandoned feelings, emotions, and unmet longing.

As we enter into the relational field with the other, committed to staying close to the immediacy of their experience, we will be invited to engage with them as an authentic, unique, and sacred person in their own right, traveling on the path of integration. We will be asked, at least temporarily, to set aside our diagnosis and evaluation and dare to see them as whole, rather than someone who is depressed, hopeless, confused, "lost in their ego" falling apart, a total mess, stuck in traumatic response or a "low vibration," bipolar, passive-aggressive, schizophrenic, or even insane. This is not to say there is no room for diagnostic engagement. But for one moment, before all that, see them as the raging and unique expression of spirit that they are.

Let us hold the hand of our friend and go directly into the darkness with them, if that is what love is asking (remaining ever mindful of our own capacities and abilities), willing for our hearts to be shattered and put back together with them, over and over again. Let us allow the other to matter, cry with them, join them in the unfolding, get on their side, and do whatever we can so that when they look into our eyes they feel us fully with them. Let us not forget that many have never had their inner experience validated or had their emotional world held in a way that did not pathologize the feelings and sensations that were moving within them. We can stay close and show them that we care about the way they have come to organize their experience and make meaning of their lives, and that we will help them make sense of their experience and create new organization if this what they wish for.

Let us join with them and with the entire phenomenal world in proclaiming that no mistake has been made, that they are not broken, flawed, or a project that needs fixing. That the mere presence of emotional intensity, confusion, and despair is not evidence that something is wrong with them but is confirmation that they are alive. Together, we can discover that all states of mind are valid, workable, and contain a certain type of intelligence, a unique form of guidance coming from the psyche in its attempt to reveal new levels of wholeness. Let us realize together, once and for all, that sadness, anger, and grief are not pathology but path.

To the degree that we can stay with the very hot, sticky, disturbing energy as it surges—cradling our own hopelessness, confusion, depression, and fear—it is to this degree that we will be able to meet and hold another and not be overwhelmed by the unconscious drive to fix them. Instead, we can create a sanctuary together where our experience can be illuminated and the transformative energies of love can flood the space between.

Forgiveness Is Not Something You "Do"

As discussed earlier, it is possible for our engagement with spiritual belief and practice to serve a defensive function, appearing at times to help us move closer to a certain aspect of ourselves or our experience, while in fact keeping us out of some very sticky, messy, raw emotional wounding. This is not necessarily a fault of the spiritual system or approach, which may never have been designed to work with that particular band of the developmental spectrum; no single teaching can address the fullness of the human heart. Again, we do not need to shame, blame, or judge ourselves or our beliefs and traditions in the face of what we might discover, but rather use our findings to catalyze our inquiry and commitment to know what is most true.

Using spirituality to avoid some really messy human experience is something that I have some personal experience with, and like many I initially reacted to this discovery with a stream of judgment, shame, and blame—which of course only deepened the grooves of self-abandonment. I became convinced I was just not devoted enough, disciplined enough, or wise enough and that if I became more extreme in my spiritual longing and practice I would finally break through the illusion of the ego and its emissaries of delusion. If I just spent a few thousand more hours in silent meditation, wandering the forests of India, translating sacred texts, and bathing in holy rivers (I promise I tried) … alas, I would finally be home. But in rejecting and abandoning my inner experience, I only further entrenched myself in a war that I could never win.

As an integral part of any journey of healing, at some time or another we are all asked to investigate and come to terms with forgiveness. As a therapist working with those interested in spirituality and inner transformation, I have spent much time exploring and working through the nature of forgiveness and its role on the path. One of the things I've discovered in my own life and in my work with others is that when someone has deeply hurt us, in the rush to do the "right" spiritual thing—sending them love, kindness, compassion, or forgiveness—we can act impulsively, before we're ready to do so in a deeply embodied way. We think that if we can engage in an outer act of compassion or forgiveness we will heal faster, but if by doing so we reenact old strategies of denial and self-abandonment, the whole process can backfire. And we can end up confused and struggling with our ability to *truly* forgive, shaming ourselves for failing yet again.

Of course, we want to replace our painful feelings of aggression, anger, and hatred with those noble qualities of love, kindness, and understanding. We want to transform the negative into the positive and move on with our lives when we feel stuck. We do not want to hold grudges, blame others, or engage in emotions we believe are destructive. This is natural. None of us wants to hold these darker energies in our hearts, our psyches, and our bodies. Nor do we want to unwittingly act them out in our relationships. But when we move straight to forgiveness, compassion, or acceptance without first metabolizing the underlying feelings of shame, pain, and grief inside us, we can easily shortcut the unfolding of the healing process and create more pain for ourselves and others. When we first digest the deep hurt we have felt, resisting the temptation to transcend it or even heal it, we cut into a lifetime's organization of turning from the fire of our direct experience.

We do not need to ostracize our pain, orphan it, and send it away as part of our spiritual journey, for all is welcome in the open embrace of what we are. There is plenty of room for our hurt, our feelings of abandonment, our anger, our jealousy, and our fear. While it may be tempting to impose a conceptual timeline on the process of grief, acceptance, healing, and forgiveness, we must set this aside and allow the process room to breathe and unfold naturally, according to the timeline inside the heart. This energy or movement of forgiveness, which is of course a significant and honorable one, has a way of arising naturally on its own when our pain, grief, and hurt are metabolized in our hearts and bodies, when we allow them to be touched by the light of our awareness. In this sense, forgiveness is not so much a "practice" that we *do* or even the result of an intention we've made. We might come to see that it is an organic, somatic process—effortless in a sense. As our pain and grief are processed in a deeply embodied, alchemical way, forgiveness waits on the other side, not as the result of a belief that we *should* forgive but as a natural by-product of the process of metabolization.

It might be helpful, then, to reframe our understanding of forgiveness, no longer wedded to it as something we "do," or try to do, with the idea that if we are able to forgive (and usually quickly), this is evidence that we're a good spiritual person—implying that our resistance or struggles to do so is very clear counterevidence that we're just not doing it right, that we've fallen short yet again. Many I have spoken with have concluded that they have failed at the spiritual path because they have not yet forgiven a particular person in their lives. They feel intense shame that they are not worthy spiritual practitioners, that somehow the mere presence of sensations and feelings such as anger, rage, or grief indicate that they have lost their way. It can be a great act of self-compassion to spend some time exploring these issues and inquiring into them with openness and curiosity, aware at all times of the tendency to reenact an early organization of unworthiness.

Forgiveness is not something we need to take on as a project. With our eyes and hearts wide open, we may see that there are times when forgiveness is *not* the most skillful response in a particular situation, nor is it the most intelligent or kind to ourselves or others. It is very important to explore this in our own experience. Setting clear boundaries, embodying a forceful *no,* consciously engaging in conflict, asserting needs, the expression of healthy aggressive energy ... these may be the most wise and loving responses we can offer, despite the fact that they may not appear "spiritual" on the outside. This is where the artificial dividing line between "spiritual" and "nonspiritual" (whatever that might be) begins to fall apart. This call toward a "nonforgiving" response can be acknowledged and respected, and by doing so, we can honor these other types of responses as just as "spiritual" as forgiveness. They may even be more so, especially if the "forgiveness" serves an avoidant function in keeping us out of actual feelings that are emerging to be integrated, or is being utilized as a tool of further shame and self-aggression.

In other words, we must remain deeply aware of whether we are "forgiving" another not out of genuine compassion and care but as a way to avoid or do an end run around our own pain and unresolved emotional wounding. In this way, forgiveness can become yet another instrument of self-abandonment in the service of an outmoded organization that we are unworthy of empathy and love.

It is a profound act of self-kindness to open to the possibility that the anger, shame, hurt, embarrassment, jealousy, grief, terror, and fear that are "still" present in the context of our relationship with another are intelligent and are expressions of guidance and wholeness. And rather than seeing how quickly we can move beyond them and transform them into other, "purer," and "more spiritual" qualities, recognizing that they in and of themselves offer a unique key to our healing and the healing of those around us. Often, in our rush to forgive and accept before the time is right, we lose touch with these important allies and the profound gifts their embrace has to offer us, thereby losing touch with our own hearts.

If you feel so inclined, you could take some time to explore whether this invitation is resonant with your own experience.

Drama in the Relational Field

We all have ways of engaging with and even catalyzing drama in our interpersonal relationships. If we look carefully, we may discover that the drama often serves some sort of distractive function. As it captures our attention and provides an exit ramp away from some really vulnerable feelings, we can find ourselves at times feeding conflict and making use of shame, blame, and complaint to escape messy human emotion and feeling. During such times, especially if we have a partner who is ready and willing to join us in the movement toward distraction, it can appear that we are moving *toward* one another and stepping more deeply into the aliveness of the emotional world while in actuality we are moving *away*. On the outside it may look like we are staying close to what is surging in our bodies, our hearts, and the relational space around us, but we may be ensuring that we never actually have to get too close. Given our early histories, for many of us this behavior is natural and makes sense. Rather than judge and shame ourselves as we become aware of how we may be reenacting outmoded strategies of denial and self-abandonment, we can become curious, open our hearts, and make the choice to move toward what is most true.

The energies of complaint, resentment, blame, and drama can, without our conscious knowing, provide a defense against the inherent openness of the relational field and just how raw and exposed we are when we step into this environment with another. Unmet feelings, unmetabolized sensations, and previously disavowed emotions lie just under the surface, longing for holding and integration, awaiting the right time to arise for a moment of our attention. Especially when we allow another to matter to us and share our vulnerability, we are likely to step into some pretty shaky territory, unsure of whether it is safe to continue. Of course, this shakiness is where all the action is, the portal in fact to the aliveness, intimacy, and connection that so many of us are yearning for. But the hardwiring to protect ourselves and remain as far away as we can from the possibility of an avalanche of feeling may always co-arise with the longing to feel alive. In response to the threat that this sort of activation portends, we move back to safe ground, doing what we can to cut into the uncertainty, nakedness, and risk lest we become overwhelmed with the anxiety underlying such exposure.

Of course, much of this activity occurs beneath the level of conscious awareness. We may continue to remain quite convinced that we are stepping all the way in, leading with our vulnerability, and not holding anything back, all the while remaining at least partly out of touch with the previously sequestered, survival-level material lurking under the surface. It is a great act of kindness to do this work—not only for ourselves but for everyone we come into contact with. To allow ourselves to dance freely in relationship while remaining fully committed to the reality that we are also separate beings unlocks the door to the transformative crucible that intimacy is.

The Longing to Be Seen

To whatever degree we have not psychologically, emotionally, and somatically metabolized unmet feelings of abandonment, loneliness, grief, shame, and rage, we can count on our partners to continue to offer this opportunity to us in a seemingly endless number of ways. This can be excruciating, but we might come to see this invitation as the unique gift of the beloved, his or her fiercely compassionate summons into the crucible of intimacy, vulnerability, and healing.

We each come into adulthood with a bias toward connection, separateness, or disorganization. These strategies loosely correspond to an early environment where caregivers were inconsistently available, engulfing, or abusive, respectively—corresponding as well to avoidant, preoccupied, and disorganized attachment styles. As nearly all of our emotional wounding arose in relationship, many believe that it is best untangled and unwound within a relational matrix. Solitary practice is immensely helpful in this area, yet many have come to discover that it is not enough, realizing that most contemplative practice was simply not designed to work with this level of the developmental spectrum, intertwining with the unfolding of subjectivity, trauma, and narrative. This is not a fault of the meditative traditions; they are excellent at what they do—introducing and deepening the realization of one's true nature as unconditioned awareness. Many have found it helpful, skillful, and compassionate, however, to explore pre-personal, personal, interpersonal, *and* transpersonal dimensions of what it means to be a human being, honoring each and not overemphasizing one at the expense of the others.

The notion that a "good" or "healthy" relationship is one where we are consistently seen and "met" by our partners is fascinating and spans multiple levels of inquiry (somatic, psychological, emotional, and neurobiological). As infants, we come to know who we are through having our experience mirrored back to us. Through consistent and attuned contact to our developing subjectivity, we are able to acquire a sense of confidence, trust, and cohesion in our sense of self and our place in the world. While we carry forward this longing for mirroring into our adult lives, we may discover that it is not possible for another to fully provide this function for us, and the (often subtle and unconscious) expectation that they do is quite a burden to place upon them. As long as we rely on our partners to mirror back to us our essential lovability and self-worth, we will not be able to fully open to them; it is just too risky because we have given them so much importance in our own psychic development. Nor will we be able to see and love them as subjects in their own right—not merely objects and functions in ours—or enter all the way into the shaky territory that radical, transforming intimacy will always require. If we take this dependency to the extreme, of course, we end up in the very complicated territory of codependency and the profound pain it can ensnare us in.

This is *not* to say that we cannot or should not ask for help from our partners and request support along the way. Of course we can and should, while simultaneously taking ultimate responsibility for our own experience, knowing they will not always be able to meet our needs. It is reasonable, healthy, and intelligent to ask our partners to be kind—to make contact with us and our emotional world while not fusing with and impinging upon it—and to provide us the space we need for our experience to unfold, illuminate, and transform[5] on its own. These qualities of contact and space are the exact qualities that grow babies' brains and nervous systems, and are likewise supportive of us as adults who continue to mature, individuate, and move into deeper levels of awareness and sensitivity.

May we make the revolutionary commitment to offering a true holding environment—for ourselves, our lovers, and our fellow travelers—and above all else to practicing a wild and uncompromising kindness as we walk the path of love together. For it is a radical and astonishing path that will demand everything from us, but offers fruit that is worthy of our deepest gratitude and awe.

---

5. Thank you to psychoanalyst and philosopher Robert Stolorow, founder (with colleagues) of Intersubjectivity Theory, for his articulation of the therapeutic process as one involving the illumination, unfolding, and transformation of relationally configured, affect-laden unconscious organizing principles.

Therapeutic Companionship

Beyond all the theories, conflicting approaches, interventions, and strategies, for me therapeutic companionship is a process of bearing witness to the life of another as they come to befriend themselves in a way that was not possible until now. To excavate meaning where there was none, to find purpose in the core of purposelessness, breath where there was no breath to be found.

This befriending is not ordinary or passive, not always flowing and peaceful. It is fierce, on fire, and an act of revolution. It is the light shining out of the core of the dark night, the outrageousness of the human spirit, and the basic goodness of the human heart.

To walk into the dark wood, into the disorienting and hopeless places, without knowing where the journey will lead, whether we will make it out in one piece, or where new life will be found. Making sense together of where they have been, who they see themselves to be, and what they are longing to become. To illuminate what matters most to them and cradle it in our shared heart. To help them gather the pieces of the broken world.

To proclaim their experience as utterly valid, their feelings as ragingly honorable and intelligent, and that they are worthy of love as they are. That despite the pain of the present, the traumas of the past, and the fragmented dreams of the future, we will dare together to reclaim the aspects, parts, and pieces of the soul that have been turned from and are now longing to return home.

We will assert together that pain is not pathology, that they need not be "cured" in order for us to stay near, that their suffering is authentic, that their hopelessness well founded. Even their doubt is holy when allowed into the inner sanctum. What they are is not some project to be improved, but a mystery to be lived.

And then, from that foundation of companionship and bearing witness to the sacredness of what a human being truly is—including profound grief and despair, and moments of great joy—we are able to turn together into the unknown and bow before its immensity.

It is awesome, in the truest sense of the word, to bear witness in this way. To fall to the ground in the beholding of God in action, of the unstoppable wild bravery of the human spirit, and the relentlessness and creativity of love as it makes its way into form.

9

The Invitation of True Intimacy

Preparing for a Healthy Relationship

WHAT IS THE BEST WAY TO PREPARE FOR A HEALTHY, DEEPLY SATISFYING intimate relationship? How can you attract the right partner for you? Someone who can accompany you on the path of the heart, a fellow traveler who is genuinely interested in exploring relationship as a transformative, modern-day crucible of healing and awakening?

There are many responses to these sorts of questions: workshops to attend, lists of ten "secrets" to attract your perfect soul mate, twelve steps to manifesting your twin flame, and so forth. It can be important to experiment with any approach you feel drawn to and that is resonant with your longing and your experience.

The suggestion I usually make, however, is not nearly as sexy or compelling, or all that fun or flashy, or even overtly "spiritual": *learn how to take care of yourself.* Practice radical self-care, self-kindness, and self-compassion; train in these transformative arts that in many ways have been lost in our world. Start there and you will lay the foundation for a rich, meaningful, and deeply nourishing relationship with another. For it is the degree to which you are able to take responsibility for your own vulnerability and core emotional wounding that you will release your partner(s) from this burden, which is not theirs to carry. As long as there is a subtle (or not so subtle) expectation that your intimate partner's role is to enact the archetype of the "good other" that was missing in earlier developmental times, you will not truly be able to love them or harness the incredibly transformational energy of intimacy and relationship.

So what does it mean to "take care of yourself" in this context? It means becoming very curious about your emotional triggers, the feelings you do not want to feel, your most tender vulnerabilities, and the unique behaviors you engage in to distract yourself from emotional experience that you'd just rather not engage in. Spending time in deep inquiry around all of this and getting clear about your expectations in relationship and your primary motivations for being in an intimate partnership is an act of kindness, toward both yourself and your partner. To what degree do you believe another person will fill the void for you, make the emptiness go away, relieve you from feelings and limiting beliefs you do not want to confront, and protect you from the unattended ghosts of your unlived life?

In order to explore this territory in an integrated way, it can be helpful at times to be willing to travel underneath the narrative, below the very compelling storyline of what happened (or didn't happen) so you can make experiential contact with those embodied parts of yourself that you may have lost contact with and may be seeking reunion with in a partner. As we've discussed, as young children we made the difficult choice to disconnect from certain inner qualities in the effort to fit in and maintain critical ties to important attachment figures around us. While doing so served an important adaptive function at the time, these aspects remain sequestered in the shadow. But as the psyche always moves toward wholeness and integration, this material will continue to find ways to emerge into our lives, usually in less-than-conscious ways.

One of the most evocative ways is in the area of intimacy and attraction to certain people. For example, if we observe carefully, we may discover that we tend to attract—and be attracted to—those who either express or reject those qualities or aspects that we have disconnected from in ourselves. The psyche longs for reunion with what we have previously split off from and will look out into the relational world for a match.

While the work of reintegration is not easy—and requires a commitment to knowing what is true more than feeling good or consistently safe or certain—you can make the intention to get curious when you notice yourself complaining about your partners and the abandoned feelings they inevitably trigger within you. While this reminder may come with a surge of irritation and annoyance, you might also come to see it as a great gift, a (sometimes thundering) mindfulness bell to bring you back to your inquiry with loving kindness. We all want to be open and kind to our partners and close friends, but the only way we can do this is by first caring for and tending to the difficult feelings our relationship with them is sure to activate. There is just something, well, uncanny about the relational field to remind us of *everything* we have yet to integrate and work through within us.

As long as we are looking to our partners to fulfill those functions that were not offered to us as young children, it will be difficult to come into a fulfilling, loving relationship that is not riddled with the pain of projection. Your partner is here to help you, support you, and make the journey by your side as a loving, caring fellow traveler of the path. But they are not here to (re)parent you or take care of your unlived life for you, for this is your sacred work and it would be unkind of them to attempt to take these holy tasks from you. They are here to encourage and walk *with* you (not *for* you) as you turn toward, meet, and offer safe passage to what has been knocking at the door of your heart for so long.

When all is said and done, perhaps there is no secret to co-creating a fulfilling, supportive, mutually beneficial intimate relationship, as it is always in the end a movement of the unknown. Healthy intimacy is not something you will figure out one day by way of some checklist or magical formula, but something you are asked to live in each moment, in all its chaotic glory. By learning to take care of yourself, you are creating a foundation upon which the mystery of intimacy can come alive within the relational field, and offer a crucible like no other for the great work of healing and individuation that you have come here to embody.

The Unwanted Lover

It is so natural to long for deep relationship with another, for a fellow traveler with whom we can explore the mysteries of intimacy. Someone you can walk together with into the uncharted lands of the body, the heart, and the psyche, unsure where the journey will lead but driven by passionate curiosity and the love of the truth.

"I want to share the burning," you call out! The tenderness, the shakiness, the joy, and the aliveness of what it means to enter into partnership with the holy other. There is a readiness to no longer hold back, to give everything to remove the last remaining shreds of separation, to no longer postpone what you know is possible. This yearning is pure and can be honored for its authenticity, power, and transformative potential.

In response to this primordial cry, alas, the "other" appears. Sadness rushes quickly onto the scene: "But when will you practice intimacy with me?" Loneliness is next, pleading for a moment of your undistracted attention. Anger, despair, grief, self-loathing, confusion, jealousy, fear, and shame: "We as well! Please do not abandon us! Please do not forget and relegate us to the dark, cold forest. We are here, now, and longing to share our essence. We have arrived. Your prayer for true intimacy has been answered!"

Um … ah, okay, but this is not what you expected. This response simply does not conform to your fantasies of the way you thought it would be. Where is the soul mate? The twin flame? The "good other" come to remove the existential flatness, the unbearable loneliness, the penetrating emptiness. Out of your genuine yearning for communion, the ancient companions will *always* respond, though in ways that may remain bewildering to a mind bent on resolution, certainty, and finding a safe landing place that is free from vulnerability, heartbreak, and disillusion. But it is important to remember that these ones come not as enemies but as *true* lovers, seeking just one moment of your presence, your compassionate communion, and the light of your holding and care. While they remember the ways in which they have been rejected in the past, they continue to come nonetheless, never giving up, never losing faith in the undivided condition of your true nature.

As you go deeper with this inquiry, you will encounter a profound truth along the way: you will never be able to be more intimate with another than you are with the unwanted lovers within. If you have not provided shelter for the unmet within you, how will you ever contain the wholeness of the beloved?

A Devastating Act of Love

While there are many valid reasons for being in relationship, it is possible to use the full-spectrum nature of intimacy to come closer to ourselves, if that is in fact what we want. It is okay if we want something else: no shame, no apology. It is no secret that intimate relationship is one of the great amplifiers of the unlived life. We can count on our partners to relentlessly illuminate everything that is longing for wholeness within us. Not because they have some agenda to do so but simply by the nature of the crucible that forms when we allow another to truly matter to us.

We come to our relationships with an already-existing patterning that formed long ago, crafted of both personal and collective material. While this template can be updated and longs for reorganization into more integrated forms, until reconfiguration it has a way of coloring our perception. It functions like a time machine: when activated, it is as if we have left the "here and now," crossed the liminal, and found ourselves back in the "there and then." Aspects of ourselves are aching to come out of the shadows and into the warmth of holding awareness, not to harm but as forerunners of wholeness. There is nothing like a close relationship to remind us of the orphaned emotions, feelings, and vulnerable parts that have lost their way in the tangle of cognitive and somatic pathways. They are exhausted from a long voyage to reach us, but they have not given up. The reminder of this truth can at times be agonizing, as the beloved may seem to have extraordinary powers to open the raw, tender, and naked dimensions of our being. But this achiness is sacred and its embodied exploration is holy. Inside the ache is a jewel. Go there.

Please be kind to your partners in response to the inevitable conflict that will arise as you make this journey together. Learning how to harness the energy of conflict and to engage it directly, skillfully, and with an open heart is essential on the path of intimacy and requires the encoding of new circuitry. The transformative art of rupture and repair is quite profound, revealing that relationships of endless depth and meaning are *not* free of conflict but flourish where conflict is embraced as a *path,* as a unique and transmutative vessel of purification, love, and healing. This is a difficult and alchemical realization to come by, one that is unfortunately not popular in a world that has forgotten the gold buried in the dark. But here we are. It is up to us to bring these fruits into the collective.

From this perspective, the promise of intimacy is freedom and wholeness, *not* a life where there is no negativity, conflict, or vulnerability. The offering here is not consistent positivity, continuous feelings of connection, and uninterrupted respite from a stressful world. In the crucible that intimacy is, *everything* that has been abandoned lies in wait for the conditions to be ripe in which it can present itself for holding and integration. At times, love will come as peace, connection, and flow; at other times as a flood of rage, separateness, and conflict.

The Invitation of True Intimacy

While it is difficult to reconcile this with a mind yearning for certainty and consistency, love will use whatever energies it must to reach us.

As we remove the burden from the "other" to take care of what we have disowned in ourselves, we step inside the gates of the sacred world. For to return this task to us is the most tender, most devastating act of love that they could give.

The Achy Yoga of Intimacy

The often achy, always challenging journey of intimacy provides an electrifying, alive, and unique opportunity to turn toward and provide safe passage for everything that has yet to be fully held and metabolized within you. Whether you're in a relationship, moving out of one, or in contact with a deep longing for a partner with whom to share the journey, the activity of the beloved is always present, appearing in your life as the archetypal play of separation and union, broken and whole, and one and many.

Yes, this love that you long for involves tremendous risk and at times requires an unbearable sort of exposure and an uncompromising willingness to move into some pretty shaky, vulnerable, and uncertain territory. Given your early history, it may be neither easy nor natural to allow another to matter, not just in a surface way but in a way that opens you to the crushing potential of heartbreak, disappointment, and deflation that intimacy is uniquely designed to activate. But opening in this way, and truly stepping into this risk and its implications, is one of the true essences of relational work as well as a foundation of a healthy and nourishing intimate connection. While it is a simple concept to understand, it is a revolution in practice and requires a new level of commitment to staying close to yourself in the face of an inevitable confrontation with those feelings and aspects that you split off from at an earlier time.

The invitation of the beloved, in all of his or her manifestations, is to step fully into the vessel of relationship where you do not limit the mystery of love's expression, resisting the temptation to have the fires of love conform to your preconditions and requirements. And to open to the reality that the most sacred function of love and intimacy is not to provide consistent feelings of safety, surety, and certainty—or to meet all of your needs—but to introduce you to the eternally creative terrain of the unknown and the vast, limitless depth of your true nature.

Acknowledging this potential and what is truly being asked of us on this path, let us remove the burden from our partners to metabolize our unresolved feelings for us, taking such good care of ourselves that we release them from this sacred work, which is ours to engage. Perhaps there is no greater act of love, to retrieve this task from those we have given it to—for ourselves, others, and a world that has forgotten the holy path of intimacy and what it truly offers.

It is important to remember that our partners are neither the "good" nor the "bad" parent that we never had (or had too much of) but will regularly evoke these archetypes to unleash the activity of integration. At times we may feel overwhelmed, impinged upon, smothered, and trapped; in the next moment abandoned, rejected, misattuned to, and forgotten. The beloved is at work, spinning and swirling his or her tools of wholeness, doing what he or she must to reach us and remind us of how vast we are. No matter how disturbing what is evoked may be, we can commit to turning toward it and receiving the secret offering of the lost pieces of our bodies, hearts, and minds and of the creative journey being born within the relational field.

Perhaps surges of heartbreak, fear, anger, jealousy, shame, and irritation will always arise in the intersubjective field of friends and lovers. Let us renew an old vow we once made to meet each of these archaic guides with an open mind and tender heart, daring to consider the possibility that each is a doorway back inside the jeweled palace of our bodies and the gateway to the aliveness and transformation we so deeply long for.

Though you may never know the actual route or destination, and though you are sure to be taken into the dark wood with no real promises or guarantees, stay close to yourself and your beloveds as you make this journey together. Above all, please be kind to yourself and your partners if you decide to take up the achy yoga of intimacy, knowing that it will take everything you have to navigate. And while it may never conform to the hopes, dreams, and fantasies you have been taught about what it *truly* offers, it is a doorway beyond imagination and an endlessly rich and luminous portal into the mystery.

Into the Alchemical Vessel

Why is intimate relationship such a provocative, alchemical vessel for personal growth, emotional healing, and spiritual transformation? When we step into the crucible with another, our intelligently crafted strategies to avoid exposure, which may have once worked well, break down and we are no longer able to shield ourselves from the open, raw exposure that true intimacy always evokes. It's as if the "other" is playing the role of a sacred enzyme that dissolves our protective barriers and armor, revealing the tender material beneath. What was once a reliable pathway of escape no longer seems to be within reach or effective. On the one hand, this is horrible news for that part of ourselves that wants and needs to know where the escape hatch is, where we can get away if things get too naked. On the other, we sense that intimacy provides a unique pathway into wholeness, one that is difficult to access outside the relational field, and we can only go so far on our own.

One of the great insights of relationally oriented depth psycho-therapy is that nearly all of our early trauma and wounding arose in an interpersonal context. Because of this, it is often most excruciatingly triggered, illuminated, and unwound within a relational field. Our partners, especially as we risk allowing them to matter to us, appear in and *as* this field, which accounts for the great opportunity that intimacy affords us. In addition to providing a transformational container in which we can come to know ourselves at deeper and deeper levels, the connection is also sure to activate profound feelings of exposure, aban-donment, rejection, jealousy, irritation, and annoyance (in addition, of course, to the soothing energies of affection, care, companionship, and rest). The field of intimacy is whole and includes everything.

If you have a partner who knows your early history, is intimately familiar with your core vulnerabilities, and is compassionately attuned to your unfolding and illumination, you are teetering on the edge of a cliff. But it is a cliff of grace. On the one hand, a portal has been opened; your guide has appeared as a mirror into everything that you are, including all of the qualities and aspects that you have split off from in your developmental journey. This sort of relationship offers a bridge into wholeness, but most of us have no dependable or accurate reference point for this sort of full-spectrum holding, and we very naturally react to such openness with hesitation, contraction, and the very compelling pull to return to safe ground. Even for those interested in intimacy as path, we can utilize teachings on tantra, vulnerability, gods, and goddesses as subtle distancing mechanisms from the true fire of the beloved, who has no interest in our fantastic list of spiritual accomplishments or fantasies of untouchability. For hers is the way of the moon, of deflation, of removing the rug from underneath even the most enlightened personas and safe constructions of awakening.

The beloved, in his or her function as tour guide of the inner landscape, is a true emissary of the unknown. Perhaps he or she is mad crazy in love with you but may never fit your historical requirements and ideas about the true implications of having a beloved in your life. If you follow this one into the inner places that have been denied the light of holding awareness, your world as you have come to know it will unravel. The beloved sees you as you are and this is terrifying. On the other hand, this is what you have always longed for. When you are seen as utterly worthy and complete as you are, this can at first be anxiety provoking and feel unbearable. You just can't believe it, for it upends decades of conditioning and organization that something is wrong with you that must urgently be repaired before you will be deserving of love. Stepping into this charged environment, you will likely come face to face with the greatest fear you've ever known but have never been able to articulate: that you *are* loved. For when you are truly loved, when you are entirely seen, when you are fully held, it is the end of your world as you know it. You will never be the same. You will never again be able to pretend that you are other than perfect and complete as you are. This can be disorienting.

You long to be seen, to be held, and to be loved as you are, but please know that the implications of this are immense. They are cosmic in proportion. To allow yourself to be embraced in this way, a part of you must die. Everything you thought you *weren't* must be surrendered. You have no choice but to let go of the stories and deep convictions of the unlovable one, the broken one, the unhealed one, the imperfect one, the flawed one, and the lonely one. You will no longer be able to lean into these ones to keep you safe and secure on the sidelines, and out of the raw fragility of your own vulnerability. But who will you be without these familiar companions?

In this warm, provocative, and unprecedented territory, the beloved will ceaselessly remind you that your heart is at risk of breaking open in any moment, and perhaps never being put back together again—at least not in the same way. But in your willingness to fall apart, to let love reorganize your hopes, your fears, and your dreams, he or she will also reveal that you were never "together" to begin with. You are much more majestic than all this. You are that open, spacious presence in which "together" and "apart" dance with one another, weaving the relative world into being with your open, tender heart as your offering.

What Is the Beloved?

I am often asked about the use of the word "beloved" in my writing. What is the beloved? Is it a person? Is it something transcendent or divine? Is it simply yourself in disguise? Only you can answer this question from inside your own direct experience. This mystery can never be fully revealed to you by another.

The beloved is what reveals to you the inside of your own heart. He can appear as an intimate partner, which is one of his most evocative forms, but he would never limit himself to this expression. Her essence is taking shape as your longing and as the sunrise on a new spring day, as the nectar in the blooming lilies and as the holding of the moon as she rises to greet a weary world. She emerges through dreams and vision and color and image. Look carefully and you will see her everywhere.

But he is also weaved into the darkness, alive in your sadness, wild and dancing in the core of your loneliness, and unfolding himself in the center of your despair. Your eternal friend, the beloved will use the entirety of the phenomenal world to find you and will never, ever give up on you, even when you have given up on yourself. She is equally prepared to take the form of duality, multiplicity, and separation in order to come alive inside you, for she has no bias toward one mode of being over another. All are her cells, her organs, and aspects of her pure essence.

As you come to know the forms of the beloved in your own life, the question of whether she is "outside," "inside," or simply the "you" that you have forgotten … these fall away, for the beloved has no interest in you resolving her mystery but only fully participating in it. Hers is the greatest invitation, into her body, her psyche, her pathways, and her being. Sink into the *question* of what he or she is, where all the energy dwells, as the *answers* are flat, dead, secondhand, and worn out. Rest in the reality that you will never resolve her activity; it is just too high voltage and creative and will always be bewildering to a mind longing for a place to land.

It is important to remember that the activity of the beloved does not become unleashed only by way of the other *people* in your life, via the so-called "external" other, but also through what I mentioned earlier as the "internal" other, those unmet and split-off qualities and aspects of the body and psyche that are longing to be reintegrated and available in the crucible as raw material for the unfolding of the heart. It would appear that the beloved has no bias and is equally prepared to take form internally or externally—whatever it takes to awaken you to the mystery of his or her presence.

As you become more and more willing to provide a home and sanctuary for the entirety of your emotions, feelings, and inner experience—and practice compassion and kindness to whatever appears—the beloved will come alive within you. She will dissolve the dream of separation and dance eternally in the contradictions, for this is her secret home. And even if you are unable to accept the way you are, "stay in the now," or maintain a consistent state of "high vibration" or spiritual bliss, the beloved is equally there, resting and moving within you. She will take form as the past, the future, a "low vibration," and the dark night of the soul if that is how she must reach you. For when you are able to offer safe passage for the dark *and* the light, you will become a clear vessel for love and its activity here. It is then that you will know her, and she will know you, and you will dance together into eternity.

Relationship as the Royal Road

It is no secret that relationship is, for many, the royal road to profound (and often excruciating) revelation about where we really are in our lives, to the endless mysteries of the path, and into the full-spectrum nature of the journey. Intimacy has a unique way of very quickly revealing what remains unmetabolized within us, the ways we're holding on and holding back, and the intricacies of how we defend and guard against the unyielding realities of the heart. When all is said and done, we really don't want to be too exposed. Maybe a little bit here or there, on weekends or vacations, as long as we can remain connected to a reliable escape route by which we can return to safety and predictability in a moment's notice.

One of the challenges of intimate relationship for those committed to spiritual growth is that the true beloved has very little interest in our great enlightened accomplishments, the states of invincibility and invulnerability that we've constructed, or the mythical spiritual journey we believe we've "completed." These are all dust at her feet. But inside these particles of dust are the alchemical gold.

Over the years, people have asked me: You've met and worked with so many teachers and authors behind the scenes, in their most vulnerable, unscripted moments. Who among them are really, truly awake? And who maybe aren't quite as enlightened as they come off in their public roles? I usually find myself cringing at these sorts of questions, looking for a nearby window out of which I can hurl myself in the hopes of avoiding having to answer. Perhaps playfully, but in a way that is also somewhat serious, I usually offer a response along the lines of "If you really want to know how awakened someone is, don't ask them. Don't ask their students or disciples. Don't look to their books to tell you. Don't watch them on stage responding to questions from devotees in sacred silence. *Ask their intimate partners. Or their kids.*"

This response is often met with an uncomfortable, forced chuckle. And then an awkward sort of silence. Things just sort of fall apart after that.

We have so many ideas about relationship that we've picked up from our families of origin, teachers of all kinds, the media, books, television, and movies. What is relationship, anyway? Is it a feeling? A sense of security? A warmth in the heart? A content knowing that there is someone to share the journey with? Is relationship, like love, a vast enough field to contain aliveness, flatness, waves of joy, feelings of irritation, and sensations of disturbance? Can we sit in the fire of intimate relationship knowing that all of our fears, fantasies, anxieties, and vulnerabilities may continue to surge and will likely never be resolved into some neat, tidy, safe package in which we can take permanent refuge? There is something about intimacy that by definition is mysterious and unable to be pinned down, which in fact is why it is so transformative. It's more a question than an answer, more a verb than a noun. Most of us have had the opportunity to become painfully aware of the seemingly miraculous power of our partners to touch our sore spots and elicit the most unexplainable and outrageous reactions within us.

A rich area of intimacy to explore is the degree to which we're willing and able to allow another to deeply matter to us. What is it like for us to take that sort of risk, to expose ourselves to the very alive potential of devastating heartbreak, rejection, and abandonment as we open to a new romantic partner, friend, therapist, or colleague? Many of our childhood biographies, in one way or another, present a very unstable situation, a precarious reality where it was not all that intelligent to let another become too important. As innocent little ones, new to the reality that this life consists of both the light *and* the dark, we naturally allowed others to deeply matter, in many cases quite quickly. Yes, we say! Yes to relationship, to connection, to stepping all the way in, quite sure we will be taken care of, attuned to, and treated kindly. Of course, that's just the way it works, right? This is just who we are as relational beings. At least for a while. This sort of exposure comes with tremendous risk, however, and many of us learned the hard way the shattering consequences of letting someone all the way in. Nonetheless, we move forward, we keep opening, we try again, at least for a while. As young children, we can't really help it; we're wired to connect.

As an adult exploring a variety of close relationships, you will come up against this notion of allowing another to matter. There may always be some hesitation, some sense that you can just take care of yourself and some idea that you don't really need another person anyway—you're all good. Yeah, it would be nice to spend some time with them, but if they're not into it, or if they don't see me quite like I see myself, or they're not going to enter into an agreement that we don't get *too* close, that's fine. Whatever. You can so quickly dismiss how important relationship truly is to you and use your distancing and overcompensating self-reliance to keep you from confronting your own impending vulnerability. On the one hand, you long for this intimacy with another in the core of who you are; on the other hand, you're terrified of it and will actively defend against even the possibility of having to encounter old feelings of rejection, abandonment, and heartbreak. This is quite natural and nothing to shame yourself about or use as evidence that you are unworthy of love, crazy neurotic, or lost in fear. Rather, you can use these experiences to *deepen* your inquiry, to befriend yourself and get to know yourself at deeper levels, vigilant to the ways you may be holding back. As you discover the ways you are defending against the full-spectrum nature of intimacy, without any shame, judgment, or apology you can commit to an embodied, open-hearted exploration of all this with loving, caring, yet penetrating awareness. You might have to push yourself a bit and step slowly and in small ways into some of the anxiety that guards the gates of your heart. For to fully enter into the crucible and allow another to matter *will* bring to light what you have not yet met and integrated. This seems to be nonnegotiable.

How is it, then, that just by being themselves, our partners seem to have the most annoyingly unique ability to trigger an avalanche of emotion within us? We can become convinced quite quickly that it is them who is *causing* us to feel so bad, to be so unsure of ourselves and overwhelmed with old material we thought we had healed. Before we realize it, it's as if we are back in the organization of a young child, terrified of rejection and abandonment, and with the urgent sense that our survival is somehow at risk. Something simple like them not returning a text right away, not paying us a compliment when we expected one, not prioritizing our needs over a friend's, some annoying behavior we interpret as evidence they do not really love us … it gets hot and claustrophobic, the heart races, the throat constricts, the face flushes, a nauseous sensation appears in the stomach, images and thoughts begin to swirl as if coming at us from the outside. Oh, god. Here we go again.

It's them, isn't it? They are clearly doing it, making us feel this way. If they would just meet us, show up according to our agreement, and stop breaking all the promises and contracts we were sure we had, then we wouldn't be feeling like this. Right?

We may chuckle when reading this on paper, but in a moment of activation—when we are hooked into the narrative and sensations of rejection, abandonment, shame, resentment, and blame—these are the archaic conclusions that present themselves when we are triggered and activated in the relational matrix. Perhaps the reactions are left over from an earlier time, or are arising fresh in the moment, or they're not even ours at all but some remnant of Mom or Dad, or another attachment figure or important person from our past. We can't really know for sure. But nonetheless we are in the thick of it and it can feel as if there is no escape. We spin out into response, guided by our early attachment templates: anxiously moving toward the other in the hope that they will regulate our internal world for us, or moving back into the cocoon—never mind, I'll just do it myself, I don't need this relationship anyway. I'm good. I'm a spiritual being and am fine on my own; I don't need anyone's help. We find ourselves swirling around the spectrum of anxiety and avoidance, fight or flight, separate or connected, unsure where we will find relief and whether intimacy is really for us after all. While these moments are deeply painful and unsettling, they are profound opportunities to encode new circuitry, to replace the self-aggression, self-abandonment, and complaining, blaming, and resenting with new pathways of slow, attuned self-care. But it takes practice and tremendous courage and a wild storm of kindness to turn toward the fire and make use of the ever disturbing, alive, and naked field of intimacy as a crucible of awakening and healing.

These moments can feel so sticky and gluey and panicky and urgent. Clearly, they don't respect us, they speak unkindly, they don't understand us, they don't show up, they don't keep their commitments, they're never there when we really need them, and they just can't quite connect with who we are at the deepest levels. Just one glance, one failed returned phone call, one reminder of how they are just like Dad, one small bit of criticism ... and then there's the big one, the king and the queen of relational failure: *they just don't meet our needs.* Of course there is likely some relative truth in each of these observations and they are worth exploring. It is an act of kindness to care for yourself, to dialogue with your partner, to make requests of them, to assert your needs, and to *unconditionally reject* an environment of abuse or neglect. Just to be clear, that is not what we are addressing here, where the "inner work" you are being asked to do would condone or excuse any situation where there is abuse and violence. Absolutely and unconditionally not. Rather, what we're speaking about are those ordinary, relatively reasonable, and to-be-expected moments that arise when we allow another to matter to us, which seem to hold extraordinary significance and trigger a reaction on our part that seems way beyond the actuality of what is occurring in the moment.

We might come to see that just by being in relationship, we will likely be forced to feel feelings that we really don't want to feel and that we have been able to stay away from while on our own. This seems to be one of those truths about relationship that, from one perspective, just sucks. Really? Does it have to be that way? How can he trigger me just by looking at me like that? How can she provoke primal abandonment by not returning my email, by preferring her friends over me, by going to the gym instead of having dinner with me, by not noticing the ways I've been working on myself? But from another perspective—if we are called to use the inherent contradictory, confusing, unresolvable tensions that are wired into the intimate field for personal healing and spiritual growth—we can reframe the way we have come to see the situation and realize just how rare and precious the opportunity is that we've been given: to both *wake up* and *grow up.* Intimacy is one of those rare vehicles in the contemporary world that provides the raw materials to work not only within the personal and interpersonal bands of development but also at the transpersonal. As many have discovered, the yoga of intimacy is truly full spectrum and demands our vigilance, awareness, and compassion at multiple levels.

At the risk of repeating myself, but just to be *crystal clear,* I'm *not* talking about withstanding an environment of abuse—emotional, physical, or otherwise—in the name of "sticking in there" and doing your "spiritual work," where standing up for yourself and enacting clear boundaries are evidence that you have failed or are "lost in your ego" or "just need to surrender more." Let's make sure we're on the same page here. What I am inviting awareness of, however, is that unexplainable power of our partners, bordering on the magical—just by being themselves and acting in a *relatively reasonable and innocuous way*—to hook us into a surge of disturbing and dysregulating thoughts, feelings, and behaviors. It's not so much that our partner is doing something *to* us but that when we open ourselves to the transformative activity of intimate connection, all of those previously unmet aspects of ourselves that have been lurking in the unconscious seeking the light of day tend to come erupting to the surface.

As we slow down and more carefully observe our experience— guided by a slow, non-urgent, yet fiery, alive kindness—we will begin to sense the ways in which we organize our lives around the avoidance of certain feelings. As I touched on earlier, this organization is an activity that is maintained in the present and requires upkeep (albeit it usually unconscious) in the here and now. While our early adaptive strategies very likely have historical roots, they are not autonomous and capable of self-maintenance; they require our participation to remain alive. This is very good and hopeful news, though, as we cannot change the past. But we *can* slow down and investigate how we are avoiding certain aspects of our emotional landscape, and then become more conscious about whether we'd like to engage in a different way. To discover these strategies and bring them back into conscious awareness can be illuminating but simultaneously confusing, and it can trigger us even more, catalyzing a secondary activation that can deepen the conclusion that something is fundamentally wrong with us. In the wake of these discoveries, it is easy to become aggressive toward ourselves, falling into the old pathways of judgment, self-hatred, and shame, which, incidentally, also take us out of underlying feeling and somatic states we have come to believe we are not able to hold and provide safe passage for. In relationship, as many have discovered, everything comes roaring forward, seeking light, seeking awareness, seeking attention, and showering us with invitations to come closer.

In this way, intimacy catalyzes a certain kind of *sacred claustrophobia,* where we can no longer hide out, duck around the corner, or fantasize that we've somehow come to a fundamental resolution or resting place with it all. We start to see that engaging in intimacy as a yoga will not support our dreams of a life of safety, certainty, and a consistent flow of positive feelings.

Sure, if we become adept at certain practices, when we're alone it's not so difficult to set things up to simulate a type of control over our external environment and even over our inner world. If something disturbing or something that does not confirm our personal sense of identity arises when we're alone, we can dissolve it back into the Absolute, back into God, back into space, or give it all to the guru. We've gotten pretty good at that. Disidentifying with arising narrative, emotion, and sensation can be a helpful practice, and the capacity to not identify with what is not ultimately true is an important milestone on the journey. However, like all practices, we can use witnessing and disidentification to bring us *closer* to ourselves and to the truth or to defensively avoid or take us *further away,* falling into dissociation disguised as spiritual realization. To learn to discern between these two movements in consciousness is a critical development on the path and it often takes the guidance of an attuned other to help us. We have to care enough and take the time to see for ourselves our deepest intentions for engaging in our practices, especially if we're doing so in response to a disturbing inner feeling triggered within the relational field.

In contemporary culture, an intimate relationship, in my opinion, is one of the most profound vehicles we have for waking up, for growth, and for healing—but should we choose to approach it in this way, we must acknowledge the difficulty of such a journey and the uncertain, chaotic terrain that we will be asked to navigate, taken apart at times piece by piece in the crucible where love is alive. While this dismemberment and reassembling may sound exciting and seem to be something to look forward to, it is important to allow in the possibility that when it comes right down to it we may have very contradictory thoughts and feelings about the whole thing. The path of love requires this sort of authenticity and self-honesty. We may think twice and choose to return to safe ground, only to jump into the fire again at another time. It's okay. Let us hold the contradictions close, allowing the mystery and paradox safe passage and room to move within us. We're never going to figure it all out, or pin down the creative activity of the beloved, as her ways operate outside conventional understanding. What a relief! To finally just be who we are, beginners on the path of intimacy, open to being astonished by the forms the beloved will take—external forms such as our outer partners, friends, and teachers and inner forms by way of the holy unmet "other" within, emerging as lost aspects and pieces of soma and psyche.

At some point along the way, we will be invited to reframe our view of neurosis and disturbance, where it is embraced not as something to be discarded, transcended, or transformed but as ongoing revelation. This may sound like madness to the mind and to a world oriented toward five quick steps to manifesting positivity and resting in permanent bliss. In order to engage intimacy as a path of *wholeness* rather than primarily as a way to remedy our own loneliness, sense of unworthiness, and existential despair, we must come to see the true potential of the relational field. It is not to make us *feel better,* produce certain emotional states, or protect us from the ongoing reality of potential heartbreak, deflation, and disappointment. Nor is it designed to provide us with some eternal resting place that is free from disturbance, conflict, or our historic core vulnerabilities. Rather, we are asked to open to the possibility that the energy of intimacy has come into our life to unfold and reveal the creativity of the unknown, to introduce us to the wholeness that we are, and invite us into the mystery where we're never quite sure how it will all turn out. In this totality, along with the sweet fruits of the intimate life—connection, closeness, companionship, and comfort—we will also be met with reorganizing feelings, heart-wrenching vulnerability, and a seemingly unbearable nakedness and exposure. Nowhere to hide. The only way out is through, into the arms of the beloved, in whatever form he or she happens to take. Into our own arms, and into the irresolvable paradox of separation and union.

When we view intimate relationship in this way—as an alchemical, at times relentless crucible for our own healing and awakening—we send out an open invitation into the seen and unseen places, beckoning all that seeks further integration to come out of hiding. All of those lost aspects of ourselves, the unmet inner family members, the sequestered hopes and fantasies, the buried somatic feelings, visions, dreams, and the full retinue of emotions and abandoned parts, summoning them all back into the light of conscious awareness. Just by being around the other—without any active doing on their part, if we have allowed them to truly matter to us—will be sure to amplify this process and illuminate the darkness.

The only way out is through, unfortunately … or very fortunately, depending on how you see it. The invitation is to slow down and call on all the guidance and help you can find to support you as you approach your inner world in a radically new way, honoring how challenging this work is and how much wisdom and compassion are required to rewire the old patterns. As you continue to practice the revolutionary yoga of kindness and caring self-friendship, you may even start to feel grateful for the opportunity to update the way you have previously organized your experience in relationship. Yes, it can be painful and achy, and it is deeply humbling, but it is a turning point in your life to know deep within you that you have the capacity to reauthor a new world. What grace that you're able to see this now, as an adult, with capacities you once did not have, to make more conscious, embodied, real-time choices as to how you would like to engage, remaining committed to turning *toward yourself* in times of activation, when you need yourself more than ever, and away from the old, worn-out path of self-abandonment that once paradoxically served you. But let's not kid ourselves: the organization of avoidance is deeply embedded—neurobiologically, emotionally, and psychically—and it will take time, practice, patience, and courage to illuminate and unravel.

Intimate relationship is a yoga because *it cuts into this organization.*

The Invitation of True Intimacy

In that way it is a rare form of *sadhana,* or spiritual practice, in the modern world. For some, it is its own temple and as holy as any other. You may be able to avoid certain feelings, vulnerabilities, and aspects of yourself when you're on your own or in relationships where you've contracted with the other to stay safe on the sidelines (and we *all* do this, by the way), but with true intimacy, alas, you're not so lucky. Or are you? Inside the crucible, the "other" will *always* push up against that which is unresolved within you. How fortunate! How painful. What grace.

May you hold those you're in relationship with, including yourself, by committing to taking love's journey with them, knowing nothing about the route or the destination. And more than anything, may you be kind to yourself and your partners if you decide to truly take up the yoga of intimacy together, knowing that it will take everything you have and are to navigate it.

The Magic of Attunement

On a flight from Denver to Oahu, I sat next to a lovely couple who must have been in their early to mid-70s. I was struck by how attuned they were to one another: the slightest cue from one was received by the other and responded to. I could literally feel in my body each time they experienced this linkage, right-brain to right-brain holding in all its purity. At other times, they would return into their own individuality, weaving together and dancing in the middle, totally connected and totally separate simultaneously. It was like magic.

As soon as I thought they had lost contact, they would meet one another's glance spontaneously, as if to behold together the unspoken holiness of the relational field itself. No words needed. It was as if I could feel their mirror neurons coming online together, empathically in resonance, attuned to one another's arising emotional subjectivity. They were alive to what was needed in a given moment, but not more. Intimacy without fusion. Communion without impingement. All in a perfect flow of mutual co-regulation.

For some reason their dance, their play, their love ... it really touched me, so much that I found myself weeping a bit. I didn't want to cause a scene or make them uncomfortable so kept to myself as much as I could.

After a little more time passed, they pulled out their video player and were going to watch a movie together. I was curious how they would be able to remain connected as there was only one headphone jack on their iPad. Would they alternate? Knowing them (as I had for about an hour now), I was sure one would just sacrifice the sound for the other, and they'd switch periodically, trusting they would be able to dialogue about the film after it was over, catching each other up to what each of them had missed.

Before I realized what was going on, the man pulled out a metallic-looking Y-shaped device that allowed them to both plug their headphones in at once. I lost it. It was so perfect, and so them. Just more attunement and connection, this time taking shape as some weird-looking modern electronic contraption. The tears flowed even more, reveling at their sweet yet powerful connection.

They finally glanced over at me, my intention to not create a scene lost to the crushing power of love that flows between two people. They both smiled and the man patted me on the shoulder, his eyes near bursting into tears himself. He understood. We understood together. No words. We stepped into some sort of crucible outside time and space where the veil parted and only love remained. I was so grateful that they allowed me into the sanctity of their love-world for a moment, and into the mystery of lover and beloved as it unfolds here, into eternity.

Just before landing, I shared this writing with them. The three of us just sort of silently wept together, holding hands as we descended into Waikiki—three new friends, held by the beloved and her mysterious ways, and the sweetness of a Hawaiian sunset. There is truly never any such thing as an "incomplete" moment.

I feel quite confident I could die now. To know even one sliver of this love. I've been given so much more than enough.

Appendix

A Love That Assembled the Stars

I SPOKE WITH A FRIEND WHO SHARED WITH ME HOW HER SPIRITUAL life had given her so much: the many ways it had helped her open her heart and experience a depth that she had been longing for since she was a young girl. She had also become aware of how her engagement with spirituality, in subtle ways, enabled her to avoid aspects of her emotional life and unmet pain from the past and kept her split off from feelings she did not want to feel.

While her practices at times brought her closer to herself, which she was deeply grateful for, she saw that at other times she was actually using them to escape from herself and abandon some of her most vulnerable experience. She was in such a raw place with it all: such appreciation on the one hand while also knowing that she needed to look anew at *everything,* be willing to start over fresh with beginner's mind and the amateur's heart, as she was being called deeper. I just listened … and felt honored to be able to bear witness to such intelligence, such unfolding wisdom, such genuine passion for the truth, such darkness, such raging light.

As she continued her inquiry in the relational field unfolding around us as we sat together, she noticed some grief that she had touched at an earlier point in her life but, for whatever reason, had not been able to stay with at the time, and as a result had covered it over along the way. As the grief (and accompanying shame and sadness) poured out, it was like a firestorm of energetic possibility, all of this unmetabolized material in her psyche and in her heart, unleashed in an eruption of reorganization.

She wasn't sure she could do this; she would dive in for a couple of minutes and then retreat, only to head back in once she felt it was safe enough to return into the fire. I told her I knew she could go deeper, that I trusted the intelligence of her process, and assured her we would stay close regardless of what appeared, with no shame, no blame, and no pathologizing what emerged into the holding environment we had found ourselves in together.

We made the commitment to go wherever she was guided, into the utter darkness and emptiness if that was what was required, into the black hole inside her that she was beginning to touch, as well as into the light that was attempting to break through. We would dare together to hold all of her symptoms and experiences as pure information and guidance, honoring them as the attempt by her psyche and her heart to reach her and reveal wholeness. While she had quite a bit of doubt and fear about how much she could actually hold, I felt confident that she could tolerate and contain a lot more. She trusted that I would push her in a way that was provocative and on the edge, but not so far that she tipped into overwhelm or fell too far outside her established window of tolerance. I explained that, in my experience, confronting anxiety, groundlessness, and uncertainty could be supportive as long as we stayed close and attuned in real time to what was unfolding. She remained unsure and shaky, acknowledging that some fear was present. But somehow she kept going.

As she allowed her experience to unfold and remain for short periods of time inside the core of the intensity, things slowed way down in a way neither of us fully understood and she touched something she had not quite known before. Something new was emerging from deep

Appendix: A Love That Assembled the Stars

within her body and her unconscious apart from what had historically revealed itself. In this place, she discovered a cosmic sort of permission in which she could allow herself to go into the unknowing, despite the fear, and allow herself to fall apart a little, removing the pressure to hold it all together and maintain *any* image or idea of herself. This felt somewhat risky, but despite the trepidation she was curious and almost excited. For the first time, she was able and willing to see clearly the ways that she did not feel seen and loved at the most primordial level. She had thought she had been to the depths of this wounding and was surprised to find even more. And even more.

And so it goes on the path of love ... always more. We realized together that there is no ending to the depth of the heart. No final landing place in which all of its wisdom has been given. Always another layer, another revelation.

She sensed that it was possible for her to meet and directly experience these long lost soul parts of grief, hurt, unlovability, and abandonment—and that until she worked through this material in a deeply somatic way, the realizations she had experienced would always remain on the surface, never able to fully penetrate her most deeply embedded conditioning and somatic armoring. As part of her inquiry, she also had a deeply embodied intuition that she could never truly love another until she offered a home and sanctuary where the perceptions, emotions, and bodily sensations could become conscious and be illuminated in her loving awareness. She saw so clearly how this yet-to-be-metabolized material was not and had never been "obstacles" to her healing and awakening but each a certain type of ally on the path. As she continued to share all of this with me, I couldn't help feeling such awe and love for her, for her (our) journey, and for the immensity and implications of what it truly means to be a human being.

As she continued to open—not all at once, but in many short bursts, followed by periods of quiet and rest—she discovered that she could meet this ancient sorrow *directly* rather than orbiting it by focusing solely on her thoughts *about* it. And that it took a lot of awareness and concentration to make this discernment in her immediate experience. What appeared as "moving closer" was often not that, but more of a conceptual approach to her experience that was still serving to keep her out of the fire and at a distance. As we went deeper into this, she discerned that she could practice intimacy with her feelings while not falling inside them, not tumbling down the rabbit hole, and not becoming fused or identified with them as who she was in an ultimate sense. *Intimacy, without fusing*—that was the alchemy she was exploring. She was experimenting with sending awareness and warmth into what was happening in her body at the level of felt sense and raw sensation, and how these affective and somatic experiences colored her perception by way of a subtle narrative that grew around them.

Additionally, she had deep insight into how these various levels of experience (perception/emotion/sensation) intertwined and inter-penetrated one another. Without our conscious awareness, they tend to fall into a looping pattern, playing off one another, on automatic pilot with a seeming life of their own. But as she slowed down and made experiential contact with each level of the spectrum, something else revealed itself. What this was we could not name, necessarily, but it seemed to catalyze a wave of freedom, as well as compassion for the tender complexity of the human experience. More than anything, more than needing to pin it down into some conceptual framework, at least for *this* moment, we wanted to touch the mystery of what she was in its entirety. A partial communion was just not going to do. Not for her!

In some ways, what she was encountering was so very personal, but in other ways she was touching the sorrow that dwells in the collective, that all sentient beings have met at some point. In this way, inner work is never for the individual alone and is intergenerational and transpersonal in its implications, reaching back into the past and forward into the future to untangle the knots of the cosmic heart and reveal greater meaning and purpose.

As she continued her exploration in an embodied way, descending beneath the density of the narrative about *why* the sorrow was there, *who* caused it, *how* it originated, and the urgency around transforming it, she began to cry, shake, and tremble. Her breath became shallow and she was struggling to hold it all together. Something was reorganizing and she wasn't sure she would make it through to the other side. Even though she was feeling anxious and fearful, I reminded her to breathe deeply and ground her awareness into the earth, and that together we could go a bit further. At times she pulled back and we rested together, feeling our feet on the ground, looking up at the sky, listening to the birds nearby. When she approached that place of near overwhelm and shutdown, we would stop the active part of the work, sink into the sensual world together, look at one another, and reaffirm that everything was actually okay—and then she would return into the fire.

Memories streamed in of when she was a little girl, gazing out the window while her mother and father drove away, leaving her alone and helpless at a young age. "You'll be fine," Mom admonished; "Stop being such a baby," said Dad. She remembered wondering what she had done wrong to cause them to abandon her, to reject her, and to need to spend private time without her. She saw images of herself crying in her bedroom, totally alone, longing to be touched, to be seen, to be held, and to be validated as a unique, living, breathing being. It was the most profound feeling of existential aloneness and despair.

After staying with her deep sadness and grief, we were both a little shocked as these feelings yielded to a wild, untamed sort of rage at consistently being discarded and unseen. In an instant she went from sorrowful and sweet and transformed into Kali, goddess of the dark. There must be *something* she was doing wrong that triggered her sense of core rejection but she couldn't quite pin it down. The only truth she could access was that no one was listening. No one *wanted* to listen because she was so wretched and unlovable as she was. The rage intensified in the wake of this perception.

"Where the fuck *was* everyone?" she yelled. "And by the way, where the fuck are they *now?*" She thrashed around and screamed at the top of her lungs, all the while eyeing me carefully to see if I would reject her, invalidating her rage, shame, blame, and turn from her, which had been the pattern in her family during times of emotional intensity. As I discussed earlier in the book, in our families or origin there were certain feelings and ways of expression that were allowed and others that were strictly forbidden. In some families, for example, anger was okay, but not sadness; in others, the expression of dependency led to anxiety and disruption, while showing independence was honored and rewarded. We learned (often the hard way) that certain emotions, styles of vulnerability, and personality structures were safe and led to increased affection and attunement while others were disastrous, triggering withdrawal and profound anxiety in those around us, leading to aggression, rejection, and neglect of all kinds.

In this particular case, she was never allowed to be angry or sad, or to create any sense of disturbance. Dad was too busy with work and Mom was an alcoholic and depressed. Any emotional expression was treated as an attack on the family, and asserting any sort of need was interpreted as an utter lack of gratitude for everything they'd given her. She learned that retreating to her bedroom and burying her feelings was her only chance to stay safe in an environment that was simply not able to contain the intensity of a fragile little girl. The sensitivities get buried, the vulnerability squashed, the emotional intelligence thwarted. It's not difficult to see the untoward consequences of such dismissal in our lives and in our world today.

Fortunately, she felt safe *enough,* held *enough,* and heard *enough* to continue, though I wasn't sure where we were headed. This is always a very delicate time in relational work, when the unknown is clearly in charge, something is breaking through, and there is no clear road map to follow. Psyche is clearly in the lead. During these times, which are liminal in nature and feel as if we are in between birth and death, the intensity can become too much and the temptation is to quickly return to safe ground, a natural response to prevent disintegration and re-traumatization. To fill the space with some meaningless conversation, to cover over the embarrassment, rage, fear, and despair, anything to counteract the open nakedness of the groundless ground.

Appendix: A Love That Assembled the Stars

While there is some intelligence guiding the process of when to pull back and turn from the intensity, at the same time dousing the fire too soon can interfere with the unfolding of some very high-voltage guidance and information, where who we are at the deepest levels is trying to break through an old internal working model of partiality and reorganize in a way that is more integrated and a more transparent reflection of our wisdom nature. Again, it is uncertain, complex, and contradictory territory, and it doesn't easily yield to conceptual analysis and the timelines we have laid upon the healing journey. Unless we're careful and in very close touch with what is appearing for integration, we can unconsciously remove ourselves from the cauldron, defending against and splitting off from the jewels that are attempting to emerge from the darkness. It is so easy and natural to slip into distractions of all kinds at this point and it is helpful to remind one another of this tendency and renew our commitment to stay in the fire, if we can.

In that moment of rage, she hated God, she hated me, she hated herself, and she was in total revolution against a reality that refused to see her, left her alone to sort it all out and somehow make sense of a world that didn't care, one that deemed her deserving of rejection and profound neglect. No matter where she looked, she could not locate any "good other" to rest in who would provide confirmation and containment, no one to idealize and look up to for presence and wise guidance, and no one to mirror her experience back to her.[1] And why was she not able to find this good other? Was it because her parents were simply too consumed in their own struggle and suffering, and were limited human beings doing their best with the training and resources they had? No. Not even close. There was only *one* explanation that made any sense to a young developing brain and nervous system: *she was unworthy of such contact and that level of care.* She was wretched at her core, fundamentally flawed and broken. Something was wrong

---

1. I am grateful to Heinz Kohut, founder of Self Psychology, for his articulation of the importance of mirroring, idealization, and twinship in the developing sense of self, especially as it expresses itself in the transference relationship.

with her and that is why no one was there to witness or be curious about her unfolding subjective experience. It was really that simple.

As the organization of a young girl presented itself in the field between us, she had enough awareness to know that she had stepped into the time machine of the "there and then," which had replaced the immediacy of the here and now. She "knew" on some level that her parents had offered all they could, that they were not trained in this work; they did not attend mindfulness retreats or yoga classes. They did not have the luxury of a therapist who cared deeply about them and did not have access to writings and teachings by elders on the path who had made the journey before. Just as she acted in unskillful, unwise, and non-compassionate ways—as the result of her own pain, suffering, and struggle—so had her parents. At this very human level, they really weren't all that different. Just stepping into this reality for a moment sent waves of freedom, forgiveness, and clarity throughout her being, and washed into me as we continued to hold her experience within the healing crucible of the relational field.

This realization in no way *excused* her parents from the neglect she encountered, but it placed it in a larger context, allowing her to begin to transform the unconscious organizing principles[2] that had colored her perception as someone utterly unworthy of empathic attunement. She could begin to reauthor the narrative of what happened and make new meaning of it, weaving a more integrated and nuanced story of her early life and its relationship to her journey as an adult. The limitation of her parents' awareness, empathy, and compassion that were the root cause of the misattunement, and not her own wretched, flawed nature that was the culprit. Just allowing this in sent shock waves throughout her body.

This moment of discovery was in no way calm, peaceful, or free of the eruption of very powerful and disturbing feeling states, as together

---

2. Thank you (again) to psychoanalyst and philosopher Robert Stolorow, founder (with colleagues) of Intersubjectivity Theory, for his articulation of the therapeutic process as one involving the illumination, unfolding, and transformation of relationally configured, affect-laden unconscious organizing principles.

we touched, contained, and held the rage, panic, and fear of a little one on the brink of decompensation. She had enough awareness and self-kindness to allow me to help her titrate the intensity so she didn't fall into a completely dissociated freeze state, which we both sensed was a real possibility if we were not skillful. She had gone there before and remained committed to staying awake. We did everything we could to keep her within her window of tolerance while still pushing her some, not knowing for sure where the boundaries of overwhelm might lie. Despite the intensity, there was a sense that everything was okay, that even in the face of dysregulation and periodic erupting emotional disturbance, the process had its own intelligence, it could somehow be trusted, and it was being guided from a deeper place of wisdom than ordinary consciousness.

As the fire passed after a few minutes, she came to a deep realization and was able to develop some perspective regarding her lifelong quest to be seen and beheld as a person worthy of love; she saw that she was special and unique, unbroken, and whole as she was. She even saw how this pursuit had played out in her spiritual life and how it filtered down through everything, including her most intimate relationships, and formed a template for how she related to her close friends and family. She saw how it even impacted her relationship with her own body, which had been something she had struggled with since her teenage years.

I was quiet and empty; we were both really raw. We breathed deeply. It was as if we had taken a journey out to the farthest star and returned, only to be shot back out again. In some sense, nothing had changed, but everything was different. We had started with the intention to provide sanctuary for the entirety of what she was, for those parts, aspects, feelings, and limiting beliefs to finally be provided safe passage in a warm holding environment where they could be illuminated at the deepest levels. We wanted more than anything to stay close and in communion with her unfolding subjective experience in all its messy glory. We met so many perceptions, core self-narratives, emotions, and vulnerabilities along the way as they arose and passed, each an important messenger of held trauma from her past.

Through all of this, she came to know at the deepest, cellular, quantum level of her being that she would not die if she allowed this material in, that if she dared to be who and what she was and stayed true to what she knew was most true, she could trust unconditionally in the validity and intelligence of her unfolding subjective experience. And that even if the panic, the fear, and the dysregulating anxiety, shame, and rage threatened to take her down, it could never truly destroy who she was in an ultimate sense. She had faith that she could return to that true nature that had never been in need of healing, that had never been broken, and that was never untransformed—if and as such inquiry was in service to her, and not in a way that denied or bypassed the very alive emotional and somatic wounding or the developmental effects of chronic and consistent empathic failure and misattunement.

She realized in a deeply embodied way that she had capacities as an adult in the here and now that were simply not available to her as a young girl in the there and then. She saw that beneath the compensatory and deeply embedded stories and narratives that held it all together was the direct experience of the darkness of not being loved: the black hole in the center of the heart that we have all spent so much of our sacred life energy turning from at all costs and covering over with our defenses, addictions, numbing, and avoidant strategies of all kinds. While it was intense and disturbing and even shocking, she came to see, finally, that this material was not an enemy coming at her from the outside. It was *her,* all of the lost pieces and aspects of herself that had become split off at an earlier time, now longing to be integrated and allowed back into the inner family.

She further discovered that not only could she *tolerate* the intensity, but she could practice *honoring* it: moving *toward* the fear, the sorrow, the grief, and the rage, not because she "liked" it or it felt good, but because it held a tremendous truth that had the potential to untangle her body and her heart like no other. While at times it seemed as if she could not stay, that she would be taken down and overwhelmed, she knew she could practice and return over and over again for short periods of time. She did not have to go in all at once, urgently scrambling to understand or shift something. This holding was the work of a lifetime, ever deepening and more subtle, and there was no urgency to transform the feelings, to replace them with some other more "spiritual" experiences, or on the deepest levels even to "heal" herself. She saw that the mere presence of previously unmet rage, sorrow, shame, and grief was not evidence that something was wrong with her, that she had failed, or that she was "unhealed." Rather, the direct, heart-guided confrontation with this material was evidence that she was alive and whole, and that who she was at the deepest levels would always be seeking this wholeness in greater depth, including its integrated, embodied expression in her outward life.

She trusted that she could find the right balance, with my help and that of other attuned friends, between staying in the alchemical fire of metabolization for contained periods of time and coming back out to rest. She could alternate, pushing herself to the edge where growth takes place but without any agenda that she storm her body and psyche in the name of "healing." She could engage in this work in a way that challenged her; it was provocative and growth inducing but not in a way that pushed her outside her window of tolerance and into dysregulating, sympathetic arousal on the one hand or parasympathetic freeze and dissociation on the other. There was another option, a sacred middle territory that is unique for each of us. She had touched it and knew she could return to it at any time, no matter how intense the inferno that was burning within her.

Once she had soothed the fire some with the cooling waters of her own presence, attunement, and loving self-compassion, she was able to return and inquire into the overall situation from a more centered place, exploring the organizing narratives that had formed the lenses through which she had been perceiving herself, others, and the world. Because she had worked through the highly charged emotions and feelings first, she was able to come back to the narrative in a slower, more grounded, and less urgent way. By first calming her sensitive nervous system—which had been spinning in fight-flight for relief and to ensure its own survival—she could then rely on and orient from the spaciousness of other, wiser, more integrated capacities as she inquired into the limiting beliefs, templates, and working models that had been shaping her perception.

As her exploration deepened, alternating between clarifying and updating the narrative on the one hand and periodically going back into the feelings and sensations on the other, she very organically circled back to her relationship with her spiritual life, which was where this had all started. She wanted to clarify how she was relating to her beliefs and practices and how they fit into the entirety of her life. Even the language she used was deeply influenced by her relationship with her spiritual path. It had become such an important part of her identity, how she spent her time and energy, who she spent that time with, and the way she had been making meaning and finding purpose in her life. She felt a lot of gratitude for her community, her teachers, and the ways the journey had facilitated new levels of awareness and had helped her open her heart.

Along with this, she also started to see that her beliefs and practices were serving a defensive function, working alongside her earliest protective strategies in helping her avoid certain parts of herself. She wasn't blaming the teachings or the traditions or even the teachers for this, but saw that there were certain aspects of her journey that were not most skillfully addressed—were sometimes even devalued—by her spiritual practices. Her body, emotions, intimate relationships, meaning and life purpose, her uniqueness as a separate being. Especially in the area of emotions, she discovered that in her relationship with spirituality she had learned to diminish—and thus dissociate from—powerful feelings such as anger, fear, jealousy, and heartbreak. In some way she had come to believe that these were "unspiritual" and obstacles on the path that must be meditated or prayed away and converted as quickly as possible to more "awakened" emotions and feelings. She wasn't overtly asked to distance herself from these feelings (well, maybe anger, which is the king of all "unspiritual" feelings in many traditions), but in subtle ways the emotional and somatic landscape was not all that honored, nor were the body or relationships or even her unique life purpose. Somehow the feminine principle had been neglected, abandoned, even abused in a more masculine rush to transcendence. She longed at an intuitive level to integrate more *yin* energy into her practice, as it had become overly *yang* in its movement away from her sensitivity and vulnerability, in the quest to transcend the messiness of the human condition. She sensed that an integration was possible and that her spiritual life *had* to include the *entirety* of what she was. This was an important contemplation for her. She sensed there was something here and she wanted to get to the core of it.

She let all of this sink in and we took a short break from where she had been and from the intensity of her inquiry. We rested together, reconnected with the natural world and our senses, and just took some time to come back together to the here and now, providing some respite from how far she had traveled.

After some time, she asked if we could continue for a little while longer. Something was bubbling up and she didn't want to lose the thread. She was discovering that in her family she had so rarely experienced being loved or appreciated as she was. In order to receive love, affection, and attention, she first had to adopt a secondary, compensatory identity structure. Without this substitute identity, she felt ignored, unseen, and abandoned, convinced that she was unworthy in her nature. Unless she could figure out who others wanted and needed her to be—and quickly shift and adjust her outward expression—she concluded that she was without value and uninteresting, and deserved to be discarded.

As a result, like many of us as young children, she learned very quickly which feelings, emotions, and behaviors, even which body language and manner of speaking, were most likely to result in the receipt of affection, attention, and the emotional holding that she so longed for. On the contrary, she also learned which of these same manifestations would result in responses of neglect, mis- or malattunement, and even abuse. Her ability to sort and spin and shape-shift was both intelligent and creative, but it came with a price tag: splitting off from half of what she was, leading to chronic anxiety, feelings of flatness and depression, and a deeply embedded conviction that there was something wrong with her.

In a way that didn't *blame* her parents—while at the same time allowing and integrating the profound rage and grief that surfaced in reaction to aspects of their behavior—she saw the ways in which she was an *object* in her parents' reality and rarely held as a *subject* in her own right, with her own feelings and ways of organizing her experience. She and I shared that it was important to not hold these memories as some exact, objective recovering of the past but more about the way she had come to make meaning of her early life. Whether the memories and associated details were objectively "true" wasn't what was most important; rather, what was germane was the way she had come to organize what happened to her, and even more importantly, how she was continuing to live out this organization in the present.

This is hard for any of us to do, as it requires that we step beyond the role of victim and take responsibility for ourselves, as adults in the here and now. Of course we were influenced by the past, but now the invitation is to stand courageously in the reality that we are no longer young, powerless children in a misattuned holding space. We have capacities we once did not have, and we are being called into new levels of organization and perception.

We consciously long to move forward, to step out of the tangles and limiting perceptions of our early lives, but we may also have an unconscious investment in holding on, in a strange way, to the familiar and the identities we have spent so much energy maintaining. Paradoxically, they still serve a function and protect us from our vulnerability, our sensitivity, and the painful feelings of unworthiness and abandonment that have been buried in the body and the psyche. Holding the tension of these opposites—of genuinely wanting to heal and not wanting to confront what we know that healing would require—is a critical art to learn on the path of wholeness, and an important alchemical milestone along the way.

In the course of her inquiry, she shared memories of how hard she tried to be seen as special, as unique, as worthy of being loved just as she was, all centered around her profound yearning to receive the empathy, mirroring, and attunement that she did not believe was available unless she became someone else. And how she had transferred this very same relational template onto her adult life and relationships with lovers, friends, family, coworkers, and spiritual teachers. And in the spirit of classical transference, how she related to me from this template and how this organization colored our relationship. She and I spoke about this always being a two-way street with the therapeutic couple, as my own unconscious organizing principles and complexes interacted dynamically with hers, forming my own countertransference contribution to the intersubjective field and crucible that existed between us. We had talked about this before, but where we both were now—vulnerable, shaky, a little fragile, but so alive—it took on new, embodied meaning.

As we explored this template together—and the ways it was impacting her current relationships, including our own—in a really embodied way, she met this deep wound of unlove in the center of her chest and felt it expand out into her throat and into her belly. She touched it in a full-spectrum way, sending her awareness and holding into its cognitive, affective, physiological, and behavioral manifestations. This was not easy for her and we had to stop and start as periodically she would begin to travel outside her window of tolerance into overwhelm. But slowly, over some time, she was able to tolerate, then contain, and then in the most miraculous way practice kindness toward this old material. It was personal, yes, but also had transpersonal and collective implications, describing how she (and all humans, and perhaps other sentient beings) had come to organize her life around avoiding or remedying this wound of unlove, including her relationship with her spiritual life and community.

She went on to share with me that it strongly felt as if she had lost a part of herself, a piece of her soul, to this trauma of unworthiness, that it had been taken from her by some sort of being who represented the qualities of shame, wretchedness, and unlove. At times, she took this image literally, describing to me these archetypal beings of unlove and what they looked and felt like, which I associated with the wrathful *herukas* of Tibetan tradition, such as *Vajrakilaya* or *Yamantaka*.

At other times she related to it metaphorically as a bundle of thoughts, feelings, and emotions that had become tangled within her. But what was most fascinating to her in the course of this part of her inquiry was that she clearly saw how an important part of her intention to be an "awakened" person and to become "enlightened" was avoidant in nature, organized around defending against this primal wound of unlove. Of course, this avoidance didn't account for the *entirety* of her spiritual aspiration but it was a part that she had never recognized, and from her perspective it was significant and worthy of further exploration.

In some ways, it explained so much and made so much intuitive sense to her; this realization really unlocked something in her psyche and deep within her body. It was exhilarating for her to see, while simultaneously raw and painful. It was as if she was completely naked before the universe, with no idea what was to come next. Who would she be without this compensatory identity as the unlovable one? How would this change her intimate relationships, her work in the world, her friendships, and her relationship with the spiritual journey?

Rather than attacking her defensive organization as "unspiritual," neurotic, or evidence of some sort of "personality disorder"—being careful not to reenact the misattunement she had felt so often growing up—she and I worked together to reframe the realization and open to being grateful for the protection and feeling of safety that her avoidant strategies provided, while at the same time acknowledging that she was ready to take the next step: organizing her experience in a new way. Yes, she would have to come face to face with all the unmet emotions and aspects of herself, those hidden core vulnerabilities and feelings of unlove that her protective strategies had more or less successfully defended her against. But she knew that this was where she was being called. And while it was unlikely that she would be "perfect" at it or would be able to feel safe all the time or in a consistent state of flow and joy as she did this work, this was her journey. She believed that this was why she had come here, to do this work, not just for herself but for all beings everywhere. I was in awe of her courage, dedication, vigilance, and her relentless love of the truth.

As she re-embodied those feelings, sensations, and soul parts that she had lost touch with over the years, and allowed them to penetrate the deepest levels of her body, psyche, and heart, I could feel the opening and expansion in and around her. Just being with her allowed me to touch many of these same places in myself, and I was grateful. As she led me through the open door, we touched the preciousness of this life together, the sweetness, the chaos, the heartbreak, and the glory. We had traveled into the darkness and the light and the pain and the bliss, where stars and galaxies were born and died. We were left in awe of the unbearable magnificence of this human body, these senses, the fragility and sensitivity of this brain, heart, and nervous system, and with a raging gratitude beyond words for the mystery that is this journey, for the love that assembled this universe, star by star, cell by cell.

Acknowledgments

I WANT TO THANK THE HUNDREDS, IF NOT THOUSANDS, OF COURAGEOUS men and women who have shared their journeys with me and who have allowed me to accompany them on their wildly unique voyages of individuation and wholeness. I am in awe and forever honored to have been a part of such bravery, dignity, wisdom, and compassion.

A special thank you to Sheridan McCarthy, my editor, and to the exceptional work and care I received from Meadowlark Publishing Services.

And to the following dear friends and loved ones, without whom my own journey into the darkness and light would never have been possible (please forgive me for not being able to name everyone): Noah Licata, Charles Licata, Nancy Licata, Krista Ahlfors, Debbie Gordillo, Tami Simon, and the infinite retinue of seen and unseen guides around and inside me.

An extra special offering of gratitude to my dear friend and fellow traveler Jeff Foster for all your support over the years and for your kind foreword.

About the Author

MATT LICATA, PHD IS A PSYCHOTHERAPIST, WRITER, AND TEACHER, counseling individuals and offering retreats worldwide. For over twenty-five years, he has been immersed in the exploration of consciousness, healing, and transformation through the intersection of contemplative spirituality, relational psychotherapy, and the poetic imagination. Editor of A Healing Space blog, he is based in Boulder, Colorado. To learn more about his work, please visit www.mattlicataphd.com.

Made in United States
North Haven, CT
17 August 2023

40416307R00157